Politics Without Stories
The Liberal Predicament

Liberal candidates, scholars, and activists mainly promote pragmatism rather than large and powerful narratives – which may be called "alpha stories" for their commanding presence over time. Alternatively, conservative counterparts to such liberals tend to promote their policy preferences in alpha stories praising effective markets, excellent traditions, and limited government. In this face-off, liberals represent a post-Enlightenment world where many modern people, following Max Weber, are "disenchanted," while many conservatives, echoing Edmund Burke, cherish stories borrowed from the past.

Politics Without Stories describes this storytelling gap as an electoral disadvantage for liberals because their campaigning lacks, and will continue to lack, the inspiration and shared commitments that great, long-term stories can provide. Therefore Ricci argues that, for tactical purposes, liberals should concede their post-Enlightenment skepticism and rally around short-term stories designed to frame, in political campaigns, immediate situations which they regard as intolerable. These stories may help liberals win elections and influence the course of modern life.

David Ricci is Professor of Political Science and History at The Hebrew University. He's the author of several books, including *The Tragedy of Political Science*, *The Transformation of American Politics*, *Good Citizenship in America*, and *Why Conservatives Tell Stories and Liberals Don't*.

Politics Without Stories

The Liberal Predicament

DAVID RICCI

The Hebrew University, Jerusalem

CAMBRIDGE
UNIVERSITY PRESS

CAMBRIDGE
UNIVERSITY PRESS

One Liberty Plaza, 20th Floor, New York NY 10006, USA

Cambridge University Press is part of the University of Cambridge.

It furthers the University's mission by disseminating knowledge in the pursuit of education, learning, and research at the highest international levels of excellence.

www.cambridge.org
Information on this title: www.cambridge.org/9781107170841

© David Ricci 2016

First published 2016

Printed in the United States of America by Sheridan Books, Inc.

A catalogue record for this publication is available from the British Library.

ISBN 978-1-107-17084-1 Hardback
ISBN 978-1-316-62183-7 Paperback

For Tamir, Dudi, Yuval, Tom, Yasmin,
Galia, Adam, Assaf, Ori, and Gili

Contents

Introduction

Imagine this scene. Hillary Clinton is giving a campaign speech sometime during 2016. She is energetically addressing a crowd of people who hold up signs that say "Fighting For Us." She wants to become President of the United States of America. It is a worthy ambition.

Quick, now. No fudging. Do you know what she stands for as a candidate? Do you know which values she admires? Do you know how she thinks the country is doing now and where it should go in the future? Or, to restate the matter, does Clinton, who hopes that American citizens will elect her to the White House in November 2016, believe in a great and inspiring story about herself and the community to which she belongs? And has she projected that story so clearly and forcefully that you know all about it? And has she shared that story with other members of the Democratic Party, to the point where she and they stand together?

If you answered all these questions with: "Well, give me a moment to think about that," you have met the liberal predicament. Hillary Clinton did not create that predicament. But it exists, it hinders her campaign, and it will live on after she leaves public life. Her competitor in the Democratic Party this year, Bernie Sanders, does not seem to labor under the same disadvantage. But that is a point to which I will return in a Postscript added to *Politics Without Stories* just before going to press.

The Liberal Predicament

The liberal predicament flows from a storytelling gap in American politics. Conservatives tell long-term political stories while liberals do not. Instead, liberals promote immediate policy proposals. Therefore, rightists such as Ronald Reagan – actor, television host, and politician – proclaim that, now and forever, from long ago and far into the future, markets are terrific, tradition is wonderful, and government, for the most part, should be small. At the same time, leftists such as Paul Starr – professor, sociologist, and co-editor of *The American Prospect* – insist, in recent years, with considerable passion, that modern medical care, a complicated business with costs and administration that no one understands entirely, should be regulated according to the Patient Protection and Affordable Care Act of 2010. This is a 906-page law that few Americans, including the members of Congress who voted for it, have read or understand.[1]

Of course, short-term partisan issues line up variously from one election to another. For example, in recent years Democrats and Republicans have quarreled over how Washington should relate to immigrants. But the principled difference in starting points between conservatives and liberals creates a storytelling gap that disadvantages liberals because, when they do not frame public life within what scholars call "narratives" – such as the conservative tale of excellent "free" markets – candidates to public office on the Left may fail to inspire enough voters to lift them to victory.

Some readers will disagree with what I just said. They will say that liberals *do* tell stories. These are about empowering minorities, preserving Social Security, growing the middle class, blaming the 1 percent, saving us all from climate change, and recommending that elected officials and government agencies work together – that is, in a sort of perpetual New Deal – to confront many difficulties in American life.

In Chapters 1, 2, 7, and 8, I will challenge whoever believes that there is no storytelling gap. Therefore, I will only say here that, yes, liberals *do* tell stories. And liberals *do* talk about the things I just mentioned. We all see that, and Bernie Sanders is telling a political story as I write these lines. But the *kinds* of stories that liberals tell are not the large and persistent kind that I have in mind, the kind that deserve to be thought of as signature "narratives" or – as I shall explain – the kind that constitute "alpha stories." I will say more about all of these later, starting in Chapter 1 and continuing until, as promised, I will comment in a Postscript on what Sanders and Clinton have been doing in 2016.

Meanwhile, here is the liberal predicament. Often, their lack of large and persistent stories forces liberals into having to come from behind

---

[1] See Paul Starr, *Remedy and Reaction: The Peculiar American Struggle Over Health Care Reform* (2011).

in electoral combat. This sort of poor positioning does not necessarily condemn them to failure at the polls. But the need to play catch-up hampers one of the country's two great political parties and thereby constantly influences the state of public policy in America. I discussed some aspects of this situation in *Why Conservatives Tell Stories and Liberals Don't: Rhetoric, Faith, and Vision on the American Right* (2011). Afterwards, I decided that storytelling is so central a part of modern politics as to warrant further reflection.

The Basic Dichotomy

During that reflection, in what follows, I will assume that most of American politicking emerges from two camps: one more liberal and one more conservative, one more left and one more right, one more Democratic and one more Republican.[2] This is a simplistic proposition, which streamlines a complicated reality for the sake of isolating something important in it. After all, despite dividing up public life so starkly, I do not intend to suggest that there are no significant differences of opinion within those camps. Everyone can see that, over time, standard bearers such as George W. Bush, Richard Cheney, John Boehner, Paul Ryan, Ted Cruz, Marco Rubio, Rand Paul, George Will, Sean Hannity, Dinesh D'Souza, and William Kristol sometimes disagree on facts and aspirations. Similarly, Barrack Obama, Joe Biden, Hillary Clinton, Bernie Sanders, Elizabeth Warren, Nancy Pelosi, E. J. Dionne, Alan Wolfe, Michael Walzer, and Paul Krugman occasionally clash on how Americans should appraise the world and try to improve it.

This point about details, some of which are crucial in the short run, is obvious but worth emphasizing here for a moment. Democrats don't all agree with one another. Neither do Republicans. Neither do liberals, conservatives, people on the Left, or people on the Right. *The American Conservative* is not the *National Review*. *Dissent* is not *The American*

---

[2] On Republicans being mostly conservative and Democrats being mostly liberal, see Nolan McCarty, Keith Poole, and Howard Rosenthal, *Polarized America: The Dance of Ideology and Unequal Riches* (2008), pp. 3–5. On how the polarization started among elites and spread to voters, see Matthew Levendusky, *The Partisan Sort: How Liberals Became Democrats and Conservatives Become Republicans* (2009), and Hans Noel, *Political Ideologies and Political Parties in America* (2013). On how the polarization moved instead from the bottom to the top as Americans increasingly practiced "self-expression" and segregated themselves into homogenous rather than pluralistic groups, see Bill Bishop, *The Big Sort: Why the Clustering of Like-Minded America is Tearing Us Apart* (2009).

Prospect. The Family Research Council is not the American Enterprise Institute. The Institute for Policy Studies is not Planned Parenthood. The Claremont Institute is not Citizens United. People for the American Way is not the Center for American Progress. *The New Criterion* is not Encounter Books. Hillary Clinton is not Bernie Sanders. Jeb Bush is neither Lindsay Graham nor Carly Fiorina. Donald Trump is like no one else. And so on.

Nevertheless, while leaving many details aside, I will overlook most differences between occasionally bickering allies in order to focus on how some Americans tend to tell – or endorse, or allude to – large political stories while others do not. On this score, there exists a pattern of political behavior that stands somewhat apart from people on the right and left who, as compatriots, may argue on any given day about what is happening and hold differing views on, say, what to do about Wall Street or how to deal with climate change. My point is that, in this pattern, the Left (roughly speaking) suffers electorally from a long-term handicap.

The Impasse

There are liberals – and we will meet some of them – who know that telling stories would help their camp electorally. However, as we shall see, they do not manage to create the necessary stories. That they fail to do so means that something about liberal convictions holds them back, no matter how much changing circumstances may call out for inspiring narratives.

The bottom line here is this: if there are liberals who know that in order to win more often they *should* tell stories but *don't*, the storytelling gap is not a consequence of overlooked needs. Rather, it is somehow inherent in American politics. Because that is so, I will not conclude this book by proposing a "solution" to the liberal predicament. No proposal that I know of can eliminate the narrative imbalance because – as I will explain later – when some people tell large political stories while others do not, they are acting out a philosophical standoff that has vexed Western life since at least the eighteenth century.

In fact, there exists here a dilemma that Max Weber, who I will discuss, associated with what he called a modern, post-Enlightenment inclination to "disenchantment." I will describe this dilemma and explain why I believe we cannot resolve it. I am convinced, though, that we should address it soberly –which I will try to do especially in Chapter 10 – not because its solution is in sight but because we should ponder this and other political dilemmas in order to live with them as successfully as possible.

This aspiration, to which I will return, can be simply framed. Troublesome situations can be described as "puzzles" or "problems."[3] Puzzles are situations in which circumstances can be managed so deftly that a "solution" emerges. For example, puzzles are like when you buy a box containing 500 pieces of a jigsaw puzzle that adds up to a Mickey Mouse picture, spread the pieces out on a table and, after hard work, put them together. If you assemble the pieces properly, into a picture of Mickey, you have solved the "puzzle." Problems, on the other hand, are situations wherein circumstances cannot be arranged decisively and consequently the problem cannot be solved. Problems are like when you buy a 500 piece jigsaw puzzle of Mickey Mouse, spread the pieces out on a table, and work vigorously to put them together – but to no avail. Consequently, you realize that someone at the factory mistakenly filled the box with 250 pieces portraying Mickey Mouse and 250 pieces portraying Donald Duck. At that point, you understand that you must live with a situation having no solution. That situation is a "problem."

The example sounds trite. Nevertheless, it has great implications for public life, in which intractable "problems" – using the term in this special sense – are often present and in which, even if you can't "solve" them, you should avoid making them worse. Thus using hard drugs is dangerous to individuals and society – but making drugs illegal may in some respects be even more costly. Similarly, the war in Syria is dangerous to everyone in the Middle East – but sending American troops to fight there might turn out to be as counterproductive as when President George W. Bush decided to overthrow Saddam Hussein in Iraq.[4]

Two Disclaimers

In the following chapters, I will leave aside two matters of great contemporary concern. One is the role of money in politics, especially after the 2010 Supreme Court decisions in *Citizens United v. F. E. C.*[5] and *SpeechNow.Org v. F. E. C.*[6] that effectively permit wealthy people and

---

[3] On puzzles and problems, but not via these examples, see T. D. Weldon, *The Vocabulary of Politics* (1953), pp. 75–83.

[4] See Richard Cohen, "The Enigmatic War," *Washington Post* (June 23, 2014): "Obama's caution [with regard to Syria] serves us well here. This is not a crisis made by a man or even men. It is made by movements. It's like a flu. The challenge is to not make it worse."

[5] *Citizens United v. Federal Election Commission*, (January 21, 2010).

[6] *SpeechNow.org v. Federal Election Commission* (March 26, 2010).

groups to sponsor parties, candidates, and policies without financial limit. Another is the impact of social media, which has transformed most American lives. On that score, if you use a smartphone today, as the song says, "You'll never walk alone."[7] Almost instinctively, we feel that these technical factors – the first for paying expenses and the second for transmitting opinions – must hugely affect public life. Thus we fear that at least some individuals and organizations hand out political money in return for receiving favors, and we assume that people spend so much time looking at their phones and computers that something coming out of both must powerfully affect their minds.

More specifically, money seems to us important for marketing candidates and their political platforms, and we know that social media carries campaign information even to voters who are little interested in receiving it. As such, whoever raises large sums can peddle his or her message widely and frequently, and whoever's campaign organization works hard at social media operations – email, blogs, websites, YouTube, Twitter, Facebook, LinkedIn, Reddit, WhatsApp, and so forth – will reach more voters than politicians and news media did in the past.

Political scientists, however, who intensively study elections, remind us that having plenty of money does not guarantee electoral success, because sometimes candidates who raise and spend more money than their opponents lose.[8] Jeb Bush fell into that category in the 2016 primary elections. We could call this "the Edsel effect" after the Ford car which, between 1958 and 1960, was lavishly advertised but rarely purchased. Furthermore, no one knows exactly how social media messages do or do not sway the people who receive them, because it is not just the number of messages that counts but also their content. For example, as I write these lines in April of 2016, Donald Trump seems to be doing well on Twitter. But the thrust of his messages – a sort of one-man reality show – may eventually lose rather than gain him votes.

The bottom line here is that, obviously, money and social media surround us in public life. Equally obviously, liberals and conservatives, Democrats and Republicans, and Americans on the Left and the Right use them both. But knowledgeable people who think systematically

---

[7] This musical insight comes from Susan Jacoby, *The Age of American Unreason* (2009), p. 256.

[8] Political science calculations about money and politics, along with substantial bibliographies, appear in Larry Bartels, *Unequal Democracy: The Political Economy of the New Gilded Age* (2008), and Martin Gilens, *Affluence and Influence: Economic Inequality and Political Power in America* (2012).

about such matters – scholars, think tankers, activists, journalists, and more – do not agree among themselves on exactly how either influences politics. Therefore, rather than supporting one plausible view or another, I will explore in this book only what the two camps are saying – with stories or without – rather than the ways in which, and the wherewithal with which, they promote what they believe in.[9]

Political Science Findings

While I will not explore the political impact of money and the social media, I also will not emphasize what political scientists have said about the division between left and right, liberals and conservatives, Democrats and Republicans. My political science colleagues agree that the division exists – but they do not agree on why. As one of them says, there is no "smoking gun."[10] In which case, even though political scientists have collected a good deal of evidence relating to partisanship, campaigning, voting, and law-making, nothing would be gained by me – an amateur in this field – taking sides in their professional debate, which is as yet inconclusive, about the meaning of that evidence. Therefore I won't.

On the other hand, because my colleagues have thoroughly analyzed "polarization," I will occasionally cite their findings. Political science research on polarization is an important project, especially because its practitioners have shown how polarization is increasingly accompanied by hostility to adversaries rather than a willingness to compromise across the aisle, to the point where American governments are less and less able to deal with matters of public concern as they arise.[11] On this score, many polarization researchers fear governmental "gridlock," for example, as it affects presidential appointments, federal and state budgets, and issues such as immigration, climate change, education, and foreign policy.[12]

---

[9] There is a serious analytical issue here. One might argue that if money rules politics – in election campaigns; in policy making; in legislative behavior; in support for think tanks and policy institutes; in media outlets, and more – then the liberals and conservatives who appear in those events or places don't really "think" but instead simply parrot opinions held by their financial masters. Whether that is true or false, readers who are curious about money in American politics will find much of it tracked by organizations such The Center for Responsive Politics and Common Cause.

[10] Boris Shor, "Polarization in American State Legislatures," in James Thurber and Antoine Yoshinaka (eds.), *American Gridlock: The Sources, Character, and Impact of Political Polarization* (2015), p. 203.

[11] Thomas Mann and Norman Ornstein, *It's Even Worse That It Looks: How the American Constitutional System Collided with the New Politics of Extremism* (2012).

[12] James Thurber and Antoine Yoshinaka (eds.), *American Gridlock: The Sources, Character, and Impact of Political Polarization* (2015).

In all of this, for my purposes, the big question is why some people feel more comfortable on the political left while others prefer the right. Some scholars cite personality factors – such as a penchant or disdain for authoritarianism – which cause partisans to line up on different sides of various issues.[13] Assuming that those factors exist, other scholars contend that they are biologically determined, maybe helping humankind to survive, and perhaps hard-wired into our brains to process information and evoke emotions.[14] Ergo, it is not clear to political scientists exactly where basic impulses for being on the Left or the Right come from.

Therefore, in a way, my thesis – which is that leftists and rightists differ in their attitudes towards stories, whereas those stories laud certain values and frame particular approaches to various political issues – is a fresh effort at locating an underlying disposition that can be said to cause polarization. Of course, my argument is not definitive, because even if it is true that the presence or absence of stories accompanies conservatives and liberals, I cannot say for sure why some people seek and promote stories while others do not. Nevertheless, the argument helps us to understand something important about how many political confrontations in America unfold and why. It is from this understanding that, in Chapter 10, I will recommend some operative conclusions.

My Inclinations

The storytelling gap weighs heavily upon liberals, and that worries me because, in most respects, I am liberal. Conservatives remind us that all societies need *stability*. I agree, partly because I believe that law and order, in the best senses of both, are necessary for civilization to flourish. Life in Iraq and Syria demonstrates that. However, one person's order may be someone else's oppression, in which case societies sometimes need *change*. Therefore I admire liberalism for helping America to evolve. For example, I am proud that liberals since the Great Depression have drummed up

---

[13] Marc Hetherington and Jonathan Weiler, *Authoritarianism and Polarization in American Politics* (2009), and Jeffery Mondak, *Personality and the Foundations of Political Behavior* (2010). See also Noel, *Political Ideologies and Political Parties* (pp. 42–45), which describes ideology as a matter of issue preferences and claims that those arise from both personality and interests.

[14] John Hibbing, Kevin Smith, and John Alford, *Predisposed: Liberals, Conservatives, and the Biology of Political Differences* (2014). See also psychologist Jonathan Haidt, *The Righteous Mind: Why Good People Are Divided by Politics and Religion* (2012), and anthropologist Avi Tuschman, *Our Political Nature: The Evolutionary Origins of What Divides Us* (2013).

support for labor unions, civil rights, unemployment compensation, old-age pensions, disability benefits, racial tolerance, feminism, gender equality, environmental protection, and, most recently, national health insurance.[15] And I would like to see the country achieve some of the goals – in higher education, health care, clean energy, and electoral reform – that President Obama set forth in his last State of the Union message.[16] Accordingly, if something weakens liberalism, that something worries me.

On the other hand, if conservatism gains strength, that also worries me. Around the world, America exports powerful political ideas, although it does not always do so consciously. Demands for democracy and civil rights at Tiananmen Square in Beijing (1989) and during the Arab Spring in Cairo (2011) show us something about how this works. In my view, the downside to such exports is that not all ideas are worth adopting just because they come from America. For example, in the last half century, some ideological products have been promoted by Republican conservatives, such as Ronald Reagan, Newt Gingrich, Richard Cheney, and George W. Bush. Consequently, in their dedication to full-tilt capitalism – as during the run-up to the Crash of 2008 – and in the throes of climate change, such people refrained from worldwide efforts to regulate private markets and globalization constructively.

Furthermore, even while conservative ideas went abroad, they also took hold so strongly at home that some ostensibly liberal or "progressive" Democrats, like President Bill Clinton, endorsed "neoliberal" views. And those views, when driving large economic projects, differed little from what politicians, thinkers, and activists on the right have long promoted.[17] This was the case, for example, with the North American Free Trade Agreement (NAFTA). Clinton acclaimed this agreement, and the Senate ratified it in 1993 by a majority that included 34 Republicans and only 27 Democrats. In the House, 132 Republicans supported NAFTA as opposed to only 102 Democrats. Subsequently, the number of American manufacturing jobs rapidly declined.[18]

[15] For liberal accomplishments, see Michael Kazin, *American Dreamers: How the Left Changed a Nation* (2011).

[16] See Barack Obama, "Remarks of President Barack Obama – State of the Union Address As Delivered" (2016).

[17] For descriptions of neoliberalism, see David Harvey, *A Brief History of Neoliberalism* (2005), and Manfred Steger and Ravi Roy, *Neoliberalism: A Very Short Introduction* (2010). For how neoliberalism arose since the Great Society out of conservative resistance to liberal calls for racial tolerance, women's rights, sexual liberation, and environmental protection, see Robert Self, *All in the Family: The Realignment of American Democracy Since the 1960s* (2012).

[18] John MacArthur, *The Selling of "Free Trade": NAFTA, Washington, and The Subversion of American Democracy* (2000).

It was also the case that neoliberalism triumphed when President Barack Obama appointed pro-business advisors such as Secretary of the Treasury Timothy Geithner and Director of the National Economic Council Laurence Summers. Obama and those advisors then presided over a Wall Street bailout, endorsed by most congressional Republicans and Democrats, which transferred hundreds of billions – if not trillions (estimates vary according to who is adding up the figures) – of taxpayer dollars to huge banks and insurance companies. At the same time, millions of American homeowners got little mortgage relief, and Congress, even when Democrats controlled both of its Houses in 2009–2010, did little to rein in "too-big-to-fail" banks – now even bigger than before the Crash of 2008 – which might again pile risk upon risk to produce another meltdown in the future.[19]

In many circumstances, I worry about the results of pro-market conservatism and its offspring: neoliberalism. I won't say much about the extent of my regard for either in this book, because that is not my subject. I will say now, though, that I believe that America and the world face enormous social and economic challenges, some of which flow from private enterprise and will not be resolved only by more of it. It follows that I hope writing about the liberal predicament will help liberals to swing Washington's ideological pendulum towards where it was before the rise of Ronald Reagan. If that will happen, I believe that America will become more prosperous at home and will do more good abroad than it does today.

---

[19] Many books analyze how Wall Street caused the Crash and how Washington responded to it. Among them are Justin Fox, *The Myth of the Rational Market: A History of Risk, Reward, and Delusion on Wall Street* (2009); Simon Johnson and James Kwak, *13 Bankers: The Wall Street Takeover and the Next Financial Meltdown* (2011); Ron Suskind, *Confidence Men: Wall Street, Washington, and the Education of a President* (2011); and Neil Barofsky, *Bailout: How Washington Abandoned Main Street While Rescuing Wall Street* (2013). For the conservative view that Washington caused the Crash, see John Allison, *The Financial Crisis and the Free Market Cure: Why Pure Capitalism is the World Economy's Only Hope* (2013), and Peter Wallison, *Hidden in Plain Sight: What Really Caused the World's Worst Financial Crisis and Why It Could Happen Again* (2015).

I

Political Stories

Cognitive psychology has shown that the mind best understands facts
when they are woven into a conceptual fabric, such as a narrative, mental
map, or intuitive theory.

Steven Pinker, "College Makeover" (2005)

On the way to exploring who tells or does not tell political stories, and
to considering why that happens, we may start with the last presidential
election. Barack Obama's win in 2012[1] was modest compared to those
of most recent, re-elected incumbents.[2] Furthermore, his margin of victory, which was smaller than in 2008,[3] probably came more from the
President's get-out-the-vote organization than from his liberal platform,
which wandered from issue to issue and did not project a powerful narrative of where America was, whether that was good or bad for its people,
and how the country should proceed.[4]

---

[1] Obama won with 332 electoral votes (compared with his rival's 206) and 64 million
popular votes (compared with his rival's 60 million).
[2] The re-elected incumbents were Franklin D. Roosevelt in 1936, Eisenhower in 1956,
Nixon in 1972, Reagan in 1984, Clinton in 1996, and Bush in 2004. Of these, only Bush
in 2004 won by a smaller margin than Obama in 2012, and this was more apparent in
the Electoral College than in the popular votes. The electoral votes were: 1936 (523 vs.
8), 1956 (457 vs. 73), 1972 (520 vs. 17), 1984 (525 vs. 13), 1996 (379 vs. 159), and 2004
(286 vs. 251). The popular votes were: 1936 (27 million vs. 16 million), 1956 (35 million
vs. 26 million), 1972 (47 million vs. 29 million.), 1984 (54 million vs. 37 million), 1996
(47 million vs. 39 million), and 2004 (62 million vs. 59 million).
[3] In 2008, Obama won with 365 electoral votes (compared with his rival's 173) and 69 million popular votes (compared with his rival's 59 million).
[4] On Obama's 2012 campaign, see William Crotty (ed.), *Winning the Presidency, 2012*
(2013); Larry Sabato (ed.), *Barack Obama and the New America: the 2012 Election and*

Friendly journalists complained all along that the President needed an attractive narrative – or "story," in popular terms. Thus Thomas Friedman wrote in 2009:

I don't think that President Obama has a communications problem, per se. He has given many speeches and interviews broadly explaining his policies and justifying their necessity. Rather, he has a 'narrative' problem. He has not tied all his programs into a single narrative that shows the links between his health care, banking, economic, climate, energy, education and foreign policies. Such a narrative would enable each issue and each constituency to reinforce the other and evoke the kind of popular excitement that got him elected.[5]

Or, as Paul Krugman wrote in 2011: "What have they done with President Obama? ... Who is this bland, timid guy who doesn't seem to stand for anything in particular? ... Arguably, all he has left is the bully pulpit. But he isn't even using that – or, rather, he's using it to reinforce his enemies' narrative."[6]

At the same time, Mitt Romney's candidacy in 2012 was weak. The former Governor went very far right during the Spring primaries. Moreover, in a leaked parlor talk to potential Republican donors, he offended many independent voters in the Fall by characterizing 47 percent of Americans as "takers" from government and therefore automatic supporters of Obama.[7] Consequently, Romney would probably have fared even worse if his campaign – which portrayed him as a family man and successful businessman – had not resonated with large and familiar conservative narratives, or stories, about traditions, markets, and limited government. In other words, if Romney had fielded a stronger election day organization and had been more charismatic as a candidate, the President's missing narrative might have cost Obama the election.

Two Questions

In light of the 2012 campaign – but also in view of the polarization of American politics since William Buckley, Jr., Barry Goldwater, Howard

---

the *Changing Face of Politics* (2013); and Richard Wolffe, *The Message: The Reselling of President Obama* (2013).

[5] Thomas Friedman, "More Poetry Please," *New York Times* (November 1, 2009).

[6] Paul Krugman, "The President Is Missing," *New York Times* (April 20, 2011).

[7] Romney's parlor talk to potential Republican donors, which characterized 47 percent of Americans as "takers" from government and therefore automatic supporters of Obama, appeared as "Full Transcript of the Mitt Romney Video," in *Mother Jones* (2012).

Jarvis, Jerry Falwell, and Ronald Reagan set the Republican tone in national life – this book asks two large questions:

1. *While conservatives tell stories (in the sense of narratives), why don't liberals like Obama do the same? That is, what holds them back?*
2. *Furthermore, if liberals don't tell stories (again in the sense of narratives), what do they do instead? That is, how do they inspire voters to support liberal projects?*

While answering these questions, I will write mainly about "stories," because to do so is grammatically and stylistically easier than writing about "narratives." Even stories are difficult to discuss, because they are nebulous objects that cannot be investigated and described exactly. Nevertheless, stories impact importantly on politics. Therefore I will try to write about them here *plainly*, even if no one can write about them *precisely*, as we shall see in a moment.

The Electoral Problem

Now, what is the problem? News reports and campaigning are dominated by television and social media. Those forums prefer to highlight not "talking heads" but large and far-reaching "stories" – that is, tales, parables, myths, themes, chronicles, extended metaphors, and so forth. Consequently, those stories can often, but not always, generate electoral success. Therefore, failure to tell them constitutes a political liability for liberal candidates to public office.[8]

This liability appears not only at election time but also between elections in the realm of governing. That realm is not my target, so I will not dwell on it here. However, its link to stories can be explained in terms suggested by political scientist Rogers Smith. As he says, politics takes

---

[8] This point is made colloquially by Stanley Fish, *There's No Such Thing as Free Speech, and It's a Good thing, Too* (1994), p. 58:

> Complexity does not play well in Peoria or anywhere else. People don't want ... to think about Columbus, sexual harassment in the workplace, date rape, the war against smoking, the dilemmas of the AIDS crisis, the spiritual malaise of modern life, the budget deficit, the trade deficit, the plight of the homeless, the media explosion, the information revolution, the interplay between educational and political policy, the impossibility any longer of separating the life of the mind from the life of the legislature and the marketplace. (p. 58)

They prefer stories (p. 59).

place in an arena shaped by two factors. The first is "coercive force," where rules and regulations, ordinances and laws, rights and privileges, and duties and obligations are laid down by government and, if necessary, backed up by sanctions administered by soldiers and the police. The second is rhetoric, or what Smith calls "persuasive stories." This rhetoric can come from government, but it can also arise from other sources. It surrounds citizens and channels their energies into shared opinions, convictions, and aspirations.[9]

Rhetoric is an intangible power, as expressed, for example, with verbal hammer and tongs in Thomas Paine's *Common Sense* (1776). With that power, it can challenge or complement more concrete instruments of political will, such as armies and bureaucrats.[10] Accordingly, we should not forget that, in the realm of governing, when democratic leaders want to promote a policy proposal, such as national regulation of health care, they know that clothing it in powerful rhetoric – that is, a persuasive story – can help them to enlist the political support necessary for enacting that proposal into law, even if rival leaders and a substantial part of the American population may oppose it.[11]

Returning, however, to the subject of elections, what hampers liberals is that candidates who offer no large and lasting stories – we will return to "large" and "lasting" shortly, when discussing "alpha stories" – must recreate their public image every time they run for office. Thus psychologist Drew Westen, observing the Democrats in *The Political Brain: The Role of Emotion in Deciding the Fate of the Nation* (2008), says:

the left has no brand, no counterbrand, no master narrative, no counternarrative. It has no shared terms or 'talking points' for its leaders to repeat until they are part of our political lexicon. Instead, every Democrat who runs for office, every Democrat who offers commentaries on television or radio, every Democrat who even talks with friends at the water cooler, has to reinvent what it means to be a Democrat, using his or her own words and concepts, as if the party had no history.[12]

In other words, voters look for disciples of a particular worldview, which – via consistent stories from one election to the next – conveniently labels

---

[9] Rogers Smith, *Stories of Peoplehood: The Politics and Morals of Political Membership* (2003), pp. 43–53.

[10] The power of Paine's prose is foreshadowed in *Proverbs 29:19*: "Where there is no vision, the people perish."

[11] Again, there is a biblical insight. See *1 Corinthians 14:18*: "For if the trumpet gives an uncertain sound, who shall prepare himself to the battle?"

[12] Westen, *The Political Brain*, p. 169.

candidates who espouse that view. In *Talking Right: How Conservatives Turned Liberalism into a Tax-Raising, Latte-Drinking, Sushi-Eating, Volvo-Driving, New York Times-Reading, Body-Piercing, Hollywood-Loving, Left-Wing Freak Show* (2006), linguist Geoffrey Nunberg highlights what happens to candidates who fail this test:

Since the late 1960s, the right's appeals have rested on a collection of overlapping stories about the currents of contemporary American life – stories that illustrate declining patriotism and moral standards, the out-of-touch media and the self-righteous liberal elite, the feminization of public life, minorities demanding special privileges and unwilling to assimilate to American culture and language, growing crime and lenient judges, ludicrous restrictions on permissible speech, disrespect for religious faith, a swollen government that intrudes officiously in private life, and arching over all of them, an America divided into two nations by differences in values, culture, and lifestyle. With occasional exceptions like Bill Clinton's 1992 campaign, Democrats and liberals have not offered compelling narratives that could compete with those. And to the extent that our basic political vocabulary is fleshed out by narratives, it's no wonder that the right has been able to dominate it."[13]

Collective Action

"Social choice theory" explains what liberals lack on this score. Thus, in *Narrative Politics: Stories and Collective Action* (2014), political scientist Frederick Mayer writes that "free ridership" is a major factor in public life, because individual citizens may calculate that their votes are so numerically negligible that they may as well stay home and stand aside – that is, ride free – while other citizens invest the time, energy, and money necessary to unite and produce "public" or "collective" goods such as clean air, parks, and public transportation.[14]

In those circumstances, the key to successful collective action is not a rational parsing of expected benefits but the projection of sweeping "narratives" – which Mayer sometimes calls "schemas" – which are capable of defining "shared interests" so powerfully that citizens will rally and work together to achieve them.[15] In literature, this point was foreshadowed long ago – albeit more floridly – by British-Prime-Minister-to-be Benjamin Disraeli in his novel *Coningsby, or the New Generation* (1844):

"Pray what is the country?" inquired Mr. Rigby. "The country is nothing; it is the constituency you have to deal with. And to manage them you have to have a good

---

[13] Nunberg, *Talking Right*, p. 35.
[14] Mayer, *Narrative Politics*, pp. 1–29.
[15] *Ibid.*, pp. 39–49.

cry," said Taper. "All now depends upon a good cry." "So much for the science of politics," said the Duke.[16]

The Categorical Heuristic

Technically speaking, the tendency to vote with stories in mind flows from citizens applying a cognitive shortcut which we may call a "categorical heuristic," where "heuristic" equals, roughly speaking, a rule of thumb. The point here, from behavioral psychology, is that in a world of incomplete information, bounded rationality, "satisficing,"[17] and adequate but not optimal decision-making, any candidate who tells a familiar story is likely to be remembered by voters on election day as a person embodying whatever virtues that story promotes.[18]

Some voters may relate to a candidate via an instinct for "name recognition." That instinct responds to personal qualities, real or assumed. For instance, the name of a latter-day Robert Kennedy III or IV reminds us of the martyred president and his fallen brother. However, aside from assuming personal qualities from candidates' names, other voters are spurred by the categorical heuristic. Therefore they recognize the candidate via stories, as part of a category that bears a collective appellation and denotes shared beliefs. For example, they see the candidate as a Christian, an Australian, a conservative, a philatelist, or a vegetarian.

Conservative Stories

Conservatives today are not hard to categorize. Day after day – for example, on Fox News and in the *Weekly Standard* and *National Review* – their talk moves from subject to subject, proposal to proposal. Nevertheless, right-wing advocates over the years – such as publicist William Buckley, direct-mailer Richard Viguerie, talk show host Rush Limbaugh, Congressmen Tom Delay, Senator Ted Cruz, think-tanker

---

[16] Disraeli, *Coningsby, or the New Generation* (1844, 1962), pp. 110–111.

[17] Herbert Simon, *Administrative Behavior* (1997), pp. 118–120.

[18] Thus Mayer, *Narrative Politics*, p. 39:

[To] a very great extent, human thought is schematic rather than analytic. It is structured by pre-existing schemas, "data structures for representing the generic concepts stored in memory." Schemas organize our world into categories, things sufficiently similar to constitute a type: a "car," a "tree," a "liberal," and so on. Associated with these types are certain attributes. "Lumberjacks" are people who wear flannel shirts, live vigorously, and like their beer. Understanding, therefore, is essentially an act of recognition, of slotting the unfamiliar in familiar patterns.

Myron Magnet, and Heritage Foundation president Edwin Feulner – have promoted and continue to promote, repeatedly and consistently, concepts that together add up to stories praising traditional values, free markets, and small government.[19]

For example, on "values," we can note George W. Bush's "First Inaugural Address" (January 20, 2001):

We have a place, all of us, in a long story – a story we continue, but whose end we will not see. It is the story of a new world that became a friend and liberator of the old, a story of a slave-holding society that became a servant of freedom, the story of a power that went into the world to protect but not to possess, to defend but not to conquer. It is the American story – a story of flawed and fallible people, united across the generations by grand and enduring ideals. The grandest of these ideals is an unfolding promise that everyone belongs, that everyone deserves a chance, that no insignificant person was ever born. Americans are called to enact this promise in our lives and in our laws. And though our nation has sometimes halted, and sometimes delayed, we must follow no other course. Through much of the last century, America's faith in freedom and democracy was a rock in a raging sea. Now it is a seed upon the wind, taking root in many nations. Our democratic faith is more than the creed of our country, it is the inborn hope of our humanity, an ideal we carry but do not own, a trust we bear and pass along ... While many of our citizens prosper, others doubt the promise, even the justice, of our own country. The ambitions of some Americans are limited by failing schools and hidden prejudice and the circumstances of their birth ... We do not accept this, and we will not allow it. Our unity, our union, is the serious work of leaders and citizens in every generation. And this is my solemn pledge: I will work to build a single nation of justice and opportunity. I know this is in our reach

---

[19] Thus Richard Viguerie, *The New Right: We're Ready to Lead* (1980), p. 11:

[A] conservative believes in six basic things: (1) a moral order, based on God; (2) the individual as the center of political and social action; (3) limited government; (4) a free as contrasted to a planned society; (5) the Constitution of the United States, as originally conceived by the Founding Fathers; and (6) the recognition of Communism as an unchanging enemy of the Free World.

Or, Newt Gingrich and Richard Armey, *Contract with America: The Bold Plan by Rep. Newt Gingrich, Rep. Dick Armey, and the House Republicans to Change the Nation* (1994), p. 4: "five principles ... describe ... the basic [conservative] philosophy of American civilization: individual liberty, economic opportunity, limited government, personal responsibility, security at home and abroad." For similar lists of conservative principles, see William Buckley, "Publisher's Statement" and "Credenda," *National Review* (November 19, 1955), pp. 5–6; Frank Meyer, "Conservatism," in Robert Goldwin (ed.), *Left, Right, and Center: Essays on Conservatism and Liberalism in the United States* (1966), pp. 5–8; Myron Magnet, *The Dream and the Nightmare: The Sixties' Legacy to the Underclass* (1993), p. 227; Rush Limbaugh, *The Way Things Ought to Be* (1994), pp. 2–3; Tom Delay, *No Retreat, No Surrender: One American's Fight* (2007), p. 5; and Edwin Feulner, *Getting America Right: The True Conservative Values Our Nation Needs Today,* (2007), pp. 2–3.

because we are guided by a power larger than ourselves who creates us equal in His image.[20]

On "markets," many conservatives argue that "free enterprise" permits Americans to exercise freedom and personal responsibility, in which case efficiency will be generated by making and selling, getting and spending. In the market, private wealth is generated and helps to keep citizens strong against potential political tyrants. Moreover, the private division of labor facilitates scientific and technological innovation that leads to progress (railroads, electric lights, skyscrapers, penicillin, and computers) and economic growth, which is assumed to promote wellbeing because, as the aphorism says, "a rising tide lifts all boats."[21] Above all, a market-driven society seems justified to conservatives because of their conviction that, in a free market, justice is served and virtue rewarded. As Milton and Rose Friedman put it, "In a free trade world ... The terms at which any transaction takes place are agreed on by all the parties to that transaction. The transaction will not take place unless all parties believe they will benefit from it. As a result, the interests of the various parties are harmonized."[22]

Then there is conservative praise for "small government." People on the right regard such government as a corollary of free markets in the sense that government must be limited so that (among other things) markets can thrive. This point was famously elaborated on January 20, 1981 by Ronald Reagan in his "First Inaugural Address" (my observations are added in brackets):

In the present crisis, government is not the solution to our problem; government is the problem ... If we look to the answer as to why, for so many years, we achieved so much, prospered as no other people on Earth, it was because here, in this land, we unleashed the energy and individual genius of man to a greater extent than has ever been done before [*here is the market*] ... It is no coincidence that our present troubles parallel and are proportionate to the intervention and intrusion in our lives that result from unnecessary and excessive growth of government ... In the days ahead I will propose removing the roadblocks that have slowed our

---

[20] Bush, "Inaugural Address."

[21] The aphorism is associated with the idea that economic growth will benefit all citizens. This distillation of market fundamentalism is based on Milton Friedman, *Capitalism and Freedom* (1962); George Gilder, *Wealth and Poverty* (1981); Michael Novak, *The Spirit of Democratic Capitalism* (1982); and Thomas Sowell, *Basic Economics: A Common Sense Guide to the Economy*, (2010).

[22] Milton Friedman and Rose Friedman, *Free To Choose: A Personal Statement* (1979, 1990), p. 51. On some of the ways in which "free trades" are neither free nor just, see Jodi Dean, *Democracy and Other Neoliberal Fantasies: Communicative Capitalism and Left Politics* (2009), pp. 49–73.

economy and reduced productivity ... It is time to reawaken this industrial giant, to get government back within its means, and to lighten our punitive tax burden ... It is my intention to curb the size and influence of the Federal establishment [*here is the preference for small government*] and to demand recognition of the distinction between the powers granted to the Federal Government and those reserved to the States or to the people.[23]

Reagan summed up these sentiments a little less famously – but very vividly – in 1986, when he declared that the nine "most terrifying" words in the English language were: "I'm from the Government, and I'm here to help."[24]

The Liberal Shortfall

In sum, rightists tell stories about values, markets, and government size. What leftists stand for is harder to say, because most liberals don't tell stories in the sense of together offering the public a broad vision or overarching narrative.[25] This is the storytelling gap. Some liberals may tell small tales (say, anecdotes) or recount a personal odyssey (say, Obama's life story) for specific occasions. However, those don't add up to a large and shared narrative. Obama's story, for example, tells us little or nothing about where Hillary Clinton came from and what she stands for.[26]

But wait. It seems obvious that some liberals – such as Martin Luther King, Jr., and other social justice activists – are now, or have been in the past, inspired by great stories, including some of religious origin. I will say something about these people later on, and then we will see that most articulate liberals – such as John F. Kennedy – set the tone for expressing their camp's views on public issues but do not address the nation via stories of the large and shared kind.[27] Therefore, I want only to stipulate

---

[23] Ronald Reagan, "First Inaugural Address."

[24] Ronald Reagan, "News Conference."

[25] Therefore Lionel Trilling, *The Liberal Imagination: Essays on Literature and Society* (1953), p. viii, said that liberalism is "a large tendency rather than a concise body of doctrine."

[26] One can argue that Obama fitted his personal story into a wider tale of American exceptionalism, where pluralism is the basis of national unity. This is the central contention in Stefanie Hammer, "The Role of Narrative in Political Campaigning: An Analysis of Speeches by Barack Obama," *National Identities*, 12:3 (September, 2010), pp. 269–290.

[27] For example, Kennedy feared losing electoral support in the South and therefore did not set the rhetorical or political stage with a great narrative that would free African Americans from juridical segregation in America. See the early chapters in Todd Purdum, *An Idea Whose Time Has Come: Two Presidents, Two Parties, and the Battle for the Civil Rights Act of 1964* (2014).

now that – for the most part, and in most cases – liberals don't have a
narrative which they promote with other liberals and repeat over time.[28]
I will return to this contention.

Defining Stories

Before exploring the storytelling gap, I should address the issue of exactly
what I am writing about, which is stories. Defining research terms can be
difficult, because sometimes a real-life issue that is important and worthy of exploring relates to something that is not tangible enough to be
pinpointed and studied precisely.[29] For example, modern scientists are
increasingly able to map out tangible parts of the brain, but are still
unable to say exactly what they mean when they talk about the existence
of "thoughts" and the "mind." In this case, I searched for but did not discover a scholarly vocabulary that can pinpoint the kind of "stories" that
I wish to explore. In other words, I have yet to discover a definition of
things popularly described as political stories, narratives, or visions that
would be satisfactory for my purposes.

The Problem of Power
The difficulty arises in the first place because the sort of stories that
intrigue me unfold in the realm of politics, which is a matter of power.

---

[28] Repetition is a crucial rhetorical tool. For example, it reinforced Reagan's speeches.
Thus his "A Time for Choosing" speech (1964), his "First Inaugural Address" (1981), his
"Second Inaugural Address" (1985), and his "Farewell Address to the Nation" (1989),
were all essentially the same speech, with fresh anecdotes provided for successive editions so that those editions would project one basic story as powerfully as four separate
gospels.

[29] For example, before writing about the history of American political science in David
Ricci, *The Tragedy of Political Science: Politics, Scholarship, and Democracy* (1983),
I searched for a scholarly definition of academic "disciplines," each of which I understood to be a scattered entity composed of thousands of colleagues interacting vocation-
ally and intellectually, mostly in colleges and universities. I hoped that such a definition
would help me to arrange what I wanted to say about professors who study politics.
However, I did not find what I was looking for. Sociologically speaking, each academic
discipline was obviously a large *organization* of people working together. But that organization was neither located in a particular place (like the Treasury Department), nor run
by a formal hierarchy (like the Catholic Church), nor held together by production imperatives (like General Motors), nor dedicated to a distinctive mission (like the Strategic Air
Command). Therefore, in *The Tragedy of Political Science*, I wrote about what happens
professionally among political scientists but could not line up my observations according
to a convenient scholarly model.

But imprecision on the subject of power simply cannot be avoided.[30] After all, who can measure the "power" of one story as compared to the "power" of another? Is *Uncle Tom's Cabin* more powerful than *The Red Badge of Courage*? Is *The Brothers Karamazov* more powerful than *1984*? Is *All My Sons* more powerful than *Invisible Man*?

Moreover, if we do somehow decide that one story is more powerful than another, or not, why is that so?[31] Is power a matter of the author's style or the audience's susceptibility? That is, could someone like Hitler, with his ferocious rendering of stories about the Aryan race, have gotten elected to lead the United States? Furthermore, metaphors pervade stories. Yet – to restate somewhat the question on power – who can know why a particular metaphor appeals to some people while another leaves the same people cold? For example, why would a liberal like Michael Grunwald, in *The New New Deal: The Hidden Story of Change in the Obama Era* (2012), compare Barack Obama to Franklin D. Roosevelt, while a conservative like Jonah Goldberg, in *Liberal Fascism: The Secret History of the American Left, from Mussolini to the Politics of Change* (2009), would believe that he is more like Benito Mussolini?

The Mystery of Resonance

Beyond metaphors, the difficulty of measuring "story power" can be phrased by regarding stories as a sort of "framing," whereby a story may resonate with some aspects of what we know and prefer, imputing to them an importance that we should consider when deciding what to seek in life and how to achieve it. Sociologists and media experts recognize much of "framing" as a technique for teaching moral lessons, such as when presidential candidate Ronald Reagan – as a conservative favoring small government and "personal responsibility" – criticized the granting of public aid to poor people with a story, actually quite

---

[30] I discuss why the power of ideas cannot be measured precisely in David Ricci, *The Transformation of American Politics: The New Washington and the Rise of Think Tanks* (1993), pp. 182–207.

[31] This is a perennial problem for advertising men and women, who are modern storytellers par excellence and know that they cannot predict whether any particular ad or jingle will persuade potential customers to buy the thing being hawked, which may be quite similar to its competitors. In which case, ad writers are artists rather than technicians, craftsmen rather than engineers, poets rather than scientists. See the Rosser Reeves anecdote in William Lutz, *Double-Speak* (1989), pp. 78–79. There, ad man Reeves says that, "The problem is – a client comes into my office and throws two newly minted half dollars onto my desk and says, 'Mine is the one on the left. You prove it's better.'"

fanciful, about a "Chicago woman" who cheated on her eligibility requirements in order to acquire $150,000 of "tax-free cash income" to which she was not entitled.[32] Nevertheless, while scholars may attribute part of what we do or don't do together in politics – sometimes called "collective action" – to the power of framing, they concede that they don't know "how frames are constructed and adopted, and, how, exactly, they motivate action."[33]

Measuring the Power of a Story

Clearly, then, the power of a story cannot be measured *cardinally* on a numerical scale. The difficulty here resembles our inability to measure the power of a metaphor. But we can consider a story *ordinally*. That is, within reason, and roughly speaking, we can compare it with other stories against which it competes for attention, affection, and influence.

Of course, to make even an ordinal comparison of the strength or weakness of a story, one must devise a rule of thumb for deciding what is to be compared – that is, what is a story and what is not. Yet the trajectory and parameters of a particular "story" may be difficult to specify exactly. Some come to us in well-known "texts." But these may appear in many variations, to the point where it is not clear what we mean by a particular story. There is, for example, a story about the omnipotent and omniscient marketplace. When did this story start? With Adam Smith's *The Wealth of Nations*? And where does it end? With Milton Friedman's *Capitalism and Freedom*? And which version, based on which details, is authoritative? Is it *The Road to Serfdom* by Friedrich Hayek? Or is it *The Financial Crisis and the Free Market Cure* by John Allison of the Cato Institute?

Furthermore, even if a specific text offers a striking version of some particular story, it seems true that the meanings which people find within

---

[32] See *New York Times*, "'Welfare Queen' Becomes Issue in Reagan Campaign," *New York Times* (February 15, 1976), p. 51:

> "There is a woman in Chicago," the Republican candidate [Reagan] said recently to an audience in Gilford, N.H. during his free-swinging attack on welfare abuses. "She has 80 names, 30 addresses, 12 Social Security cards and is collecting veterans benefits on four non-existing deceased husbands ... she's got Medicaid, getting food stamps, and she is collecting welfare under each of her names. Her tax-free cash income alone is over $150,000."

> Journalists discovered no such woman in Chicago, but Reagan's description of her was a powerful "frame" for denigrating "welfare" as a policy concept.

[33] Mayer, *Narrative Politics*, p. 47.

the text depend on what they bring to that reading.[34] Abraham's near-sacrifice of Isaac, for example, has for centuries evoked different Jewish, Christian, and Moslem interpretations.[35] Under the circumstances, no one knows how to determine the authoritative "meaning" of such stories.

Common Sense

In short, and taking various difficulties into account, I regard as stories what are *commonly known* as stories. There is a theoretical sense in which no one can know exactly what such an entity is. Still, I am convinced that – to paraphrase Supreme Court Justice Potter Stewart's remarks on pornography – we are capable of knowing, more or less, what is a story when we read, hear, or see it unfolding.[36] This is especially true if we will take into account what is commonly known about the subject. On that score, I will rely not only on my own impressions of political stories but also, from time to time, on what some other observers have said about stories in public life.

Technically speaking, this intuitive sort of recognition, common in the humanities, is what Blaise Pascal – mathematician, physicist, and philosopher – called *esprit de finesse*. This sense of things, as described by historian Jacques Barzun, "does not analyze, does not break things down into parts, but seizes upon the character of the whole altogether, by inspection."[37] Historians, for example, may use such calculations to talk about an American "culture of slavery," or a "Mediterranean mentality." What *esprit de finesse* loses in precision it gains, hopefully, in insight.

A more methodical sort of recognition, which is common in the social sciences, Pascal called *esprit de geometrie*. As Barzun said, it deals with things that "are well-defined … do not change when they are talked about and can thus be represented by numbers."[38] Economists, for example,

---

[34] See Stanley Fish, *Is There a Text in This Class? The Authority of Interpretive Communities* (1980).

[35] That Christian and Jewish interpretations of this tale differ in principle, and that their implications clash, is discussed in James Carroll, *Constantine's Sword: The Church and the Jews* (2002), pp. 263–264.

[36] See *Jacobellis vs. Ohio* 373 US 184 (1964), in which Justice Stewart admits that he cannot define "hard-core pornography" but claims that he knows it when he sees it.

[37] Pascal used these two terms in his *Pensees* (1670). Barzun recycled them in "Culture High and Dry," in Jacque Barzun, *The Culture We Deserve* (1989), pp. 3–22.

[38] *Ibid.*

use such calculations when they speak of national income, productivity rates, and global transfers of capital. *Esprit de geometrie* is, of course, the driving force underlying empirical research – for example, via survey questionnaires – which seeks precision.

I believe that Pascal's distinction, and Barzun's interpretation of it, are especially useful in relation to political stories because finesse can help us to grasp their dimensions and significance.[39] Still, to compensate for my own subjectivity, I try to take into account opinions of political scientists, historians, journalists, judges, activists, candidates, think tankers, and others who explore or participate in the public conversation. If they agree, based on available evidence, that certain stories are present or absent, I am inclined to accept their verdict.

Alpha Stories

In these circumstances, some parameters for thinking about political stories can be stated plainly (although, as I noted earlier, not precisely). To that end, I will use chiefly the term "alpha story" to explain the narrative disparity between liberals and conservatives. Here is where we come back to the adjectives "large" and "lasting" in the context of creating effective political stories.

The term "alpha story" suggests that, like the alpha wolf in a pack, there are stories which are powerful enough to trump competing tales (or allegories, chronicles, metaphors, parables, homilies, and so forth) within a political camp and which can then compete against alpha stories from rival political camps. Thus one well-known alpha story in American politics was that of Thomas Paine, who refuted monarchy with common sense in 1776.[40] His argument – that being ruled by a king is absurd – became an alpha story for rebels, but not loyalists, in the colonies. A second American alpha story was that of Abraham Lincoln binding the Declaration's egalitarian philosophy to the Constitution's structural safeguards in 1863.[41] This part of the Gettysburg Address, which described

---

[39] The assumption that common sense – as in *esprit de finesse* – should matter little to most academics is criticized as the modern "research ideal" in Anthony Kronman, *Education's End: Why Our Colleges and Universities Have Given Up on the Meaning of Life* (2007), *passim*.

[40] Thomas Paine, "Common Sense (1776)," in Howard Fast (ed.), *The Selected Work of Tom Paine and Citizen Tom Paine* (1945), pp. 3–54.

[41] In Garry Wills, *Lincoln at Gettysburg: The Words That Remade America* (1992), p. 263.

the Constitution as a moral manifesto, served anti-slavery Republicans as an alpha story.

Neither of these alpha stories consisted of fleeting impressions and frameworks. Therefore, I define alpha stories as *large* and *lasting* tales. This is because, as a matter of power alone, even small stories can take center stage in public discourse for short periods of time, trumping others by overcoming the attention paid to them. For example, what is called "news" in the Age of Television (and television-like newspapers and news magazines) is full of such stories – about desperate refugees, pollution disasters, royal weddings, medical tragedies, sporting victories, hurricane damages, sexual harassment, and more – which supersede and replace one another constantly to attract viewers and readers. Such stories are *alpha* in the sense of exercising immediate power, but *not alpha* because they do not massively and persistently convey a sense of shared identity and commitment over time.

Levels of Analysis

In other words, to speak of alpha stories is to highlight a particular level of political storytelling, to focus on it, and to consider how one political camp over time might portray itself there as different from another. That is, to speak of alpha stories is to evoke the power of some stories not everywhere but at a certain intersection of public life.

Crucially, that intersection is different from America's higher story level, which is national in scope and broader than what we are trying to understand here. Stories that were originally alpha – like those told by Paine and Lincoln – may eventually rise up the ladder of storytelling to become national stories. But that is not our concern here, because national stories are consensual. That is, they are more or less accepted by all mainstream political camps, like Republicans and Democrats, which challenge each other electorally but simultaneously agree on treasured sentiments. These sentiments infuse the large stories that maintain a nation-wide community.

National and Partisan

Consequently, several propositions about political stories seem to me reasonable. At the highest level of public consciousness, where a broad spectrum of people share common civic and cultural ties, most American citizens are inspired by *nation-wide stories*, like the biblical references, alluding to Jerusalem, which portray America as a "City on a Hill."[42] More recently, there was an American story of "the Greatest Generation," which struggled through the Depression, worked to fill the arsenals of democracy, and joined a citizens' army that defeated German and Japanese dictatorships. Manifestations of this story can be seen in books like Stephen Ambrose's *Citizen Soldiers* (1998) and Tom Brokaw's *The Greatest Generation* (1998), in films like Steven Spielberg's *Saving Private Ryan* (1998), and in the televised mini-series *Band of Brothers* (2001).

In a scheme of orderly categories, America's nation-wide sentiments inhabit a realm of what we may call "uber stories." As such, they are comparable to talk and tales – along with food, clothes, idioms, flags, holidays, songs, proverbs, ceremonies, antiquities, and more – that make French people French and Chinese people Chinese. We need not explore these high-level stories here because, while inspiring voters in every walk of life, they provide no political advantage to right-wing or left-wing activists within America. After all, if everyone contesting an election is on the same page, there can be no advantage to being on that page.

However, at a lower political intersection which is crucial to our analysis, only conservatives believe in and promote "alpha stories." These refer to *popular sentiments* – for example, commitment to individualism, freedom, religious tolerance, and so forth – which are admired by most Americans and therefore must accompany any viable candidacy on the Left or Right. Beyond that, however, alphas stories are *partisan stories* in the sense that – while compatible with higher points of national under-standing, aspiration, commitment, and enthusiasm – they divide rather than unite America's great voting blocks. Those are the stories that may generate political gains. *Accordingly, it is (1) conservative enthusiasm for (2) alpha stories that opens (3) the storytelling gap, which fuels (4) the liberal predicament.*

Liberal Testimonies

Despite what I have said so far, some readers may feel that there really is no gap, that liberals substantially agree among themselves in impor-tant respects, and that they therefore tell the same stories to justify their policy recommendations. I will return to this contention. Meanwhile, let

---

[42] Nationwide stories – narratives, myths, sagas, or epics – are sometimes explored in schol-arly works about nationalism in various countries. Those include books by Byron Shafer, *Nationalism: Myth and Reality* (1955); E. J. Hobsbawm, *Nations and Nationalism Since 1780* (1990); and David Miller, *On Nationality* (1995).

us consider testimony about the gap from several knowledgeable liberals. All of them believe that, so far as they can see, below the level of national consensus their compatriots disagree among themselves - that is, they lack shared aspirations and mutual expectations.

Charles Schumer

Thus in *Positively American: How Democrats Can Win in 2008* (2007), Senator Charles Schumer (D-NY)[43] observed that not even Democrats know what the Democratic Party stands for.[44] I interpret this to mean that the Democratic Party – which I regard, with some qualifications, as a liberal party – has no shared story, narrative, or vision that sums up its core ideals.

Second, Schumer pointed out, in 2007, that Republican Party core values can be expressed in eight words: "War in Iraq. Cut Taxes. No gay marriage."[45] Maybe the senator underestimated the number of words needed. Whatever, I interpret his claim to mean that such slogans, which may be updated from time to time, evoke larger verities, in which case Republicans have an alpha story – or mutually reinforcing alpha stories – of tradition, including patriotism, and a marketplace mostly unrestrained by government.

Third, Schumer invited readers to access his website and propose there any combination of eight words that might evoke the missing Democratic values. Then he remarked that readers of his book's previous edition already did that and suggested to him "bright and intriguing ideas," the "sheer variety" of which "underscored the difficulty of the project." Thus, even after receiving these suggestions, Schumer lacked an eight-word formula for describing the central tenets of his own party. Therefore, via a process he called "induction," he went on to solve the problem of Democrats not knowing where they stand by offering, in *Positively American*, chapter after chapter of policy proposals that express Democratic values. Subsequently, gradually, and over time, he argued, "The ideas in this book will make it clear what we stand for."[46] What this suggests (but inadvertently on Schumer's part) is that, because

---

[43] For non-American readers: senators' political affiliations and states are abbreviated and presented in parentheses throughout the book. For example, "D-NY" here indicates that Charles Schumer is a Democrat (D) representing New York (NY).

[44] Schumer, *Positively American*, pp. 13–15.

[45] *Ibid.*, p. 105.

[46] Schumer, *Positively American*, p. 121.

his readers did not agree on a storyline, Democrats still don't have an alpha story.

Alan Wolfe

These interpretations are confirmed when political scientist Alan Wolfe, in *The Future of Liberalism* (2010), describes liberalism as a complicated political outlook that cannot be summarized as an inspiring vision. As Wolfe says, the devotion of liberalism to:

> proceduralism [enthusiasm for decent laws, civil rights, separation of powers, elections, due process, fair trials, and so forth] presupposes a clash of ideas [rather than the discovery of "truth"]; its temperamental openness welcomes dissents to its own ways of thinking; and its substantive ideals are intended to be partisan and therefore subject to debate. As much as liberals ought to want to see their ideas win over their opponents ... A world in which the only ideas were liberal ideas would not be a liberal world.[47]

In sum, liberalism is such a tentative conviction that it willingly invites non-liberals to challenge and reject it.

Jeffrey Isaac

Similarly, while strongly committed to liberalism, political scientist Jeffrey Isaac concedes the political weakness of that project in *The Poverty of Progressivism: The Future of American Democracy in a Time of Liberal Decline* (2003). In his words, liberalism:

> counsels a healthy, realistic, pragmatic sense of the limiting and frustrating possibilities that currently present themselves ... Such a sensibility allows us to express our indignation, to grope for alternatives, and to take inspiration and draw hopes from successful efforts to improve our world, but without the hope of ... one coherent, 'progressive' political agenda or organized political purpose.

Unfortunately, he continues, "such a position offers little inspiration for those activists ... who would prefer a more buoyant and heroic rhetoric of opposition or reform, and who perhaps require such a self-image in order to work with such dedication against great odds." Furthermore, "such a view is too nuanced, too ambivalent, too qualified to gain a hearing in the melodramatic world of postmodern publicity, a world of simplicities and cynicisms, of slogans and celebrities."[48]

---

[47] Wolfe, *The Future of Liberalism*, p. 286.
[48] Isaac, *The Poverty of Progressivism.* All these passages are from p. 6.

Moving On

Such testimonies confirm, although not always knowingly, that alpha stories are missing in liberal discourse. So let us now extend that confirmation by moving on to look at what liberals write and don't write, what they tell and don't tell, what they put in and leave out.

2

Liberal Books

Democrats never agree on anything. That's why they are Democrats. If they agreed with each other, they would be Republicans.

American humorist Will Rogers (c.1920s)

The shortfall on alpha stories appears in typical liberal books, some of which I will now describe. So many of those are available that there is no way of drawing from them a "scientific" sample which can represent the entire class of such items. Still, to consider even a few books written by liberal scholars, publicists, and politicians, is to get a sense of their main characteristics, among which there is a certain disjuncture between the tales told by one book and another. Later, we will consider a fourth group of liberal books, suffering from their own narrative shortcomings but written by philosophers.

In all of this, some of the writings that I am about to describe, having been written years ago, may not seem much relevant to leading public issues today. However, my point is that we should highlight the coming authors not because they have made memorable contributions to modern knowledge but because, in an important way, they are not all on the same page.

Scholars

John Kenneth Galbraith

Economics professor John Kenneth Galbraith's *The Affluent Society* (1958) highlights America's passion for economic growth as defined by

Gross National Product. Galbraith argues that most people admire this growth not only because they hope to acquire more of an ever-expanding economic pie but also because they assume that growth is a virtuous public project which delivers what consumers decide they need in life. However, he says, when producers use advertisements to evoke a desire for their products that does not arise naturally among consumers themselves, it is sellers rather than buyers who decide what the economy will supply. In which case, the interests of a relatively few manufacturers and merchants, rather than those of ordinary people, will unfairly shape the way modern citizens live together.

To moderate the results of this bias, Galbraith recommends raising state and local sales taxes to provide money for public goods automatically in proportion to the number of goods purchased privately. For example, if advertisements will encourage people to buy more cars and bottled drinks than they bought in the past, more plentiful tax revenues will enable local governments to build more roads and hire more trash collectors.

Christopher Lasch

History professor Christopher Lasch's *Haven in a Heartless World: The Family Besieged* (1977) focuses on average Americans today. In previous generations, these people learned from family and friends how to conduct their lives and mold their offspring. Now, in modern times, they are encouraged to believe that they cannot know enough on their own to marry and raise children successfully. Increasingly, their familiar sources of information, such as sermons and extended family ties, are regarded as outworn and merely traditional. Once those are discounted, however, the disconnected parents who remain, plus their rootless offspring, will be manipulated by "experts" such as doctors, psychologists, teachers, sociologists, penologists, and various bureaucrats, all of whom claim to know how modern people should live together.

Lasch describes the driving force behind all this expertise as a therapeutic ethic, which plays down familiar standards of right and wrong in favor of achieving acceptable "adjustments" to social conditions and obligations that ordinary people do not control. Simultaneously, he identifies the "heartless world" as an extension of the way in which, during the twentieth century's first decades, forward-looking employers suppressed the craft skills of their workers in favor of managerial authority.

Neil Postman

Media professor Neil Postman's *Amusing Ourselves to Death: Public Discourse in the Age of Show Business* (1985) explains that, like the printing press before it, television is not a neutral instrument but an artifact that imposes specific forms of thought and behavior on any society that uses it. In the case of television, says Postman, we are in thrall to a machine whose broadcasts must be amusing because, if they are not, bored viewers will switch to other channels.

The imperative here (the agenda, so to speak, of televisions) is that, in order to become subjects for television coverage, events arising in society at large – such as funerals, elections, wars, religious ceremonies, poetry readings, parades, murder trials, art exhibitions, city council hearings, and more – must be made more entertaining than some of them deserve to be. Or, as Postman suggests, it is as if having a television in the living room tends to turn every aspect of modern life into an adjunct of show business. As a result, losses to our sense of what is truly important and why are large and pervasive. And because America's schools are a mainstream force, we cannot count on them to educate children to be unconventional enough to understand how to resist the small screen's distortions.

Robert Reich

Public policy professor Robert Reich published *Supercapitalism: The Battle for Democracy in an Age of Big Business* in 2007. In it, he describes what he calls "democratic capitalism" as a post-World-War-II regime wherein governments, corporations, and workers cooperated to maintain American prosperity and progress under fairly static social and technological conditions. Then came "supercapitalism," in which new technologies, commercial competition, and globalization offered consumers and investors new products and growing rewards.

The problem, according to Reich, is that these opportunities so enriched corporations as to enable them – for example, via campaign contributions – to unfairly influence political institutions such as parties, elections, courts, and the legislative process. Therefore, he concludes, this democratic imbalance should be redressed by voters and elected leaders promoting a considerable measure of government regulation to compel socially responsible business behavior.

Bruce Ackerman

Law professor Bruce Ackerman's *The Decline and Fall of the American Republic* (2010) highlights how various and dangerous elements of presidential power have evolved in recent decades. Some of these are electoral, such as when around-the-clock newscasts and the gauntlet of primary elections produce doctrinaire presidents who are less like average, moderate voters than they used to be. Some of these are professional, such as the tendency to employ high-ranking military officers in security jobs formerly staffed almost entirely by civilians. Some of these relate to "legitimacy," in that modern ways of conducting public life encourage what Ackerman calls "government by emergency" and "government by public opinion." And some of these emerge from personal aggrandizement, such as the increased use of presidential signing statements whereby the White House "accepts" new congressional acts but declares it will enforce them only in part.

Because eighteenth-century statesmen foresaw none of these developments, Ackerman asks the public to idolize the Founders less and understand more that the original Constitution cannot provide safe government today. Accordingly, that charter should be amended and supplemented by modern procedures and institutions designed to re-establish restraint and foster prudence.

Publicists

Naomi Wolf

Naomi Wolf's contribution to feminism, *The Beauty Myth: How Images of Beauty are Used Against Women* (1991), does not criticize women for wanting to appear attractive. But it deplores the way some men and many business people promote the notion that being beautiful should be not just one, but the main objective in life for what Damon Runyan called "dolls." Thus female CEOs, teachers, politicians, broadcasters, and homemakers are described as beautiful or not, regardless of how well they perform the job they are supposed to be doing. And thus corporations bombard the public with advertisements which associate "perfect" women's bodies – in swimsuits, for example – with products that are not naturally related to female physical attributes. And thus doctors promote plastic surgery to enhance women's curves while pharmaceutical companies peddle diet nostrums to keep their bodies thin.

Against all this, says Wolf, women must learn, perhaps together with other women, to resist such powerful images of the female gender. In short, they must insist on pursuing their own needs – including, if they want, makeup and attractive clothing – rather than seeking mainly what commercial messages tell them to desire.

Robert Kuttner

Robert Kuttner, in *Everything for Sale: The Virtues and Limits of Markets* (1998), explains that some markets are more efficient than others. For example, in the realm of food shopping, many entrepreneurs can open supermarkets, many suppliers can stock the shelves, and many buyers will throng the aisles. But there are other realms – such as the provision of health care, or banking services, or travel by air – wherein supply and demand do not lead to effective competition and where the consequent product is not offered on reasonable terms to all those who want or need it. Where that is the case, what Kuttner calls "second-best markets," involving a mixture of competition and government intervention, should be established and maintained. Such markets characterized much of American life between roughly 1948 and 1973, but their regulatory restraints, such as those over banking practices, were largely repealed after that.

Kuttner attributes the retreat to intellectual confusion, and especially to conservative thinkers not choosing correctly between Smithian, Keynesian, and Schumpeterian theories of economic "efficiency." The first promotes optimal allocation of productive resources, the second encourages maximum rates of employment and output, and the third fosters long-term technological progress. Most important, for Kuttner, Keynesian and Schumpeterian understandings of economic life justify government activity on behalf of a "social contract" dedicated to large decencies that a Smithian economist, such as Milton Friedman, can only hope will be achieved by market behavior. Therefore, it is America's recent rejection of that contract, promoted by conservatives committed to Smithian economics, which Kuttner would reverse.

Barbara Ehrenreich

Barbara Ehrenreich's *Nickel and Dimed: On (Not) Getting By In America* appeared in 2001. She describes it as an exercise in "old fashioned journalism," whereby one leaves the newsroom and searches for "first-hand experience" of something worth reporting on. In this case the subject is unskilled employment in America where, around the turn of the century, $14 per hour was regarded as a "living wage" for one adult parenting two children. At that time, about 60 percent of American workers earned less than that and sometimes earned as little as $6 to $8 per hour in stores like Wal-Mart, which in 1998 employed more than 800,000 "associates" who worked – often only part-time – without any union to protect their rights or bargain for them collectively.

To experience some of this, Ehrenreich hid her educational achievements, her professional training, and her financial resources, and set out to work successively, in different areas of the country, as a waitress, a cleaning woman, a nursing home aide, and a retail clerk in Wal-Mart. The aim was to try each job for a month and see if she could earn enough, after living frugally, to cover at least the next month's rent. In the end, she barely succeeded in doing that, or she did not succeed, or she succeeded only by working overtime or at an additional job. In these circumstances, Ehrenreich concludes that there is no justification for the widespread notion, espoused by many Republicans (conservatives) and some Democrats (neoliberals), that most poor people can escape from poverty if only they will work hard.

Thomas Frank

In 2004, Thomas Frank published *What's The Matter with Kansas? How Conservatives Won the Heart of America*. In it, he asks how conservatives manage to win elections in "red" states like Kansas even though the candidates who they vote for – who may prevail and take office in Washington – enact there "free-market" policies which encourage corporations to outsource jobs to poor people abroad and thereby increase unemployment at home. That right-wing candidates in Kansas will get elected regardless of this dynamic is due, Frank says, to a "Great Backlash," which is actually a great distraction, whereby Republicans speak not about the politics of economic life – for example, how Big Agriculture kills family farms – but about how best to fight culture wars. It is a strategy that portrays liberals as unpatriotic, arrogant, fickle, and exploiting their "domination" of many professions – including the mass media, great universities, and the entertainment industry – to preach disdain for small town life.

The Great Backlash overturns an earlier Populist Party outlook promoted by Kansans, who more than a century ago viewed the country as a project run by rich people who oppressed the poor. Now, Republicans like Ronald Reagan and Newt Gingrich encourage indignant traditionalists, who might think of themselves as "authentic" Americans – including many farmers and workers, evangelicals and small businessmen – to vote for their "values" against a "liberal elite" rather than against people who Franklin Roosevelt had called "economic royalists."

Jonathan Chait

Jonathan Chait wrote *The Big Con: The True Story of How Washington Got Hoodwinked and Hijacked by Crackpot Economics*, in 2007. The book observes that everyone knows that no political party can win permanent control over the federal government. Therefore, Chait says, conservatives since the 1970s have sought instead to control the "terms of debate," which, no matter who momentarily holds power in Washington, can shape the range of respectable policy alternatives in American public life. In this situation, a coterie of conservative thinkers – "loonies," in Chait's lexicon – hit on "supply-side economics" as their defining principle. This recipe for constant tax-cutting and perpetual underfunding of government services was promoted by men such as Arthur Laffer, Jude Wanniski, George Gilder, Ronald Reagan, Irving Kristol, and Grover Norquist.

Chait notes that these men had no intellectual standing among America's leading economists. Nevertheless, they were backed by think tanks, lobbyists, activists, and journalists, funded mainly by wealthy people who like low taxes. Consequently, many voters came to regard a minimal – or even bankrupt – federal government as preferable to any other. As a result, enthusiasm in Washington for political ideas that in the 1950s had been regarded by Daniel Bell and Richard Hofstadter as unreasonable, or even paranoid, drove moderate Republicans out of public life.[1] At the same time, via electoral pressures, it pushed many Democrats rightwards into what now looked like the political "center." Thus, in Chait's view, the country effectively became a plutocracy in which government provided few public goods and promoted little redistribution of massively unequal personal incomes.

---

[1] Daniel Bell (ed.), *The Radical Right* (1963), and Richard Hofstadter, *The Paranoid Style in American Politics and Other Essays* (1964).

Politicians

Gary Hart

Senator Gary Hart (D-UT), in his *A New Democracy: A Democratic Vision for the 1980's and Beyond* (1982), argues that Democrats in the Reagan era must campaign against Republicans on the basis of new ideas about how to solve new problems. For example, Washington should reverse the process of moving American manufacturing jobs abroad, which eventually led to what became known as "deindustrialization." In his book, Hart suggests that new thinking about these problems must build on old commitments to equal rights and equal opportunity. But it must also address new facts on the ground in policy realms such as education, taxation, industrial modernization, health, energy, security, and environmental degradation.

In the light of such facts, Hart calls for an "agenda" of suggested remedies. The list of proposals is long and includes promoting American exports, simplifying taxation, streamlining the military, achieving energy independence, expanding Washington's support for research and development, and providing vocational training for new jobs.

Barbara Boxer

Senator Barbara Boxer (D-CA) in her *Strangers in the Senate: Politics and the New Revolution of Women and America* (1994), starts by discussing Clarence Thomas's 1991 nomination to the Supreme Court, Anita Hill's sexual harassment charges against him, and the resulting surge in feminist sentiment throughout America. Then Boxer describes her tense but ultimately successful run for the Senate in 1992, and the way in which Majority Leader George Mitchell graciously welcomed five new women into the Senate in 1993.

Overall, this book is partly a memoir about surmounting gender discrimination in America and partly a paean to the way in which having women in public life contributes to increasing national concern for children, gun control, abortion rights, the elderly, health care, and the environment. In particular, Boxer wants to help needy children to live in stronger families, with better schools, in safer neighborhoods, and protected by adequate medical insurance. She is convinced that federal government allocations to these ends will eventually pay for themselves when the same children, after growing up more capable and energetic than they would have become without aid, will work effectively and steadily, consequently paying taxes that will reimburse government for whatever benefits they received earlier from the national budget.

John Kerry

Senator John Kerry's book, *A Call to Service: My Vision for a Better America* (2003), declared his intention to seek the Democratic nomination for president in 2004. Above all, said Kerry (D-MA), the country must rediscover "a sense of common purpose." Referring repeatedly to lessons about public service which he learned from his combat experience in Vietnam, Kerry argued that George W. Bush provoked bitter partisanship in Washington, abandoned the poor instead of implementing a truly "compassionate conservatism," and promoted irresponsibility in federal affairs by spearheading tax cuts that enriched the wealthy while reducing the amount of public revenue available to fund government services and initiatives.

Accordingly, in realms such as education, health care, energy policy, and environmental protection, government must lead by enacting new programs and policies. Kerry therefore proposed (among other things) creating a State Tax and Education Fund, a Corporate Subsidy Reform Commission, a College Opportunity Tax Credit, a Twenty-first Century Teaching Corps, a new Manhattan Project for creating energy independence, and a Service for College program of students working at civilian needs.

Rahm Emanuel and Bruce Reed

Congressman Rahm Emanuel (D-IL) and Democratic Leadership Council President Bruce Reed, in *The Plan: Big Ideas for America* (2006), insist that America is no longer what it used to be. As they say, Ozzie and Harriet don't live here anymore. That being the case, Democrats must go beyond Thomas Frank's scorn for red-state voters and woo them by tackling the country's problems with practical solutions rather than sparring with Republicans over mere words and slogans. That is, Emanuel and Reed recommend action rather than phrase mongering.

Theirs is a hard-nosed approach that calls for a new social contract, a return to fiscal responsibility, an end to corporate welfare, tax reform to enable more Americans to accumulate wealth, a new strategy for the "War on Terror," and energy practices that will halve the nation's dependence on Middle East oil within ten years. Thus the Emanuel and Reed "Plan" proposes – among other things – universal citizen service, universal college access, universal retirement savings, universal children's health care, middle-class tax relief, strict military procurement oversight, and government support for high-speed railroads, for universal broadband, and for a national institute for science and engineering.

The Bottom Line

Books such as these, as a sample of many that point to difficulties in modern life, highlight problems that may be worth debating and perhaps even resolving in line with what liberals prescribe. However, my aim here is not to judge the quality of liberal research and analysis but to understand the storytelling gap. To that end, it seems clear that *the liberal books we have just considered promote no shared vision of how to arrange and maintain public life.* Rather, they define, illuminate, analyze, and prescribe remedies for particular social, political, economic, and environmental situations which they regard as problems. In fact, they explore so many "problems" – by which they mean mainly what I called "puzzles" in Chapter 1 – that there is a sense in which liberals typically and continually complain about an endless variety of difficulties and dangers in modern life.[2]

Now, liberal books may suggest, here and there, the contours of a story about post-World War II America, which explains that many of the problems they regard as paramount arose together after World War II and could have been averted. For example, Jonathan Chait claims that from approximately 1948 to 1973, "democratic capitalism" promoted equality and prosperity, both of which were denied after that to people of small to middling income by "supercapitalism," according to Robert Reich. Consequently, between the insights of Chait, Reich, and many other liberals, there exists a potential morality tale about the multitude being buffeted by plutocrats and large forces, and about using government as a

---

[2] Conservatives also complain endlessly. The difference between left and right on this score is that liberals grumble about so many things that, as *Claremont Review* editor Charles Kesler implies (Kesler, *I am the Change: Barack Obama and the Crisis of Liberalism* 2012), and as we shall see in Chapter 8, one might regard them as complaining for the sake of complaining. Whereas when conservatives complain, they insist that America's great problems, from abortion to divorce to poverty to low SAT scores to drugs to lack of patriotism, flow from ignoring the lessons of right-wing alpha stories – as if government is too big and intrusive, as if citizens spurn the great values they inherit from their forebears, and as if profitable inventions will eliminate dangerous consequences such as climate change, which liberals attribute to market-oriented behavior in the first place.

democratic instrument to promote conditions, more equally distributed than today, which better the lives of ordinary people.[3]

Yes, the potential for such a tale exists. However – and here is the cardinal point – the tale itself does not quite crystallize among liberals as a shared source of inspiration. That is, it does not appear as an alpha story. Later, I will consider why liberals address many different problems and recommend many different solutions to them. For now, the political reality is simply this: liberal books link neither their subjects nor their policy proposals to a common storyline.[4] Some liberal authors tell large and commanding stories, such as when Galbraith describes the imbalance between sellers and buyers in an affluent society, or when Frank insists that many Kansas Republicans vote against their material interests, or when Wolf says that women must unite to overcome the "beauty myth" in order to achieve emotional health. However, the stories they tell separately don't add up to one – or even a few – tales that resonate across the land.

The List Syndrome

Furthermore, almost as a default setting, this failure to add up generates what may be called a "list syndrome." It appears when liberal politicians like Hart, Rahm, Reed, and Kerry, and later (as we shall see) Barack Obama string together one policy proposal after another (there are the lists) rather than organize those proposals around short and powerful statements, repeated endlessly, about what such proposals represent together and why they should be adopted.

---

[3] For example, see Sheldon Wolin, *Democracy Inc.: Managed Democracy and the Specter of Inverted Totalitarianism* (2010), p. 260, where he argues that:

> [D]emocracy is about the conditions that make it possible for ordinary people to better their lives by becoming political beings and by making power responsive to their hopes and needs … Democracy is not about bowling together but about managing together those powers that immediately and significantly affect the lives and circumstances of others and one's self.

[4] Many liberal politicians are in the same boat. Thus Senator John F. Kennedy identified himself in 1960 as a liberal in typically vague terms:

> What do our opponents mean when they apply to us the label, "Liberal?" … [If] by a "Liberal," they mean someone who looks ahead and not behind, someone who welcomes new ideas without rigid reactions, someone who cares about the welfare of the people – their health, their housing, their schools, their jobs, their civil rights, and their civil liberties – someone who believes that we can break through the stalemate and suspicions that grip us in our policies abroad, if that is what they mean by a "Liberal," then I'm proud to say that I'm a "Liberal."

See Kennedy, "Acceptance of Party Nomination."

I will return to the liberal list syndrome in Chapter 8. Meanwhile, we should keep in mind how Charles Schumer rues the liberal failure to cohere. As Schumer points out, what liberals say is not simple and memorable enough to appear on bumper stickers. Or, in our terms, the things they say are not sufficiently coherent and persistent to achieve the status of alpha stories, and thus do not come to be widely regarded as the quintessential liberal narrative or narratives.

Schumer acknowledges that he cannot solve this problem. What he does subsequently, however, is to fall into the list syndrome. Thus, after providing no liberal bumper sticker, he offers in *Positively America* twelve chapters of suggestions for enacting new government programs and fixing old ones in fields ranging from property taxes to energy independence, higher education to abortion rights, and immigration to child obesity. In which case – and here is the bottom line – the liberal camp's image problem, and the political handicap which it imposes on that camp's candidates, remain.

3

Philosophical Impotence

> Philosophers have hitherto only interpreted the world in various ways; the
> point is to change it.
>
> *Karl Marx, Theses on Feuerbach (1888)*

But why do liberal politicians tend to list remedies, rather than rally
around inspiring stories of shared principles which explain why they recommend taking steps that seem to them necessary? In fact, the storytelling gap today starts in philosophy, because liberal philosophers do not
fashion for other liberals the interlocking concepts they need to justify
activism. Consequently, those other liberals – including scholars, publicists, and politicians – lack common "truths" around which they might
rally, rhetorically, over time.

This claim requires a caveat. I am about to show how liberal philosophers do not create materials for a common liberal narrative. This does
not mean, however, that philosophers on the Left are failing to do something that philosophers on the Right manage quite well. Rather, as I shall
discuss in a moment, liberals are strong in academia. In that world, consistency is hard to maintain, because university work encourages many
professors – and especially social scientists and humanists, who include
philosophers – to maintain a constantly moving conversation, one "paradigm" after another, whereby scholars get ahead by offering new ideas
and rejecting those already in place.

Conservative Philosophers

But this is exactly what most conservative philosophers *don't* do. Instead,
they interpret and refine stories which appeared in Western society before

them and will live on there after them. For example, while many liberals criticized laissez-faire "capitalism," conservative thinkers after World War II switched to speaking of "free markets." Later, in the 1980s, conservatives like Jude Wanniski and George Gilder promoted the notion of "supply side economics" in praise of such markets.[1] Capitalism; free markets; supply-side economics: it is really all the same tale.

In Chapter 5, I will further explore the fact that conservative philosophers tend to tell old stories in updated versions. Meanwhile, we should note that the stories conservative philosophers tell – unlike the successive paradigms fashioned by liberal philosophers – tend to remain on target. One reason for this is that these stories are touted from outside of academia by people who have something to gain from perpetuating the same stories. For example, the story of a Judeo-Christian tradition as essential to America comes from theology, and there are religious leaders who want to promote this story to maintain whatever power and status they presently enjoy. In addition, the story of "free" markets as natural, fair, and perpetual is a notion promoted by business people for whom this idea constitutes a shared and self-serving "ideology," as defined by sociologist Karl Mannheim.[2] In recent years, variations on this theme include "conscious capitalism" promoted by John Mackey of Whole Foods and "philanthrocapitalism" promoted by Bill Gates of Microsoft.[3]

The Empirical Temptation

On the other hand, liberals are stymied. By research standards acceptable to themselves, modern liberal philosophers cannot validate the crucial American precept that is postulated as "self-evident" in the 1776 Declaration of Independence.[4] What the Declaration says – in a great

[1] Supply-side economics is advocated in Jude Wanniski, *The Way the World Works* (1978) – which was praised by Irving Kristol as "The best economic primer since Adam Smith" – and in George Gilder, *Wealth and Poverty* (1981), pp. 28–46 – which David Stockman described as "Promethean in its intellectual power and insight."

[2] See Karl Mannheim, *Ideology and Utopia: An Introduction to the Sociology of Knowledge* (1936, 1955), pp. 108–146. For discussion of how the business world provides new interpretations of long-running conservative stories, see Bethany Moreton, *To Serve God and Wal-Mart: The Making of Christian Free Enterprise* (2009), especially pp. 270–271 (of course, Moreton does not use the term "alpha stories"). For more on how business interests promote the marketplace story, see Kim Phillips-Fein, *Invisible Hands: The Businessmen's Crusade Against the New Deal* (2009), and Colin Crouch, *The Strange Non-Death of Neoliberalism* (2011).

[3] Nicole Aschoff, *The New Prophets of Capital* (2015), pp. 42, 109.

[4] See Edward Purcell, *The Crisis of Democratic Theory: Scientific Naturalism and the Problem of Value* (1973).

Enlightenment story of trial, tribulation, and triumph – is that political and civil rights for all men should be equal and inalienable. The country has not always lived up to that ideal. But falling short of it is not – for liberal thinkers, at least – an insurmountable problem. They can always say, for example on issues of race and gender, that Americans have made considerable progress and will probably make more in the future. This was the message on racial tolerance of Barack Obama's great eulogy for Reverend Clementa Pinckney at Emanuel African Methodist Episcopal Church in Charleston, South Carolina on June 28, 2015.[5]

However, aside from America's occasional failures to allocate rights properly, the deeper and philosophical difficulty for liberals is that the Declaration depends on "natural law" notions of morality.[6] That is what Jefferson had in mind when he wrote into the Declaration – and when the Continental Congress affirmed on July 4, 1776 – that "We hold these truths to be self-evident, that all men are created equal, with certain inalienable [natural] rights." We think today of this claim as anchored in a notion of divine order that is immune to change. That is, we view natural rights as ultimately rooted in theological, rather than scientific, justifications.[7] Yet "proof" in the Age of Science typically requires empirical evidence.[8] Consequently, because they have no proof in the modern sense for God's benevolent creativity, liberals tend to abandon their own natural rights story and its adjuncts.[9]

---

[5] See also Richard Rorty, *Achieving our Country* (1998), pp. 106–107. Rorty notes that, around 1900, few people "would have predicted the Progressive Movement, the forty-hour week, Women's Suffrage, the New Deal, the Civil Rights Movement, the successes of second-wave feminism, or the Gay Rights Movement." From this he infers (p. 101) that "You have to be loyal to a dream country rather than to the one to which you wake up every morning."

[6] On this natural law theme, see Carl Becker, *The Declaration of Independence: A Study in the History of Ideas* (1922), and Carl Becker, *The Heavenly City of the 18th Century Philosophers* (1932).

[7] Alternatively one can argue that many of the Founders were deists who believed, approximately, that natural rights were revealed by science (distilled common sense) rather than theology (metaphysics and revelation). Along these lines, see Matthew Stewart, *Nature's God: The Heretical Origins of the American Republic* (2014).

[8] For a classic example, see Galileo Galilei, *Dialogue Concerning the Two Chief World Systems, Ptolemaic & Copernican*, (1632, 1967). On the scientific demand for evidence rather than authority, Salviati tells Simplicio (p. 113): "So put forward the arguments and demonstrations, Simplicio – either yours or Aristotle's – but not just texts and bare authorities, because our discourses must relate to the sensible world and not one on paper."

[9] I am overstating my thesis on empiricism here because some scholars, and especially psychologists and economists, follow a line of reasoning based not on "facts" but on speculations known as "thought experiments." These are usually introduced with phrases such as

Examples of this preference for empiricism abound among modern scholars. Thus economist Joseph Schumpeter, on behalf of "realistic" economic and political analysis, rejected the greatest of liberal stories, which he called "the classic doctrine of democracy."[10] This doctrine was based on faith in popular sovereignty, reasonable voters, and policy mandates arising from preferences expressed by many ordinary citizens. Against this democratic ideal, Schumpeter argued that, according to studies of actual human behavior, real-life voters do not so much *instruct* politicians as they are *forced to choose* between competing candidates drawn from rival elites. Furthermore, once elite candidates are elected, they may feel free to follow their own instincts rather than those of the public.

Moreover, on behalf of what they regard as historical accuracy, historian James Kloppenberg, political scientist Rogers Smith, and various other academics reject Louis Hartz's inspiring story, as told in *The Liberal Tradition in America* (1955), of America being born free and unencumbered by Europe's unequal classes and antagonistic groups.[11] Accordingly, rather than praising an American cup they see as half full, they tend to worry about the empty half, focus attention on it, and highlight continuing inequalities – sometimes entrenched by law – in realms concerning difference, identity, and gender.[12]

The downside to such cases is that, on behalf of solid research and sound scholarship, many diligent academics and their disciples have taken lately to slighting or denying basic elements of America's collective

---

"suppose that you were," or "let's imagine a society in which," or "if we could divide the workforce into," or "all other things being equal," or "imagine that you and an accomplice ..." This sort of scholarship has influenced government activity in various areas of life, such as national defense, fiscal policy, and central banking. A recent example of such scholarship relates to what is called "the ticking bomb problem." On how this concept has inspired military interrogation practices such as waterboarding, see Sanford Levinson (ed.), *Torture: A Collection* (2004), especially pp. 31–33 and pp.191–195.

[10] Joseph Schumpeter, *Capitalism, Socialism, and Democracy* (1950), pp. 250–268. Having abandoned the popular and inspiring vision of modern democracy, Schumpeter (p. 243) admonishes his readers: "To realize the relative [uncertain] validity of one's convictions and yet stand for them unflinchingly [despite their tentativity] is what distinguishes a civilized man from a barbarian."

[11] I am emphasizing Hartz's optimism on this point rather than his gloomy sense that the liberal tradition in America occasionally expresses – as during the Palmer raids and McCarthyism – violent hostility to people who challenge conventional thinking.

[12] See Rogers Smith, "Beyond Tocqueville, Myrdal, and Hartz: The Multiple Traditions in America," *American Political Science Review* (September, 1993), pp. 549–566, and James Kloppenberg, "In Retrospect: Louis Hartz's *The Liberal Tradition in America*," *Reviews in American History* (September, 2001), pp. 460–476.

image of itself as an admirable and "exceptional" nation.[13] This especially annoys conservatives,[14] whose case against skepticism and diffidence as scholarly default settings is, perhaps inadvertently, buttressed by historian Daniel Rodgers. As Rodgers explains in *Age of Fracture* (2011), scholars in disciplines such as economics, political science, history, and philosophy have lately described America in terms that leave modern society with no persuasive vocabulary for talking about common sentiments, collective institutions, national solidarity, shared problems, and sensible solutions. For example, Kenneth Arrow's "Impossibility Theorem" of social choice claims that individual preferences cannot be combined, via voting, to express a ranked list of optimal preferences.[15] But if the theorem really describes what happens in democratic politics, it challenges the longstanding notion that American elections produce popular mandates and are therefore commendable for peacefully signaling to Washington what voters want.[16]

Philosophers

Within this broad context, and while unwilling to enlist the support of great narratives, liberal philosophers try to convince readers that "social democracy" – in the common expression – is the best regime. Their usual

---

[13] For example, Benjamin Ginsberg, *The American Lie: Government by the People and Other Political Fables* (2007). Trying to repair some of the damage to democratic faith are political scientists who celebrate the concept of "rational voting" according to which, in some versions, voters in the next election will deliberately reject leaders who disappoint us today. For example, see Morris Fiorina, *Retrospective Voting in American National Elections* (1981); Benjamin Page and Robert Shapiro, *The Rational Public: Fifty Years of Trends in Americans' Policy Preferences* (1992); and Samuel Popkin, *The Reasoning Voter: Communication and Persuasion in Presidential Campaigns* (1994). Larry Bartels, "The Irrational Electorate," *The Wilson Quarterly* (Autumn, 2008), pp. 44–50, is pessimistic about voter competence.

[14] For example, James Connelly, *The Modern Liberal Jungle: A Guide for Americans* (2012), p. 38: "Modern Liberals tell people that an intelligent person, a person with an open mind, rejects American culture and traditions. In addition, if a person is intelligent and sophisticated, according to Modern Liberals, he will scoff at patriotism and displays of flag-waving. Modern Liberals reject that America is exceptional."

[15] This theorem appears in Kenneth Arrow, *Social Choice and Individual Values* (1963), pp. 22–33. It is based on a "thought experiment," as discussed in footnote 9 in this chapter.

[16] For example, Daniel Rodgers, *Age of Fracture* (2011), p. 86, describes social choice theorizing about the behavior of individuals in works by James Buchanan and William Riker: "Under the weight of these analyses the idea of governance as an expression of the public good all but evaporated."

strategy is to use logic and verbal precision to encourage Americans to draw moderate political conclusions from "values" which, since the Enlightenment, are no longer a part of God's plan. That such philosophers believe that modern people are capable of discovering these values and acting accordingly is a reflection of "humanism," to which we will return in Chapter 4.

The Protagonists

In the academy, leading philosophical works are intensively debated in complex professional conversations. Some of these revolve around works by exceptional minds.[17] But space here permits only brief consideration of some books written by five celebrated American philosophers – John Rawls, Amartya Sen, Michael Walzer, Richard Rorty, and Ronald Dworkin – who are commonly regarded as liberals. In these books, apart from others by the same authors but too numerous to mention now, we can sense something of where these liberals and their colleagues stand, as a class, vis-à-vis the liberal political predicament.[18]

John Rawls

In *A Theory of Justice* (1971), John Rawls proposes that justice is "the first virtue of social systems." Rawls defines this justice as a matter of "fairness," where citizens will know what fairness means if they will consider,

---

[17] Amartya Sen, winner of the Nobel Prize for economics, read for Harvard University Press the manuscript of *A Theory of Justice*, which John Rawls submitted for possible publication. Later, he commented that it evoked in him the feeling that Wordsworth famously expressed about the French Revolution: "Bliss was it in that dawn to be alive,/ But to be young was very heaven!" Political scientist Douglas Rae was similarly impressed. See his "Maximum Justice and an Alternative Principle of General Advantage," *American Political Science Review* (June, 1975), p. 630: "[*A Theory of Justice* is] perhaps the bravest work of political theory written in this country since the times of Madison and Calhoun."

[18] All five of these philosophers have changed their minds and recommendations from one publication to another. Therefore, if I were to describe the full spectrum of each man's writings, I could conclude that his views varied from time to time, in which case his teachings suffered from inconsistency. But that is not the point I wish to make here. Instead, I will consider only some major works and show how the ideas expressed in those works so clash from one author to another that one cannot build upon them a *shared* liberal narrative. For example, I will explore the most famous precepts of John Rawls, as expressed in *A Theory of Justice* (1971). But I will not linger on Rawls to explain how, from emphasizing "the right" (philosophical) in that first book he later supported "the good" (practical) in Rawls, *Political Liberalism* (2005). Thus *Political Liberalism* exalted "political reason" as the cardinal democratic virtue rather than, as in *A Theory of Justice*, the very different principle of "fairness." In which case – oddly enough – Rawls did not share a narrative with himself, much less than with his liberal colleagues.

as a thought experiment, what they would do as intelligent people confronted with an imaginary situation that Rawls labels "the original position." In the original position, while ignorant of "the outcome of natural
chance or the contingency of social circumstances" which might appear
later in their lives, and while intent on not accidently giving advantage to
anyone else, rational individuals would accept "equality as defining the
fundamental terms of their association."[19]

Once the validity of this basic principle has been evoked by logical
consideration of the original position, says Rawls, additional principles
can be discovered via what many social scientists, especially economists,
call a process of "rational choice."[20] What this means is that, while fitting
moral ends to available means by a series of sensible calculations, the citizens of a well-ordered society, seeking to incorporate into its democratic
institutions the notion of justice as fairness, will proceed to agree on two
extensions of the same notion. The first requires that laws will be enacted
to assure that "the basic liberties of citizens" will be equal in the realms
of politics, conscience, free thought, and due process according to law.[21]
The second, which Rawls calls "the difference principle," stipulates that,
in a properly democratic state, inequalities – that is, differences in social
and economic circumstances – are morally permissible only if they will,
like progressive taxation, contribute to everyone's advantage.

Amartya Sen

In *The Idea of Justice* (2009), Amartya Sen claims that John Rawls so
emphasized abstract principles that he neglected matters flowing from
actual choices that individuals and societies must make. Sen agrees with
Rawls that original, or "transcendental," principles of equality should
be embodied in political institutions. But he adds that one must assure
that justice will emerge from those institutions in the form of reasonable
"results."[22] Such results can be achieved, he says, by enabling citizens to
make decisions according to the "theory of social choice."[23] This theory
calls for "basing our choices – explicitly or by implication – on ... close
reasoning (with adequate reflection and, when necessary, dialogue with

---

[19] Rawls, *A Theory of Justice* (1971), pp. 3–13.
[20] *Ibid.*, pp. 16–17.
[21] *Ibid.*, p. 61.
[22] Amartya Sen, *The Idea of Justice* (2011). The distinction between these two approaches
to justice appears first at pp. 5–8. It is later extended repeatedly.
[23] *Ibid.*, pp. 82–86.

others), taking note of more information if and when it is relevant and accessible."[24]

Extending this line of thought, Sen explains that social choice theory, which aims at achieving rational decisions, insists that "pluralist" considerations – based on many possibilities and perceptions – should inform the decisions which real people make. This means that they must look beyond a few "original principles" and take into account, among other considerations, the complex constellation of what Sen calls "unbiased principles."[25] On this score, he suggests that in any society there will exist a spectrum of sound but incompatible arguments for pursuing satisfactory courses of action or inaction. Here is a plurality of considerations. These flow, he says, from various needs, assumptions, commitments, and interests, which become food for thought when people and institutions ponder which public policies will lead to good results. Here is another plurality. For example, he points out that people belong to various groups in which they absorb, and therefore sincerely espouse, different concepts of what government should properly do under specific circumstances.[26]

Going still further, Sen observes that Rawls recommends the fair distribution of means to acquire "primary goods." Consequently, in any particular society, the degree of existing equality can be measured largely in terms of how much it costs to buy those goods.[27] The necessary money should reach everyone more or less equally. To supplement this emphasis, however, Sen asks us to consider the question: "Equality for what?"[28] That is, what will real people actually do with the fairly equal means, or resources, that Rawls recommends providing for them?

Sen's answer is that where individuals are differentially "capable" of using their means, the results for some individuals may be less just than they deserve. He then lists four "contingencies" that may lead people to "convert" their income into lives that are more or less desirable. These four include personal differences (such as age, health, and gender), environmental variances (such as climate, the quality of air, and residential location), social differences (such as access to public health care, public education, and crime-free neighborhoods), and what Sen calls "differences

[24] *Ibid.*, p. 180.
[25] *Ibid.*, p. 57 and pp. 239–243.
[26] *Ibid.*, pp. 119–122.
[27] *Ibid.*, pp. 253–254.
[28] *Ibid.*, p. 293.

in relational perspectives" (such as needing more income to keep up with the Joneses in a rich rather than poor country).[29]

The bottom line for Sen is that, rather than recommend only that a just state will maintain basic purchasing power via the right sort of democratic and economic procedures and institutions, he favors government that is committed to constantly tracking the "capabilities" of citizens and sometimes revising the existing distribution of resources so that everyone, no matter what their circumstances, will be equipped to confront his or her opportunities effectively and successfully.

Michael Walzer

In *Spheres of Justice: A Defense of Pluralism and Equality* (1983), Michael Walzer explores what he calls "distributive justice," by which he means who *actually* gets what and why, and also who *should* get what and why. It is a project that takes Walzer deeply into everyday life, because the "what" in this formulation – that is, the things that get distributed – includes a wide range of goods, services, statuses, offices, and memberships. And those can be distributed on many grounds, such as competence, birth and blood, friendship, need, merit, free exchange, political loyalty, and democratic decision.[30] Most importantly, Walzer insists that standards defining distributive justice vary from one realm of goods to another. For example, no one should rise among the clergy without enjoying some competence in theology, and no one should be appointed a military commander without demonstrating some competence at making war.

From such considerations, two implications flow. The first is that a just state cannot rest on first principles. That is, we cannot obey a fixed set of axioms when confronting practical questions of distribution, because the appropriate standards for that distribution vary from one realm of goods to another.[31] One can talk, like Rawls, about unswerving principles that should determine which rights and institutions citizens will possess. But, as Walzer points out, many issues, such as who should be granted citizenship – poor migrants? refugees? guest workers? Werner von Braun? – can be discussed only on the practical basis of what existing citizens, who succeed one another over time, want their community to look like.[32]

[29] *Ibid.*, p. 255.
[30] Michael Walzer, *Spheres of Justice* (1983), p. 4.
[31] *Ibid.*, p. 10.
[32] *Ibid.*, pp. 31–63.

The second implication of plural realms is that money can sometimes override the normal operation of standards appropriate to distributive justice in various realms. That is, "money talks," and it can help people to buy their way to rank, status, and success in some realms – even though the same people are not, despite the money they possess, morally fit to acquire those goods in such realms. It is for this reason that Walzer writes about "blocked exchanges," which he believes should prevent an unjust "dominance of wealth."[33] Laws authorizing blockage should bar the purchase or sale of people, political power, criminal justice, free speech or religion, marriage and procreation rights, emigration, exemptions from military service or jury duty, honors such as Pulitzer or Nobel prizes, and so forth.

More than Rawls and Sen, Walzer buttresses his pro-justice arguments with real-life stories about Greek cities, medieval towns, secular vacations, "robber barons," Israeli kibbutzim, Chinese mandarins, Plato's guardians, Stakhanovite workers, and more. The point, as Walzer says, is to stand not outside but inside Plato's cave,[34] constantly in touch with actual societies, using powerful examples of life in them to clarify philosophical points about politics in general.

Nevertheless, for all of Walzer's storytelling, *Spheres of Justice* does not tell one all-encompassing story. That is not surprising, because the book's tales refer to "spheres" (that is, realms) whose standards do not necessarily match those of other "spheres" and do not flow from an overall, consistent ideal of the good life. Thus democracy, for Walzer, is like an ongoing discussion among passengers of a boat who, as their circumstances and aspirations change over time, debate among themselves where the boat should go and how it should get there.[35]

Richard Rorty

In *Philosophy and the Mirror of Nature* (1979), Richard Rorty observes that many philosophers – such as Plato, Aristotle, Descartes, Locke, Rousseau, Kant, and Hegel – have assumed that our minds are like a mirror, and that what we know in them accurately reflects the world "out there."[36] Rorty suggests instead – in line with insights borrowed from Wittgenstein, Dewey, and Heidegger – that our mental

---

[33] *Ibid.*, pp. 100–103.
[34] *Ibid.*, p. xiv.
[35] *Ibid.*, pp. 286–287, p. 304.
[36] Richard Rorty, *Philosophy and the Mirror of Nature* (1979), pp. 3–13.

perceptions do not correspond to "reality" but rather reflect "language games" which change occasionally,[37] say from the days of Ptolemy to those of Copernicus, Newton, and Einstein. In current terms, Rorty suggests that these successive "games" frame what Thomas Kuhn, in *The Structure of Scientific Revolutions* (1962), called "paradigms."[38] Within these paradigms, philosophers over time do not search for some basic sort of reality that is "out there," but rather, via occasional new paradigms, leave old puzzles behind and raise questions they had not asked before.

In all of this, Rorty argues that "epistemology" is a search for shared ground among philosophical paradigms – as if we can create rules for a continuing investigation, paradigm after paradigm, whereby practitioners may hope to achieve common understandings of what they are exploring. Instead of epistemology, Rorty recommends "hermeneutics," whereby the philosophical conversation moves from one paradigm to another while the main objective is to keep the conversation going in order to achieve humanistic "edification" rather than scientific "knowledge."[39]

The bottom line here, according to Rorty, is that what we regard as knowledge, including the discoveries of science, flows from a succession of incommensurable paradigms where no one paradigm, not even those in science, has access to "the truth."[40] But if people cannot discover what is true, how can modern liberals "reason" their way to creating and maintaining a society that is truly just?

Rorty addresses this question in *Contingency, Irony, and Solidarity* (1989). There, he insists that what we "know" cannot grasp "reality" directly because what we think we know flows from the language we use to think, which itself emerges from historical and social circumstances. There is the "contingency."[41] That being the case, liberal citizens must abandon the Enlightenment conviction that we can reason our way to a "better" life based on timeless truths already or yet to be discovered. We must instead concede that the best we can hope for is a dialectical series of poetical and metaphorical descriptions of heartfelt sentiments. Over time, these will impel us as friends and neighbors to increasingly favor sympathizing with other citizens and their needs – a sort of "do unto others as you would have them do unto you" creed. There is the

---

[37] *Ibid.*, pp. 34–39.
[38] *Ibid.*, p. 263.
[39] *Ibid.*, pp. 315–394.
[40] *Ibid.*, pp. 357–365.
[41] Richard Rorty, *Contingency, Irony, and Solidarity* (1989), pp. 3–22.

"solidarity."[42] That we will commit ourselves to such a decent course is paradoxical because we must do so despite being aware that what we know is not, strictly speaking, "true." There is the "irony."[43]

Ronald Dworkin

Ronald Dworkin's *Justice for Hedgehogs* appeared in 2011. Without explicitly engaging Walzer, it denies his claim that moral principles may legitimately vary from one "sphere" of life to another. Moreover, it explicitly rejects Rorty's skepticism, due to "contingencies" of time, place, and circumstances, about our ability to discover fixed moral standards.[44] Dworkin argues instead that there is a "unity of value" which we can ascertain, that "ethical and moral values depend on one another," and that this large "philosophical thesis" is the "one big thing" that a "hedgehog" like Dworkin knows.[45]

Dworkin traces his claim about an underlying unity of values to David Hume's great philosophical insight that, no matter how many facts we may collect via science, they cannot tell us definitively how to behave. Dworkin agrees that this "is/ought" distinction is valid. He adds, though, that it should not be used to justify "skepticism about moral truth."[46] Instead, Hume should be regarded as revealing that the "domains" of science and morals are two separate realms,[47] wherein we can establish "objective truths about values"[48] not by empirical evidence in the first realm but by "adequate" moral arguments in the second.[49]

There are political implications to all of this. Accordingly, what Dworkin calls "legitimate government" must, as a matter of moral principles, dispense "justice" in two senses. The first requires rulers to show "equal concern" for all their country's citizens, and the second requires the same rulers to "fully respect" the right of each citizen to "make something valuable" of his or her life.[50] The question is, though, how to decide in a large and diverse society such as America exactly what such general injunctions require of us in specific circumstances. After all, "equal

---

[42] *Ibid.*, p. xvi, pp. 189–198.
[43] *Ibid.*, pp. 73–95.
[44] Ronald Dworkin, *Justice for Hedgehogs* (2011), pp. 59–63.
[45] *Ibid.*, p. 1. The reference is to the stolid hedgehog who knows one big thing and the clever fox who is fascinated by various things.
[46] *Ibid.*, p. 17.
[47] *Ibid.*, p. 41.
[48] *Ibid.*, p. 7.
[49] *Ibid.*, p. 37.
[50] *Ibid.*, pp. 2–4.

concern," "full respect," and many other decencies are contested notions among people who, via democratic institutions, aspire to achieve various ends and promote a wide array of public policies.[51]

To answer the question about general injunctions, Dworkin insists that in the moral domain "arguments" rather than "evidence" are decisive.[52] He does not explain exactly how to make such arguments, since they do not involve weighing tangible data systematically. But he suggests that they are a matter of "interpretation," of somehow judging means and ends, of seeing the world more like it is seen by poets and novelists than by biologists and astronomers.[53]

If constructed properly, says Dworkin, these arguments have the power to resolve many contradictions between various moral preferences that people express today.[54] Therefore the goal is that such arguments, when conducted with the help of philosophers who will clarify terms and choices,[55] will create a "network of value," which by overcoming moral contradictions will furnish Americans with a shared basis for belief about how to elect and maintain a government committed to human "dignity."[56]

Shortcomings

In an orderly intellectual world, philosophers such as these would provide for politically engaged liberals a conceptual call to arms, as John Stuart Mill did with his *On Liberty* in 1859.[57] To that end, they would fashion points of fact and principle around which their activist compatriots might rally in public life. But liberal philosophers as a class don't do that, and we can attribute their failure in this respect to, among other things, certain shortcomings in what they write.[58] To draw attention to

---

[51] On this point, on pp. 118–120 Dworkin offers the example of an occasional disparity between the ideals of kindness and honesty. His example is, in effect, an update of the Talmudic question of what a guest should say at a wedding where the bride is ugly. Should he say she is beautiful (kindness) or should he describe her accurately (truthfulness)? See *Babylonian Talmud*, Ketubot, 17a.

[52] Dworkin, *Justice for Hedgehogs*, p. 82, p. 116.

[53] On interpretation, see *ibid.*, pp. 123–188.

[54] *Ibid.*, p. 331.

[55] *Ibid.*, pp. 370–371, pp. 378–379.

[56] Dworkin uses the term "dignity" to refer to the principles of equal concern and full respect that he posits as characterizing "legitimate government." On dignity, see *ibid.*, pp. 192–218, pp. 255–270.

[57] For example, John Stuart Mill's concept of a marketplace for ideas still inspires Al Gore, *The Assault on Reason* (2007), especially pp. 11–13.

[58] Some of these shortcomings are described in Benjamin Barber, *The Conquest of Politics: Liberal Philosophy in Democratic Times* (1988), pp. 3–21.

such shortcomings is not to charge that they are defects – as if, say, liberal philosophers have failed to assess the world accurately. It is simply to observe that some aspects of the philosophical texts I have discussed can help us to understand why philosophers do not provide the liberal political camp with a steady flow of conceptual consistency, which that camp lacks.[59]

Jargon

First, there is the issue of clarity. I translated into plain English much of what appears above. I did that because many of the original texts are incomprehensible to ordinary men and women. Michael Walzer, who edited *Dissent* magazine for many years, has always avoided jargon. But most readers will not understand, for example, what a liberal philosopher like Richard Rorty means when he writes:

That special sort of subject of predication whose appearance *is* its reality – phenomenal pain – turns out to be simply the painfulness of the pain abstracted from the person having the pain. It is, in short, the universal *painfulness* itself. To put it oxymoronically, mental particulars, unlike mental states of people, turn out to be universals.[60]

Let us be fair. Such statements are grammatically correct. And they march across page after page of recent philosophy logically and precisely. But the result is a verbal density from which voters can take little inspiration or guidance. Historian Henry Commager reminds us that the Founders wrote prose – for example, in *The Federalist* (1788) – that most Americans could easily comprehend.[61] But today, even academics like me, from nearby fields, can barely understand works by many liberal philosophers, who write mainly for one another.[62]

---

[59] The proof of the pudding appears in books like James Young, *Reconsidering American Liberalism: The Troubled Odyssey of the Liberal Idea* (1996). Young analyzes the moral and political theories promoted by John Rawls, Sheldon Wolin, John Schaar, Michael Walzer, Michael Sandel, Richard Rorty, and many other liberal philosophers, all the while showing – unintentionally – that, in principle, they agree on very little.

[60] Rorty, *Philosophy and the Mirror of Nature*, p. 30.

[61] Henry Commager, *The Empire of Reason: How Europe Imagined and America Realized the Enlightenment* (1977), p. 130. For example, *The Federalist* (1788) consists of plain-spoken newspaper articles written by Alexander Hamilton, James Madison, and John Jay, in favor of ratifying the Constitution in New York. Because it is still intelligible to ordinary citizens, it can stimulate discussion of even modern public issues. Thus Sanford Levinson, *An Argument Open To All: Reading "The Federalist" in the Twenty-First Century* (2015).

[62] See Robert Bellah, Richard Madsen, William Sullivan, Ann Swidler, and Steven Tipton, *Habits of the Heart: Individualism and Commitment in American Life* (1986), pp. 297–307, on academic specialization and mutually incomprehensible disciplines.

There is nothing surprising about this difficulty. Books written by professors like Rawls, Sen, and the like reflect a problem of form that lurks on all modern campuses, because using jargon enhances professional status by making practitioners seem to know something that rank and file citizens do not. Thus a philosopher may split hairs until he or she has demonstrated, implicitly at least, that ordinary people, who use a popular and approximate vocabulary – for example, equating liberty and freedom, ethics and morals – must be misguided in their thinking about politics for not taking into account intricate distinctions that keep philosophers busy.

An element of verbal one-upmanship stands out here. It is more institutional than personal, because it extends across many disciplines populated by thousands of practitioners. The work of Amartya Sen is a case in point. In *The Idea of Justice*, Sen explores what he believes to be important differences between what he calls "membership entitlement" and "enlightenment relevance," between "reason" and "objectivity," between "closed impartiality" and "open impartiality," between "reasonableness" and "rationality," between "the opportunity aspect" and "the process aspect" of freedom, between "the institutionalization critique" and the "feasibility critique" of human rights, between the "culmination outcome" and the "comprehensive outcome" of opportunities, between "bounded willpower" and "insufficient self-command" in the realm of rationality, and between "comparative" and "transcendent" sorts of justice.[63]

While these distinctions are important to Sen, the problem is that very few people think, talk, or act politically in such terms.[64] Because

---

[63] Here is another example of the same density, in Dworkin, *Justice for Hedgehogs*, p. 122:

In science, if the physical world is as it is no matter whether there is any reason to think it is that way, we may be in irretrievable error. Our beliefs may be wrong in spite of the fact that we could find no evidence that they are wrong. We might be in fundamental and uncorrectable error about events in some other universe, for example, or about events so far away that their light cannot reach us before our universe expires. But because the truth about morality just is what the best case shows, our moral convictions cannot be irretrievably mistaken. Our culture or education or other factors of personal history may prevent us from appreciating the best case. But people with different personal histories might well discover and appreciate it. Moral truth is always within human grasp in a way that scientific truth may not always be.

From which an amateur reader might ask: Is what Dworkin says here true? Indeed, what exactly *is* he saying?

[64] Can ordinary Americans consult philosophers on matters of war and peace? Some Middle East militants use civilians as human shields. Is it ethical, in war, to assault such

that is so, most Americans, who might be impressed by the Founders, will learn little from the philosophical works of someone like Sen. To draw inspiration from his writings they would, like his students at Harvard University, first have to make great efforts to acquire his vocabulary.

Competition

Second, even when they are comprehensible, the propositions which liberal philosophers fashion are elaborated brilliantly but competitively. That is, each scholar builds for himself or herself a profitable academic niche.[65] As a result, most disagree among themselves and do not furnish common principles that can inspire consensus proposals for a liberal camp. One can move from Friedrich Hayek's *The Road to Serfdom* (1944), and Jerry Falwell's *Listen, America!* (1981), to the activism of Newt Gingrich, George W. Bush, Sarah Palin, and Paul Ryan. That is, one can move from compact conservative narratives to powerful right-wing campaigning. But the philosophical speculations of even John Rawls – sometimes regarded as the greatest liberal philosopher since John Stuart Mill[66] – are, as we have seen, not entirely accepted and amplified by his

fighters if doing so is likely, collaterally, to injure or kill civilians? Philosophers may analyze this situation in terms of "the trolley problem," which is a thought experiment in which, hypothetically, you can save five people from eventually getting run over by a trolley car if you will earlier derail the trolley by throwing a stout man under it first. The philosopher Francis Kamm says that relevant principles here include:

> ... the principle of alternate reason, the principle of contextual interaction, the principle of ethical integrity, the principle of instrumental rationality, the principle of irrelevant goods, the principle of irrelevant need, the principle of irrelevant rights, and the principle of Secondary Wrong ... [and] the principle of the Independence of Irrelevant Alternatives of Permissible Harm or the principle of Secondary Permissibility.

Kamm's terms appear in David Edmunds, *Would You Kill the Fat Man? The Trolley Problem and What Your Answer Tells Us about Right and Wrong* (2014), pp. 53–54. Can citizens keep these distinctions in mind when they consider how their soldiers should behave?

[65] We can see "niche building" when Sen (in *The Idea of Justice*) amends Rawls at length, when Dworkin (*Justice for Hedgehogs*, pp. 59–66) explicitly disagrees with Rorty and Rawls, and when Rawls (*A Theory of Justice*, pp. 35–40) politely dismisses "intuitionism" (using common sense to choose between competing moral principles), which is actually Walzer's strong point. On niche building as a social practice, see Pamela Popielarz and Zachery Neal, "The Niche as a Theoretical Tool," *Annual Review of Sociology* (August, 2007), pp. 65–84.

[66] For example, the philosophy of John Rawls enormously impressed political scientist Douglas Rae. See above, p.47, note 17, for his *A Theory of Justice*.

colleagues.[67] Therefore his work has not, and perhaps cannot, inspire liberal politicking.

Relativism

Third, while liberal philosophizing proceeds from reasoning (which is inherently contestable) rather than from stories (which believers regard as absolutely true), the same liberal philosophizing has no incontrovertible ethical anchor. Conservative critics who complain of this – such as Charles Colson, James Wilson, Dinesh D'Souza, Bill O'Reilly, and Daniel Flynn[68] – regard ethical tentativity, which they call "relativism," as a liberal weakness that cannot be repaired because, they say, as a class of thinkers liberals don't together believe firmly in anything.[69]

In a nutshell, the critics are correct.[70] Thus liberals like Robert Reich and Michael Sandel encourage us to believe – even when they cannot be certain about what to do and why in public life – that thinking things through and debating them can bring citizens closer to agreement. As Reich says, activists need passion and commitment to win political power, but "we [the liberals] have reason on our side."[71] And as Sandel says, there is no clear rule for allocating distributive justice, but "a just society involves reasoning together about the good life."[72]

In other words, in the Age of Science and empirical validation, liberals do not know exactly where they stand, together, on principles and goals. Therefore they recommend that we will "reason" our way to successful

---

[67] Prominent liberal critics included Brian Barry, *The Liberal Theory of Justice: A Critical Examination of the Doctrines in "A Theory of Justice" by John Rawls* (1973), Michael Sandel, *Liberalism and the Limits of Justice: A Critical Examination of the Principle Doctrines in "A Theory of Justice" by John Rawls* (1982), and Barber, *The Conquest of Politics* (1988).

[68] Charles Colson, *A Dance with Deception: Revealing the Truth Behind the Headlines* (1993); James Q. Wilson, *The Moral Sense* (1993); Dinesh D'Souza, *The End of Racism: Principles for a Multi-Racial Society* (1995); William O'Reilly, *No Spin Zone: Confrontations with the Powerful and Famous in America* (2001); Daniel Flynn, *Why the Left Hates America: Exposing the Lies That Have Obscured Our Nation's Greatness* (2004); and Dinesh D'Souza, *What's So Great About Christianity?* (2007).

[69] For example, Tammy Bruce, *The Death of Right and Wrong: Exposing the Left's Assault on our Culture and Values* (2003), p. 24: "Their [the Left's] values are that they have no values. Theirs is the standard of no standard."

[70] Liberals admit this. Thus Alan Brinkley, "Liberalism and Belief," in Neil Jumonville and Kevin Mattson (eds.), *Liberalism for a New Century* (2007), p. 75: "We live in an age of belief ... In this rush to certainty, liberalism quakes and at times collapses, its adherents unable and unwilling to embrace fundamental dogmas of their own and incapable of effectively challenging those who do."

[71] Robert Reich, *Reason: Why Liberals Will Win the Battle for America* (2005), p. 208.

[72] Michael Sandel, *Justice: What's The Right Thing to Do?* (2009), p. 261.

public policies and political programs, whatever those might be. Sen sharpens this point philosophically when he claims that "Reasoning is our ... ally ... The remedy for bad reasoning lies in better reasoning, and it is indeed the job of reasoned scrutiny to move from the former to the latter."[73] Yet, as conservatives observe, to recommend reasoning is not the same thing as telling us what conclusions this reasoning will produce.

Style

Fourth, much of liberal philosophy, even when it is intelligible to amateurs, is unexciting. Books like William Galston's *Liberal Purposes* (1991), and Stephen Macedo's *Liberal Virtues* (1991), do not arouse like William Buckley's *God and Man at Yale* (1951), or Barry Goldwater's *Conscience of a Conservative* (1960). Certainly they do not match the clarion salesmanship embodied in, say, Ronald Reagan's "First Inaugural Address" (1981).[74] In fact, liberal philosophy is not adequate emotionally; it does not touch what Lincoln called the "mystic chords of memory",[75] and it therefore cannot much inspire political practices.

By contrast, we should note the Tea Party's ability to galvanize Republican activists with striking propositions – right or wrong – about ruinous federal taxes, irresponsible federal deficits, runaway federal entitlements, tyrannical federal bureaucrats, and misguided federal bailouts.[76] Indeed, it is the power of Tea Party talk to occasionally trump liberal philosophy that provoked journalist E. J. Dionne to reject Tea Party views of the American Revolution and suggest an alternative and

---

[73] Sen, *The Idea of Justice*, pp. 46–49.

[74] Ronald Reagan, "First Inaugural Address," 1981.

[75] We saw in Chapter 1 that Ackerman, in *The Decline and Fall of the American Republic* (2010), exhorts readers to temper their admiration for the original Constitution and its Founders. Ackerman's advice expresses a sort of scholarly realism that encourages many academics to refrain from turning facts they discover into sweeping and politically relevant narratives. By contrast, see the fulsome praise for George Washington, William Livingston, Henry Lee, Thomas Jefferson, James Madison, and other Founders on display in conservative think tanker Myron Magnet, *The Founders at Home: Building America, 1735–1817* (2013).

[76] See former Congressman Richard Armey and Matt Kibbe, *Give Us Liberty: A Tea Party Manifesto* (2010); former Congressman Newt Gingrich, *To Save America: Stopping Obama's Secular – Socialist Machine* (2011); Congressman Rand Paul, *The Tea Party Goes to Washington* (2011); former Senator Jim Demint, *The Great American Awakening: Two Years that Changed America, Washington, and Me* (2011); and David Brody, *The Teavangelicals: The Inside Story of How the Evangelicals and the Tea Party are Taking Back America* (2012).

avowedly liberal view of American history.[77] We will return to Dionne's effort in Chapter 9.

Missing Politics

And finally, liberal philosophers have little to say about the great, blooming confusion of politics. Some of those philosophers may be known as "political theorists." But they are less interested in fashioning political yardsticks than they are in generating abstract precepts. Therefore they aim mainly at postulating basic principles, which once established may or may not enter into political conversations, thereby influencing people who are entitled to vote and/or make policy decisions.[78] The result is that liberal philosophers tend, as I wrote some years ago, to leave aside "the sticky and protracted issues of real political life, where strongly held goals clash and where some rank order or compromise must be made among them and the interests they generate."[79] It follows that, rather than discussing the hard choices which confront politicians – such as how to deal with nationalism, religion, ethnicity, identity, difference, environmental degradation, globalization, taxation, income disparities, and education – liberal philosophers often argue in favor of neutrality with regard to different ends pursued by various citizens.

Here is where, among some thinkers on the Left, "procedural liberalism" seems warranted.[80] It assumes that a certain set of institutions, rules, and rights, perhaps enshrined in a constitution, can enable citizens to compete against each other "correctly" and "fairly." Where such procedures exist, the results of political competition can be called democratic even though, in real-world politics, they might be judged disappointing.

---

[77] E. J. Dionne, *Our Divided Political Heart: The Battle for the American Idea in an Age of Discontent* (2012).

[78] Rawls, *A Theory of Justice*, p. 18, says that "The aim is to rule out those principles [of justice] that it would be rational to propose for acceptance ... only if one knew certain things [politically relevant knowledge] that are irrelevant from the standpoint of justice." In Book XV of *The Prince* (1515), with reference to Plato, Machiavelli deflated such philosophical speculations as follows:

[M]any have imagined republics and principalities which have never been seen or known to exist in reality; for how we live is so far removed from how we ought to live, that he who abandons what is done for what ought to be done, will rather learn to bring about his own ruin than his preservation.

[79] Ricci, "Epilogue on Political Theory," in *The Tragedy of Political Science*, pp. 319–323.

[80] On "procedural liberalism," see Michael Sandel, *Democracy's Discontent: America in Search of a Public Philosophy* (1996), "The Constitution of the Procedural Republic," pp. 3–119. See also the discussion of "pure procedural justice" in Rawls, *A Theory of Justice*, pp. 86–88.

Rawls sums up his philosophical preference for this apolitical stance when he says that he wants to pursue the "right" rather than the "good."[81] In everyday language, this means that he is more interested in principles than in compromises. The latter, which epitomize the endlessly tangled stuff of politics, must be set aside so that, in *A Theory of Justice*, Rawls can stipulate the simplifications – such as *ceteris paribus* – which permit him to fashion what he regards as a useful "theory."[82]

Walzer and Rorty say more about compromises than Rawls does. Walzer, in fact, is all about compromises. But he and Rorty offer no principled rule that would help decision-makers decide where, when, and how much to compromise. In fact, logically speaking, neither man *can* provide such a rule. This is because Walzer sees moral principles as differing legitimately from one public realm to another, while Rorty sees moral principles as determined by the "interpretive community" to which one belongs.[83] Rorty is quite open about this. Explicitly, he concedes that his sort of liberal philosophy is politically useless. He is, he says, an "ironist" and cannot believe otherwise. But, he notes, "I cannot ... claim that there could or ought to be a culture whose public rhetoric is *ironist*. I cannot imagine a culture which socializes its youth in such a way as to make them continually dubious about their own process of socialization. Irony seems inherently a private matter."[84]

The Gap Remains

Rorty, who died in 2007, regarded his work as a variant of pragmatism, to which we will return. He knew, admitted, and regretted that what he

---

[81] Rawls, *ibid.*, p. 31. See Robert Skidelsky and Edward Skidelsky, *How Much is Enough? Money and the Good Life* (2012). The Skidelskys criticize modern economics for, via men like Jeremy Bentham and William Stanley Jevons, reducing "good" (what is right) to "utility" (what is desired). Then they observe, on p. 92, that economics "no longer aspires to realize the Good [right] but only to create conditions in which people can realize 'the good' as they conceive it [which is utility]."

[82] Rawls, *A Theory of Justice*, p. 111.

[83] Rorty is reputed to have phrased this notion as "that is the way we do things around here." See him cited in Stephen Macedo, *Liberal Virtues: Citizenship, Virtue, and Community in Liberal Constitutionalism* (1990), p. 34, and Steven Lukes, *Liberals & Cannibals: The Implications of Diversity* (2003), p. 36.

[84] Rorty, *Contingency, Irony, and Solidarity*, p. 87. Wolfe, *The Future of Liberalism*, pp. 117–122, citing Reinhold Niebuhr and Richard Rorty, praises irony as a liberal virtue that challenged simplicity, zealotry, and ideology after World War II. But Wolfe probably does not have in mind the steady, corrosive irony that Rorty recommends in his unflinching philosophical works.

believed could not inspire democratic education and politics. But he also reminded us very eloquently of what liberals lack in this realm. Thus he declared:

Nothing would do more to resurrect the American Left than agreement on a concrete political platform, a People's Charter, a list of specific reforms. The existence of such a list – endlessly reprinted and debated, equally familiar to professors and production workers, imprinted on the memory both of professional people and of those who clean the professionals' toilets – might revitalize leftist politics.[85]

In sum, Rorty was a passionate citizen who admitted, in his own terms, that liberals acutely lack something similar to what I have called an "alpha story." It would have to reflect, he thought, a unifying platform – which he knew that he and other philosophers had not fashioned. Liberal politicians like Charles Schumer, familiar with electoral infighting, described for Democrats the missing commonality as a persuasive and shared set of ideas that would fit on bumper stickers. Schumer admitted, though, that liberal thinkers find those stickers difficult if not impossible to create. So let us now consider a deep explanation, entailing what Max Weber called "disenchantment" since the Enlightenment, for why that is the case.

[85] Rorty, *Achieving Our Country*, p. 99.

4

Weber's Disenchantment

Enlightenment is Man's leaving his self-caused immaturity.

Immaturity is the incapacity to use one's intelligence without the guidance of another ... *Sapere Aude!* [Dare to know!] Have the courage to use your own intelligence! is therefore the motto of the enlightenment.

Immanuel Kant, "What is Enlightenment?" (1784)

Much can be said about why liberals don't create the bumper stickers that Charles Schumer was looking for. We should start, however, by noting a fact that sometimes gets lost in partisan rhetoric today: *liberals are not politically retarded*. Some conservatives say or imply that they are.[1] But they really aren't. Thus many liberals know very well that they may fail in electoral politics because they don't have a clear and powerful story, told again and again, capable of uniting them and their principles.

For example, Paul Waldman insists that politics is about telling stories to frame people and issues. Then he observes that conservatives have an attractive master narrative, in which case "progressives" desperately need an "overarching story that tells us who progressives are and what they believe."[2] Todd Gitlin similarly calls attention to Newt Gingrich who, on behalf of Republicans, promotes a narrative whereby Americans from 1620 to 1965 prospered by individuals working hard and productively on private projects, whereupon the Great Society "messed everything up"

---

[1] For example, Michael Savage, *Liberalism is a Mental Disorder* (2005).
[2] Paul Waldman, *Being Right is Not Enough: What Progressives Must Learn from Conservative Success* (2006), pp. 139–167.

by funding government programs that encourage laziness, irresponsibility, and stagnation. Against the power of such a narrative, Gitlin recommends that liberals will tell voters an alternative story about how, during the course of American history, ever-widening circles of people (minorities and majorities), with occasional government help, have sought and found liberty and happiness by working together on public life – especially lately – in a "Big Tent" Democratic Party where rights and interests are discussed, compromises are concluded, and government acts to enable all citizens to prosper.[3]

Taking such arguments a step further, Eric Alterman observes that, even if Democrats temporarily promote the right sort of story, they do not necessarily stick to it. Thus he complains about Barack Obama breaking campaign promises he made to labor unions, pro-choice voters, environmentalists, strapped homeowners, and many other Americans in need. Because "the system" is friendly to naysayers and obstructionists, says Alterman, it made Obama's promises hard to keep. But the President also hobbled himself, in Alterman's view, because once he entered the White House he abandoned the "heroic narrative" of his 2008 campaign in favor of uninspiring "back-room dealings of exactly the kind … [that] candidate Obama so eloquently condemned."[4]

Disagreements

From the fact that such thinkers know what they are missing, we can infer that the problem in American public life is not that someone must discover how to persuade liberals to start telling stories, which will help them on election day. Rather, the problem is that – for reasons we have not yet considered – no matter how much they are prodded, liberals as a class simply don't see the world in terms of large shared stories. But if that is true, then no amount of exhortation – *Express your vision! Invent a story! Tell a tale!* – will produce the desired product, because liberals are driven by aspirations that place them somewhere else, without stories.

Some observers know this. For example, historian Alan Ryan does not discuss storytelling but highlights liberal disagreements on which basic principles might be used to construct a shared liberal tale. As he says:

Anyone trying to give a brief account of liberalism is immediately faced with an embarrassing question: are we dealing with liberalism or with liberalisms? It is

---

[3] Todd Gitlin, *The Bulldozer and the Big Tent: Blind Republicans, Lame Democrats, and the Recovery of American Ideals* (2007), pp. 238–249.

[4] Eric Alterman, *Kabuki Democracy: The System vs. Barack Obama* (2011), pp. 145–158.

easy to list famous liberals; it is harder to say what they have in common. John Locke, Adam Smith, Montesquieu, Thomas Jefferson, John Stuart Mill, Lord Acton, T. H. Green, John Dewey, and contemporaries such as Isaiah Berlin and John Rawls are certainly liberals – but they do not agree about the boundaries of toleration, the legitimacy of the welfare state, and the virtues of democracy, to take three rather central political issues.[5]

In this passage, Ryan comments on the disarray of liberal *theories*. But historian Alan Brinkley shows that liberal *practitioners* are no more consistent when they assess their own deeds. Thus he writes about how, in 1940, Keynesian economist Alvin Hansen remarked:

I do not really know what the basic principle of the New Deal is ... I know from my experience in government that there are as many conflicting opinions among the people in Washington under this administration as we have in the country at large.[6]

Comments such as these suggest that, even where the need for putting liberal things into order is great, one cannot reconcile liberal facts on the ground. Seeing that to be the case, political scientist Alan Wolfe in effect suggests that we cannot understand the mystery of liberalism without first understanding the puzzle known as modernity. As he puts it, "Liberalism may not have created modernity, but liberalism is the answer for which modernity is the question."[7] We will explore this link between "liberalism" and "modernity" more fully in a moment.

Skepticism

So far, we have seen liberal writers whose books do not invent a new alpha story, do not amplify an existing alpha story, and do not express an alpha story together with other liberal books. Therefore we can regard the books and authors I have described as evidence, on the surface of things, of the storytelling gap. It is time, however, to look for deeper evidence of this gap. To that end, let us consider what might be so basic on

[5] Alan Ryan, *The Making of Modern Liberalism* (2012), p. 21. For a unitary definition of liberalism, see political theorist Stephen Macedo, *Liberal Virtues: Citizenship, Virtue, and Community in Liberal Constitutionalism* (1990), p. 4:

By liberal ... I mean the tradition of John Locke, John Stuart Mill, and John Rawls. By 'liberal' I mean those political values like individual freedom and responsibility, and institutions such as the rule of law and the separation of powers, that have guided and informed the practice of constitutionalism in America and elsewhere.

[6] Alan Brinkley, *Liberalism and Its Discontents* (1998), p. 37.
[7] Alan Wolfe, *The Future of Liberalism* (2010), p. 254.

the Left side of contemporary political thought that it animates, limits, and defines most of the thinkers who we commonly regard as liberal.

Given the issues explored so far, it seems reasonable to assume that those who have recently been setting the liberal tone live mainly in a world of "skepticism," wherein they try sincerely to replace elements of subjective, uncertain, intuitive faith or opinion with empirical, accurate, rational truth or knowledge. To that end, they are committed to innovative inquiry *a la* Benedict de Spinoza, David Hume, Charles Darwin, Karl Marx, and Sigmund Freud, by which old truths are tested, challenged, and sometimes replaced.

Years ago, Bertrand Russell expressed this commitment when he emphasized the danger of "inspirational pronouncements" and insisted: "What the world needs is not dogma, but an attitude of scientific inquiry, combined with a belief that the torture of millions is not desirable, where inflicted by Stalin or by a Deity imagined in the likeness of the believer."[8] Nowadays the same commitment is epitomized academically, especially for its indifference to stories, by psychologist David Myers. As he says:

My concern ... is ... with assembling an accurate picture of reality ... I rely much less on compelling stories than on research findings ... I'm not much persuaded by anecdotes, testimonials, or inspirational pronouncements ... The truth of human experience, I believe, is better discerned by surveys that faithfully represent the population and control for complicating facts, and by careful experiments.[9]

Disenchantment

In a word, liberal thinkers who tell few or no great stories – such as John Kenneth Galbraith, Neil Postman, Naomi Wolf, Barbara Ehrenreich, John Kerry, Barbara Boxer, John Rawls, and Richard Rorty – are, in their work at least, mostly "secular." Max Weber viewed this phenomenon as part of a broad social trend toward disbelief and worldliness. He therefore argued that after the Enlightenment, which he regarded as promoting reason and rationality (as in Kant's 1784 wake-up call on behalf of both, cited at the beginning of this chapter), the hallmark of "modernity" is "disenchantment." As Weber said, "Our age is characterized by rationalization and intellectualization, and above all, by the disenchantment [*entzauberung*] of the world" – that is, indifference to old truths resting on mysterious or even supernatural forces.[10]

---

[8] Quoted in Jennifer Hecht, *Doubt: A History* (2004), p. 453.
[9] David Myers, *The American Paradox: Spiritual Hunger in an Age of Plenty* (2000), p. xiii.
[10] Max Weber, "Science as a Vocation," (1917), in Max Weber (ed.), *The Vocation Lectures* (2004), p. 30.

The Sequence

Wolfe linked liberalism to modernity in one comment among many. But Weber made that link a central point in his sociological theory. So let us take Weber's insight a little further, because "modernity" defined as "disenchantment" is crucial to the incidence of political storytelling. If Weber was right,[11] the sequence is as follows:

1. Many leading liberal thinkers today are modern and thereby disenchanted.
2. Consequently they are, by conviction, disinclined to reclaim enchantment.
3. Yet if people are disenchanted they are not likely to seek the meaning of life, or an explanation of how things work, in stories similar to those that earlier generations told in order to explain facts that at the time seemed otherwise inexplicable. Therefore, disenchanted people since Darwin will, for example, prefer the scientific theory of natural selection to the theological tale of Creationism.[12]
4. In which case, when they deal with public affairs, liberals will tend not to tell political stories of the large kind that can be regarded as partisan narratives – or, in our terminology, alpha stories.

[11] In Weber's view, the opposite of "enchantment" is "reason." Thus Ernest Cassirer, *The Philosophy of the Enlightenment* (1955), p. 6:

> The eighteenth century is imbued with a belief in the unity and immutability of reason ... From the changeability of religious creeds, of moral maxims and convictions, of theoretical opinions and judgments, philosophers of the Enlightenment believed that a firm and lasting element can be extracted which is permanent in itself and which in this identity and permanence expressed the real essence of reason.

See also Peter Gay, *The Enlightenment: An Interpretation, Vol. II: The Science of Freedom* (1969), p. 27:

> The advance of knowledge ... [during the Enlightenment] meant the advance of reason. In the course of the eighteenth century, the world, at least the world of the literate, was being emptied of mystery. Psuedo science was giving way to science, credence in the miraculous intervention of divine forces was being corroded by the acid of skepticism and overpowered by scientific cosmology.

For the historical triumph of Christian theology, metaphysics, and miracles over an earlier Greek philosophical tradition that was learning to challenge enchantment, see Charles Freeman, *The Closing of the Western Mind* (2005). For the revival of that pagan tradition in Western Europe, see Stephen Greenblatt, *The Swerve: How the World Became Modern* (2011).

[12] One of the sticking points here is that creationists usually believe that, whereas God created all living things, we should assume that He did so for good reasons because He is just. Some evolutionists say that they cannot believe in a just God who would create a process of natural selection based on innumerable violent and painful deaths. See Robert Ingersoll, *What's God Got To Do With It?: Robert Ingersoll On Free Thought, Honest Talk, & the Separation of Church & State* (2005), "Fable" (1879), p. 134, for Ingersoll's anecdote about the lethally designed stork and the helpless fish.

This sequence is essential for understanding liberalism as a frame of mind. If people are disenchanted, they will prefer facts to stories – or, in the modern idiom, science to narratives. But their preference is not something they freely choose, because in a sense they are congenitally unable, by personality, to feel that stories grasp reality more accurately than science.[13] Thus Joseph Wood Krutch, long-time drama critic for *The Nation* and professor of English, observed that "What [modern] man knows [by science] is everywhere at war with what he wants [from literature, philosophy, and theology, linked to stories]." However, "Any deliberately managed return to a state of relative ignorance, is obviously out of the question. We cannot … believe one thing and forget another merely because we happen to be convinced that it would be desirable to do so."[14]

In other words, liberal thinkers may *want* to believe in stories. But that is like wanting to believe in God for the comfort of it when one sees no convincing evidence that God exists.[15] The same liberals may even possess a talent for composing inspiring stories. Poets, novelists, admen, and lyricists possess this talent. Just think of Pete Seeger's mesmerizing song, "We Shall Overcome." But that does not mean that the liberals among them, as a class of citizens, are capable of believing together – and the "together" is crucial – even the stories that their colleagues might compose.

In short, if liberals tend to be disenchanted, they cannot (except perhaps like born-again devotees) talk themselves back into being enchanted, back into believing in stories.[16] And if a sector of the population is in that

---

[13] If some people have liberal personalities, we still do not know where such a personality comes from. In keeping with neo-Darwinist explanations, some political scientists are convinced that political personalities have genetic origins – thus John Hibbing, Kevin Smith, and John Alford, *Predisposed: Liberals, Conservatives, and the Biology of Political Differences* (2014). Furthermore, there is the added complication that some people, like Ronald Reagan, seem disposed – although we do not know why – to see the world via stories more than via "logical–mathematical" intelligence. On this point, see Howard Gardner, *Frames of Mind: The Theory of Multiple Intelligences* (1983), and Lou Cannon, *President Reagan: The Role of a Lifetime* (2000), pp. 110–114.

[14] Joseph Wood Krutch, *The Modern Temper: A Study and a Confession* (1929, 1957), p. 10, p. 13.

[15] Philosopher Daniel Garber (interviewed in Gary Gutting, "Can Wanting to Believe Make Us Believers?" *New York Times*, October 7, 2014), declares that "I can't believe [in God] because I'm not convinced that it is true that God exists. It is as simple as that. Belief is not voluntary, and there are no (rational) considerations that move me to believe that God exists."

[16] Thomas Nagel, author of *Mind and Cosmos: Why the Materialist Neo-Darwinian Conception of Nature is Almost Certainly False* (2013), criticizes materialism and neo-Darwinism for being overly rationalistic, which is to say, too disenchanted. But Nagel notes of the alternative that "My instinctively atheistic perspective implies that if I ever

situation, we should expect that they will not usually tell stories or sympathize much with people who do.

Humanism

For many years, central elements of this syndrome have led to what is called "humanism." As a matter of rejecting enchantment rather than affirming revelation or metaphysics, humanism is the historical term assigned to (roughly speaking) *philosophy* centered on human needs and *politics* driven by human creativity.[17] In general, humanism assumes that people can often overcome what political scientist Michael Sandel called social, economic, and political "encumbrances"[18] and then act, without divine inspiration and aid, to improve their lives and circumstances.

Over hundreds of years, and in numerous manifestations, Western humanism evolved as an alternative to Christian notions such as the doctrine of original sin, the great chain of being, and the divine right of kings – all of which assumed in various ways that human capacities are inherently limited.[19] Historian Carl Becker touched on these limitations when he described medieval man as believing life to be a "cosmic drama" fashioned by God, in which "The duty of man was to accept the drama as written, since he could not alter it; his function, to play the role assigned."[20]

Enlightenment Variations

We will return to humanism. Meanwhile, with respect to American liberalism and conservatism, it is useful to regard disenchantment and modernity as related. From what Weber said about it, the link is analytically

found myself flooded with the conviction that what the Nicene Creed says is true, the most likely explanation would be that I was losing my mind, not that I was being granted the gift of faith." This quotation comes from Thomas Nagel, "A Philosopher Defends Religion," *New York Review of Books* (September 27, 2012).

[17] See Wilson Coates and Hayden White, *The Emergence of Liberal Humanism: An Intellectual History of Western Europe* (1966), pp. 177–324.

[18] Sandel discusses encumbrances in "The Procedural Republic and The Unencumbered Self," *Political Theory* (February, 1984), pp. 81–96, and in *Democracy's Discontent: America in Search of a Public Philosophy* (1996), especially pp. 3–24.

[19] America's religious conservatives know this. For example, Rowe, *Save America!* (1976), p. 42: "[T]here are only two movements in history – God's and man's. God's movement has been revealed in the Holy Scriptures ... It is theocentric: God is at the center. Man's movement is humanism ... It is anthropocentric: Man is at the center."

[20] Carl Becker, *The Heavenly City of the 18th Century Philosophers* (1932), p. 9.

fuzzy. For our purposes, it is stated more exactly – if not precisely – by historian Peter Gay, who describes the Enlightenment as rejecting "mythical" (or "mythopoetic") thinking in favor of a "critical mentality" (epitomized in science).[21]

Gay's definition validates Weber's insight. But because particular thinkers during the Enlightenment sometimes mixed what Gay would have called mythopoetic and scientific propositions, it is useful to refine Weber's category of "disenchanted" people by noting recent claims in intellectual history which describe the *philosophes* as a collection of intellectuals who were divided approximately into those who were more radical and those who were more moderate.[22]

For example, in terms used by historians Jonathan Israel and Philipp Blom,[23] Enlightenment "radicals" (such as Spinoza, Diderot, d'Holbach, and Condorcet) promoted disenchantment and swept aside historical, literary, and theological justifications for government by a few. But Enlightenment "moderates" (such as Locke, Hume, Voltaire, Rousseau, and Smith), while endorsing some repair of the Old Regime, often retained framework notions of divine interest and intervention in human affairs. Therefore they sometimes claimed that superstition and tradition, but not in every historical case, are necessary bulwarks of virtuous behavior and social stability.[24]

---

[21] Gay, *The Enlightenment*, Vol. I, pp. 90–94. I treat the Enlightenment as if it were a matter of new ideas and major thinkers: that is, a sort of humanistic moment or breakthrough in intellectual history. This is the approach, roughly speaking, of Jonathan Israel, *A Revolution of the Mind: Radical Enlightenment and the Intellectual Origins of Modern Democracy* (2010), Philipp Blom, *A Wicked Company: The Forgotten Radicalism of the European Enlightenment* (2010), and Anthony Pagden, *The Enlightenment and Why It Still Matters* (2013).

[22] Americans did not have to struggle much, in their colonies and then early states, against the resistance to eighteenth-century reformist ideas thrown up by some European thinkers and institutions. On that resistance, see Wilson Coates and Hayden White, *The Ordeal of Liberal Humanism: An Intellectual History of Western Europe* (1970), pp. 52–111, pp. 169–249. It follows that, given the way in which thoughts and events unfolded differently east and west of the Atlantic Ocean, terms that describe European *philosophes* in all their variety were not exactly relevant to Americans then or applicable now.

[23] Their works are cited in note 21 in this chapter.

[24] Voltaire allegedly insisted that "If God did not exist, it would be necessary [for maintaining social order] to invent Him." This proposition was opposed by Laplace, who reputedly told Napoleon that the existence of God was an hypothesis for which he had no need. For an American example of Enlightenment "moderation," see the colonial loyalist Samuel Seabury, *A View of the Controversy Between Great Britain and Her Colonies* (1775), who accepted the tradition of English rule over the British Empire including England's American colonies.

That is, Enlightenment moderates tended not to promote *total* disenchantment, and their social thought did not condemn stories *in principle*. For example, they sometimes told stories of a "social contract." Therefore, their descendants today, – including many American conservatives, still tell and rely upon stories. In this spirit, modern conservatives like Rus Walton, John Whitehead, and Jerry Falwell insist that citizens can only be bound by moral injunctions which are absolute, in which case those injunctions can come only from God (who we know via stories).[25]

Enlightenment radicals were more inclined to humanism. That is, they tended to believe that many human beings – although not most women, paupers, non-white people, and so forth – are blessed with considerable competence and self-sufficiency and can therefore decide for themselves how to relate decently to one another. In eighteenth-century America, such radicals included Thomas Paine and Thomas Jefferson.[26] Their heirs today include Barack Obama, Sam Harris, Naomi Wolf, and Bernie Sanders,[27] although these heirs favor empowerment for many people who were formerly excluded.

Of course, modern conservatives are uncomfortable with humanism because if people can work out how to relate to one another they may decide to do so differently in different societies. The danger there is that, across the board, behavior and morals may collapse into relativism. For example, in some places people will eat snails and in other places they will eat neighbors. On behalf of the Right, political scientist James Q. Wilson played down this real-life sort of pluralism by positing an innate and consistent sense of moral sentiments as part of human nature in every corner of the world. As for snails and cannibals, Wilson argued

[25] Walton, *One Nation Under God* (1975), John Whitehead, *The Stealing of America* (1983), and Jerry Falwell, *The New American Family: The Rebirth of the American Dream* (1992). See also Paul Chamberlain, *Can We Be Good Without God? A Conversation About Truth, Morality, Culture, & a Few Other Things That Matter* (1996), Tammy Bruce, *The Death of Right and Wrong: Exposing the Left's Assault on our Culture and Values* (2003), especially pp. 39–58, and William Lane Craig, *Reasonable Faith: Christian Truth and Apologetics* (2008).

[26] See Paine, "The Age of Reason (1793)," in Howard Fast (ed.), *The Selected Work of Tom Paine and Citizen Tom Paine* (1945), pp. 285–330, and Henry Commager, *Jefferson, Nationalism, and the Enlightenment* (1975), especially pp. 182–196.

[27] See Barack Obama, *The Audacity of Hope: Thoughts on Reclaiming the American Dream* (2006), which argues that, via intelligent public policies, Americans can deliberately solve their great social and economic problems. See also Sam Harris, *The End of Faith: Religion, Terror, and the Future of Reason* (2005), Naomi Wolf, *Give Me Liberty: A Handbook for American Revolutionaries* (2008), especially pp. 125–139, and Bernie Sanders, *The Speech: A Historic Filibuster on Corporate Greed and the Decline of our Middle Class* (2012).

that the moral sense expresses itself not in universal "rules" but human "dispositions" such as sympathy, decency, and mutual aid.[28] Wilson did not introduce God into his argument. But if they are so inclined, other conservatives can easily postulate that human nature, including a moral sense, is shaped by a Creator.

European Detours

Enlightenment variations aside, until after World War II mainland Europeans were sidetracked repeatedly by romanticism, nationalism, communism, and fascism. These ideologies, buttressed by powerful stories, all assumed that encumbrances (of religion, ethnicity, class, and race) did and should shape people's lives.

With this political record in mind, Louis Hartz proposed that America was born free of many European encumbrances, although he did not use that term but observed in colonial America an absence of "feudal and clerical oppressions."[29] For example, in comparison to social arrangements in Europe, eighteenth-century writers like Hector St. John de Crevecoeur testified to a remarkable degree of colonial tolerance. Thus Crevecoeur noted that Lutheran and Low Dutch and Catholic farmers lived side by side in America, each believing what he wished without persecuting others; in which case, why should it concern "the welfare of the country, or of the province at large, what anyone believes, if it harms no one else?"[30] Thomas Jefferson was even more colloquial: "The legitimate powers of government," he said, "extend to such acts only as are injurious to others. But it does me no injury for my neighbor to say there are twenty gods, or no God. It neither picks my pocket nor breaks my leg."[31]

America's Political Moment

Hartz claimed that America's Founders managed not to sink into lives shaped by European ideologies. Instead, they went beyond the natural law inspiration of the Declaration and constructed the Constitution,

---

[28] James Q. Wilson, *The Moral Sense* (1993), especially pp. 225–230. The notion of an innate moral sense is rejected by philosopher Jesse Prinz, *Beyond Human Nature: How Culture and Experience Shape our Lives* (2012), "Coping with Cannibalism," pp. 293–329.

[29] Louis Hartz, *The Liberal Tradition in America* (1955), p. 3.

[30] J. Hector St. John De Crevecoeur, *Letters from an American Farmer* (1782, 1957), pp. 44–47.

[31] Thomas Jefferson, *Notes on the State of Virginia* (1785, 1964), p. 152.

which can be regarded as a bundle of utilitarian solutions for many problems of government.[32] In this sequence, the Founders sometimes differed among themselves on philosophy. For example, as we measure outlooks today, John Adams was conservative and Thomas Jefferson was liberal.[33] But the men who wrote the Constitution managed to agree on institution building more than European thinkers.

In this sense, America enjoyed an Enlightenment that was morally imperfect but, in many respects, politically successful. *In principle*, it embodied a belief in humanism as the capacity (although not unlimited) for immediate agency.[34] For example, writing in favor of ratifying the Constitution, James Madison proudly expressed this belief:

> Is it not the glory of the people of America that, whilst they have paid a decent regard to the opinions of former times and other nations, they have not suffered a blind veneration for antiquity, for custom, or for names, to overrule the suggestions of their own good sense, the knowledge of their own situation, and the lessons of their own experience?[35]

Alexander Hamilton agreed:

> It has frequently been remarked that it seems to have been reserved to the people of this country, by their conduct and example, to decide the important question, whether societies of men are really capable or not of establishing good government from reflection and choice.[36]

---

[32] The late-eighteenth century switch from natural law to utilitarian justifications appears in Jeremy Bentham, *A Fragment on Government* (1776, 1951), especially pp. 131–163, and Jeremy Bentham, *The Principles of Morals and Legislation* (1789, 1948), pp. 1–7.

[33] For a philosophical comparison of Adams and Jefferson, see May, *The Enlightenment in America* (1976), pp. 278–304.

[34] Americans were not total humanists. In principle, the Founders believed that *men* were inherently capable. But they did not regard *all men* or *all people* as fully capable. Thus Edmund Morgan, *American Slavery, American Freedom* (1975), pp. 363–387, but especially pp. 380–387, discusses the paradox of colonial "republicans" aspiring to "equality" but not for everyone.

[35] This passage is from Madison, No. 14, in Alexander Hamilton, John Jay, and James Madison, *The Federalist* (1937), p. 85.

[36] *Ibid.*, No. 1, p. 3. See also Thomas Paine, "Common Sense (1776)," in Howard Fast (ed.), *The Selected Work of Tom Paine and Citizen Tom Paine* (1945), pp. 18, p. 30:

> In the following pages I offer nothing more than simple facts, plain arguments, and common sense: and have no other preliminaries to settle with the reader, than that he will divest himself of prejudice and prepossession, and suffer his reason and his feelings to determine for themselves ... [in which case] when a man seriously reflects on the precariousness of human affairs, he will become convinced, that it is infinitely wiser and safer, to form a constitution of our own in a cool deliberate manner, while we have it in our power, than to trust such an interesting event to time and chance.

Accordingly, with considerable faith in human competence, the Founders chose to act decisively in 1787. Whereupon *in practice* they wrote into the Constitution federalism, separation of powers, an independent judiciary, an elected executive, and so forth, which were all products of human agency and solutions to some but not all governmental problems.[37] In light of the problems that remained, some historians have concluded that the Constitution's compromises, and especially those which perpetuated slavery, were probably the best outcome that statesmen from the South would permit at the time.[38] It would have been no consolation to the victims, of course, that in philosophical terms one might call the Constitution a triumph of the feasible but imperfect "good" over the flawless but unattainable "right."

The Liberal Tradition

On the issue of telling stories or not, Americans did not look back consistently on their founding moment. That is, American thinkers and leaders did not eventually divide up as conveniently, for analytical purposes, as many Europeans did, where liberals such as James Mill tended to promote utilitarianism[39] while reactionaries such as Joseph De Maistre continued to praise stories.[40] Instead – except for racists who favored slavery and later segregation and therefore the principle of "states' rights" – most Americans supported the same democratic regime and still do. In which case, whether or not they tell stories, Americans are generally committed to what Weber would have called a modern way of organizing society (as opposed to monarchy or aristocracy).

Yet if Americans are mostly modern – in this case, democratic – we should adjust Weber's insight a little. Let us propose, then, instead of pure Weber, that American liberals are likely to favor a Liberal sort of politics – in Hartz's sense of consensus Liberalism – for disenchanted reasons,[41] while American conservatives are likely to argue that Liberal

---

[37] On leftover governmental problems, see Robert Dahl, *How Democratic is the American Constitution?* (2001), and Sanford Levinson, *Framed: America's 51 Constitutions and The Crisis of Governance* (2012).

[38] On leaving slavery in the Constitution, see Joseph Ellis, *Founding Brothers: The Revolutionary Generation* (2001), pp. 81–119, and Richard Beeman, *Plain, Honest Men: The Making of the American Constitution* (2010), pp. 308–336.

[39] As in James Mill, *An Essay on Government* (1820).

[40] As in Joseph De Maistre, *On God and Society* (1959). This is an anthology of items that De Maistre wrote mostly during 1808 and 1809.

[41] For example, John Rawls, *Political Liberalism* (2005).

politics should be inspired by telling great stories.[42] That is, the Liberal Tradition *object* of devotion is mainly the same but the *reasons* for devotion may be significantly different.

The Present Matrix

The present political matrix crystallized around a powerful storyline. Thus, in his Gettysburg Address, Lincoln proclaimed that "Four score and seven years ago our fathers brought forth on this continent, a new nation, conceived in Liberty, and dedicated to the proposition that all men are created equal." By placing America's birth in 1776, the President in effect demolished arguments for succession and declared that the Declaration informed and animated the Constitution of 1789.[43]

It was a remarkable rhetorical achievement because, when Lincoln's vision of America's true nature became a national story, that meant that, henceforth, Americans on the Right would have to conserve a somewhat radical regime (principles and institutions) of mainly Liberal government (rights and practices).[44] A moderate conservative way – say by George Will or in the *Wall Street Journal* – of defending this support would be to note that after the Declaration and Constitution were written, ratified, and implemented they became part of history – and thus, in Burkean terms, justified as embodying accumulated wisdom. In which case, even when there are policy disputes between what are called liberals and conservatives in America, both generally support most of Hartz's Liberal Tradition even while some tell stories and some don't.

In other words, although Right and Left in America disagree on what "the government" should or should not do, their minds mainly meet

---

[42] For example, James Burnham, *Suicide of the West: The Meaning and Destiny of Liberalism* (1985), p. 291:

> Men become willing to endure, sacrifice and die for God, family, king, honor, [and] country, from a sense of absolute duty or an exalted vision of the meaning of history ... It is precisely these ideals and institutions that liberalism has criticized, attacked and in part overthrown as superstitious, archaic, reactionary and irrational.

[43] See Garry Wills, *Lincoln at Gettysburg: The Words that Remade America* (1992).

[44] Conservatives are troubled by having to preserve Liberal *institutions* while opposing many of the *policies* those institutions have produced – for example, the Supreme Court as opposed to the Supreme Court's insistence that women have a right to abortions. The dilemma is acute in view of the fact that Edmund Burke, the paragon of intellectual conservatism, urged that policies with a solid historical pedigree should mostly be conserved. Therefore Dinesh D'Souza, *Letters to a Young Conservative* (2002), p. 25, advises young rightists on how to maneuver in a Liberal society. The recipe, he argues, is to be "philosophically conservative" (maintaining a Liberal Tradition's constitution) while also "temperamentally radical" (opposing liberal policies in the name of conservatism).

on what shape "the regime" should take.[45] Thus, relatively speaking, Americans think consensually rather than quarreling constantly over regime form – as, say, monarchists and republicans did in nineteenth-century France.

Separation

At this point, let us qualify the analytically useful generalization which says that liberals are disenchanted. As I already noted, some liberals – like Reinhold Niebuhr, Jimmy Carter, Martin Luther King, Jr., and Mario Cuomo – obviously believe in large stories of the providential kind. What is striking, though, is that those religious liberals usually don't believe in using providential stories to understand, describe, or inspire the special activity called *politics*.

For example, when John F. Kennedy campaigned for his party's presidential nomination in 1960, he insisted that neither voters nor elected officials should be guided by any prelate – including the Pope.[46] And when Martin Luther King, Jr. spoke in public, he referred more to the Constitution than to natural law.[47] Given that liberals usually endorse the separation of church and state, King's choice suggested that, like many of his devout compatriots, he could set aside stories about God as unnecessary to America's conversation on public affairs. Something remains here of an apprehension entertained by radical Enlighteners in the eighteenth century. Those men were not necessarily atheists. But they aspired to foster progress by avoiding a large measure of piety and ignorance, even while both were promoted by kings and priests who persistently framed reality with self-serving stories.[48]

---

[45] This point was certified after the Civil War by the Supreme Court in *Texas v. White* (1869), when succession was finally laid to rest and the American regime was defined as "an indestructible union, composed of indestructible states."

[46] See his September 12, 1960, campaign speech in Houston, Texas.

[47] Furthermore, to the extent that King spoke of God in public appeals (not church sermons) for the protection of civil rights, he evoked more a Jeffersonian, deist God than a Bush II, biblical God. See Martin Luther King, Jr., *Why We Can't Wait* (1964).

[48] Thus Diderot is said to have insisted that freedom will be achieved only by strangling the last king in the entrails of the last priest. This as opposed to Edmund Burke, *Reflections on the Revolution in France* (1790, 1955), pp. 86–87, lamenting the unseemly, almost casual (to Burke) deaths of Louis XVI and Marie Antoinette:

[T]he age of chivalry is gone. That of sophisters, economists, and calculators has succeeded, and the glory of Europe is extinguished forever … All the pleasing illusions which made power gentle and obedience liberal, which harmonized the different shades of life, and which, by a bland assimilation, incorporated into politics the sentiments which beautify and soften private

Of course, the Founders knew that many people prefer to live according to recommendations embodied in powerful narratives. Religious people, for example, especially fashion their sense of identity from sacred tales. These are memorable even if some of them violate modern standards of right and wrong. Thus there is not much enthusiasm in America today for, say, the piety in the book of *Numbers* that inspired the High Priest Pinchas to execute the Israelite Zimri and his Midianite lover Cozbi for sinning against ancient principles of tribal purity.[49] Ditto for the biblical command in *Exodus* that "thou shall not suffer a witch to live."[50] Nevertheless, while recognizing the power of religious stories, the Founders tried to keep most of them safely out of public life by writing into the Constitution principles of religious tolerance and an intimation of separating church and state.[51] This was a *utilitarian* ploy of America's political moment, even while most of the nation's citizens believed in God.

Very importantly, this ploy still affects American politics. Conservatives like the Reverend Pat Robertson, Senator Rick Santorum, Congressman Tom DeLay, and Governor Mike Huckabee argue that Providential stories should shape public policy.[52] But even if liberals like Mario Cuomo and Jimmy Carter believe in such stories, they also believe that those stories should inspire politicians no more than personally.

Carter, for instance, writes that he believes in God but not in the specific tenets of any particular church; he sees no contradiction between science and his faith in Jesus as a transcendental presence in this world; and he would regard any government program for enforcing religious

---

society, are to be dissolved by this new conquering empire of light and reason. All the decent drapery of life is to be rudely torn off ... On this scheme of things, a king is but a man, a queen is but a woman; a woman is but an animal, and an animal not of the highest order ... The murder of a king or a queen, or a bishop, or a father are only common homicide.

[49] *Numbers* 25: 6–15. Radical Moslems still promote fierce piety occasionally, such as when Iran's Ayatollah Khomeini issued a *fatwa* in 1989 condemning to death the exiled novelist Salman Rushdie for committing blasphemy by writing his novel *The Satanic Verses* (1988).

[50] *Exodus* 22: 19.

[51] The relevant clauses are in Article VI, which forbids religious tests for public office, and the First Amendment, which forbids Congress from establishing any religion. It was Thomas Jefferson in 1802 who, in a letter to the Danbury Baptist Association, first explicitly talked of a "wall of separation between church and state."

[52] Pat Robertson, *America's Dates with Destiny* (1986); Rick Santorum, *It Takes a Family: Conservatism and the Common Good* (2005); Tom Delay, *No Retreat, No Surrender: One American's Fight* (2007); and Mike Huckabee, *Do The Right Thing: Inside the Movement That's Bringing Common Sense Back to America* (2008).

conformity as violating democracy's basic principles.[53] Cuomo was equally adamant as Governor of New York. A practicing Catholic who tries to follow the church's teachings, he said, is not obliged by his religious faith to support a proposed constitutional amendment that would ban abortion and thereby, in a pluralistic society, make "our belief everyone's rule."[54]

This reluctance separates Carter, Cuomo, and their liberal colleagues from theistic rivals in the conservative camp.[55] Consequently, it seems to me reasonable, with regard to political stories, to treat religious liberals mostly as members of a non-storytelling camp in American public life.

The Case Of Progressivism

Beyond today's religious left, however, let us note another very obvious case that may disprove the rule of disenchantment among liberals. Between the late nineteenth and early twentieth centuries, Darwin's theory of evolution – supplemented by other scientific achievements, such as those of Sigmund Freud and Albert Einstein – challenged religious storytelling as powerfully as eighteenth-century Enlightenment radicals had challenged earlier stories that supported the Old Order. In America, some citizens and institutions reacted to these new ideas by becoming Progressives.

At first, many Progressives were known for combining a commitment to good deeds and Christian benevolence, both inspired by providential stories, with what today would be approximately described – especially in reference to public projects promoted by Theodore Roosevelt and Woodrow Wilson – as a program of political liberalism. Direct liberal descendants of those early Progressives still exist today. But they do not seem to be much inspired by the original, somewhat religious Progressive vision of social reform.[56] We should therefore eventually ask why Progressivism lost its faith around World War I (in what was then called the Social Gospel) to the point where the analytical rule now is that modern liberals – unlike some, or even many, of their Progressive forebears – are disenchanted. I will return to this question in Chapter 9.

---

[53] Jimmy Carter, *Living Faith* (1998), p. 3, pp. 35–37, pp. 185–186, p. 195.

[54] See "Religious Belief and Public Morality: A Catholic Governor's Perspective" (1984), a speech delivered at Notre Dame University and reprinted in Mario Cuomo, *More Than Words: The Speeches of Mario Cuomo* (1993), pp. 32–51.

[55] See Fox News host John Gibson, *The War on Christmas: How the Liberal Plot to Ban the Sacred Christian Holiday Is Worse Than You Thought* (2005).

[56] The Protestant family backgrounds of early Progressive leaders and intellectuals is noted in Eldon Eisenach, *The Lost Promise of Progressivism* (1994), pp. 42–43.

5

Dewey's Pragmatism

The pragmatic method is primarily a method of settling disputes that otherwise might be interminable.

William James, "What Pragmatism Means." (1907)

When modern liberals don't tell alpha stories, a gap arises between liberals and conservatives on storytelling. In Chapter 2, I noted that this gap may have electoral consequences, and that two broad questions therefore seemed to me worth asking. These are worth restating now:

1. *While conservatives tell stories (in the sense of narratives), why don't liberals like Obama do the same? That is, what holds them back?*

2. *Furthermore, if liberals don't tell stories (again in the sense of narratives), what do they do instead? That is, how do they inspire voters to support liberal projects?*

What we have seen so far suggests a plausible answer to the first question. Broadly speaking, liberals are "disenchanted." Therefore they tend to adopt scientific findings rather than to use stories to understand the world. As a result, they rarely tell stories to describe and shape public life. This, then, is the storytelling gap.

But what of the second question? If liberals don't tell the kind of stories that conservatives promote, what *do* they do politically – and, in the process, contribute to public life? That is, if liberals refrain from living publicly *within* stories, how do they live publicly *without* stories? In other words, where are these people intellectually?

The answer to this second question comes in several parts, as we shall see. It starts, however, from a situation in which – instead of telling large stories and using government to achieve what those stories recommend – most liberals aim to "solve problems."[1] (We should note, of course, that they do not mean "problems" in the intractable sense but "puzzles" that can be solved.)

For example, where is there a political, social, or economic problem? If it is at point X, how can we deal with it? If it is at point Y, what needs to be done? Furthermore, if one thing doesn't work, why not try another? As Franklin Roosevelt said, "The country needs ... and demands bold, persistent experimentation. It is common sense to take a method and try it: If it fails, admit it frankly and try another. But above all, try something."[2]

Pragmatism

Franklin D. Roosevelt was certainly a typical liberal. It is therefore worth stating plainly that his approach to public affairs constituted a form of "pragmatism." Pragmatism tests public policy proposals not by weighing their theoretical validity, or rightness, but by judging their actual results, or goodness. We have already seen that these two may be different, such as when John Rawls's theory of justice describes mainly the "right" (moral) rather than the "good" (effective).

In fact, even before the New Deal, much of American behavior was pragmatic – although before the Civil War, the French visitor Alexis De Tocqueville would have called it "practical."[3] As a distinct approach to life, however, pragmatism arose in America as a descendent of Enlightenment skepticism and in response to Charles Darwin's great mid-nineteenth-century challenge to revelation. Later, in the twentieth century, pragmatism became a major project within academic philosophy, promoted in recent years by scholars such as Sidney Hook, Hilary Putnam, Richard Rorty, Richard Bernstein, and Susan Haack.[4]

---

[1] William Boyer, *Myth America: Democracy vs. Capitalism* (2003), pp. 22–44. The practical importance of defining problems and proposing solutions is highlighted in John Kingdon, *Agendas, Alternatives, and Public Policies* (1984). Problems in this formulation are not *problems* in the intractable sense, but rather *puzzles* that can be solved.

[2] Franklin D. Roosevelt, "Address at Oglethorpe University in Atlanta Georgia" (1932).

[3] Alexis De Tocqueville, *Democracy in America*, Vol. 2 (1840, 1945), pp. 3–8.

[4] On the history of pragmatism, see Cornel West, *The American Evasion of Philosophy: A Geneology of Pragmatism* (1989), Louis Menand, *The Metaphysical Club: A Story of Ideas in America* (2002), and Richard Bernstein, *The Pragmatic Turn* (2010).

In that project, intricate formulations, some of them clashing with others, accumulated in many academic works. Those formulations continue to compete against one another in university philosophy departments; they are not particularly relevant to our concerns; and we need not survey them here. On the other hand, to see where pragmatic sentiments and aspirations link up to liberalism it is worth looking at some of the principles which constitute a common – and somewhat political, rather than mainly academic – understanding of what pragmatism is about.

Charles Peirce (1839–1914)

The earliest concepts of pragmatism relate to how we know about the world and what to do in it. They were devised by logician Charles Peirce in 1877, when he proposed that there are four ways of "fixing" our beliefs.[5] The first was what Peirce called "tenacity," whereby people are sometimes simply stubborn about what they believe, in which case stubbornness keeps their beliefs firmly in mind. The virtue of tenacity is that it banishes doubt. Nevertheless, Peirce says that tenacity cannot generate adequate social relations, because it does not help a believer to find reasons that will persuade someone else to agree with him or her.

The second way of fixing belief is "authority," where people believe – often together with friends and neighbors – more or less what their opinion leaders tell them to believe. According to Peirce, authority was a potent force in the pre-modern world where – among other things – it raised Egypt's pyramids and inspired widespread piety. The problem with authority is that, like tenacity, it may not help us to persuade other people that our principles are valid. Furthermore, it may encourage us to force those principles on people who believe in something else. Europe's sixteenth- and seventeenth-century wars of religion testify to this dangerous side of authority.

Peirce calls the third way of fixing belief "rationalism," or the "a priori method." Here, we first assume that something called "reality" exists, that it is not affected by human agents, and that everyone can try to measure his or her surroundings against it. Then we reason our way to understanding that reality. This sort of philosophy worked well for Immanuel Kant and Friedrich Hegel, who used it to discover what they saw as large and impressive "truths." A major weakness of the a priori method, however, is that by encouraging us to employ what

---

[5] "The Fixation of Beliefs" appeared in *Popular Science Monthly*, (November, 1877), pp. 1–15. I will cite page numbers for that article as it was reprinted in Louis Menand (ed.), *Pragmatism: A Reader* (1997), pp. 7–25.

seem to be reasonable assumptions it leads us to think mostly conventional thoughts. In which case, says Peirce, Hegel's understanding of the world was no more advanced than that of other learned people in his day.[6]

The fourth way of fixing beliefs is "science," which collects tangible items as evidence and tests them empirically. Science is not as strong as tenacity; it is not as easy as authority; and it is not as comfortable as a priori reasoning. But it has a crucial capacity for occasionally introducing new knowledge into society, because its great advantage, says Peirce, is that it brings opinion "to coincide with the fact."[7]

William James (1842–1910)

In "What Pragmatism Means" (1907),[8] psychologist William James cited Peirce's pioneering explorations of pragmatism and then expanded on the notion of science as the hallmark of a new philosophy. What drove James in that direction was what he regarded as "absolutism" in the writings of men like Kant, Hegel, and Spencer. James claimed that their philosophies were based more on "rationalist" or "a priori thinking" than on "empiricism" or science. He thus thought that their pursuit of "metaphysics" tended to absolve us from responsibility for our own actions, because that sort of abstract analysis suggests powerful and impersonal forces – such as Hegel's "Spirit" – which rule the world regardless of our preferences and practices.[9]

James observed that absolutist philosophies purporting to describe the world may be true or false. He did not discuss which philosophies are more or less so. But in many cases, he said, such philosophies produce rhetorical disputes – such as that over the nature of the Trinity – that are "interminable."[10] He therefore recommended pragmatism, which sidesteps those disputes in favor of trying to ascertain, for each proposition about the world or life in it, what "its respective practical consequences" might be.[11] To make this recommendation seem especially useful to fellow Americans, James went so far as to suggest that testing ideas for their

---

[6] *Ibid.*, p. 22.

[7] *Ibid.*, p. 24.

[8] "What Pragmatism Means" appeared originally in William James, *Pragmatism: A New Name for Some Old Ways of Thinking* (1907). I will cite pages as they appear in the same essay reprinted in Menand, *Pragmatism*, pp. 93–111.

[9] *Ibid.*, pp. 106–111.

[10] *Ibid.*, p. 94.

[11] *Ibid.*, p. 94.

consequences might set those ideas to work within "the stream" of our "experience" and bring out their "cash-value."[12]

Most importantly, James insisted that pragmatism is a philosophy of "method" rather than of doctrines or dogmas.[13] That is, it stands for no particular results or enduring truths. Instead, it encourages people to test ideas and beliefs constantly, seeking those that will "carry us prosperously from any one part of our experience to any other part."[14]

By analogy, James described this process as taking place in a hotel corridor flanked by guest rooms on both sides. The rooms are occupied by different ideas about how to search for knowledge about the world and the meaning of life. To leave the rooms and to reach citizens outside the hotel, however, those ideas – from metaphysics to mathematics, from art to geology – must pass through the corridor in which, challenged by pragmatism, they are all equally subject to testing for acceptable results.[15]

In effect, James described pragmatism as a philosophy which resembles science and explains how science is practiced. The inference was that, in the modern world, pragmatic people – following exemplars such as Copernicus, Galileo, Harvey, Boyle, Newton, Buffon, Priestley, Hutton, Maxwell, Darwin, and Pasteur – should continually challenge old, and possibly outworn, beliefs. If they will do that, then this new method of testing, validating, verifying, and refuting will produce a steady stream of useful knowledge.

Typically American

James's pragmatism expressed various American sentiments. For example, it implicitly rejected the European notion that famous intellectuals may be entitled, by the presumed excellence of their thinking, to tell everyone else how to live. On the contrary, that Americans almost instinctively admired practicality –as exercised by Hank Morgan, the hero of Mark Twain's *A Connecticut Yankee in King Arthur's Court* (1889) – helps us to understand De Tocqueville's observation that "in no country in the civilized world is less attention paid to philosophy than in the United States."[16]

In fact, pragmatism encouraged this small regard for abstractions when James implied that any reasonable and diligent person, rather than just

---

[12] *Ibid.*, pp. 97–98.
[13] *Ibid.*, p. 98.
[14] *Ibid.*, p. 100.
[15] *Ibid.*, p. 98.
[16] De Tocqueville, *Democracy in America*, Vol. 2, pp. 3–8.

"great thinkers," could contribute to the growing fund of useful knowledge. Americans such as Thomas Edison and Henry Ford were already doing just that, as befitting a democratic society which, in principle, at least, shunned elitism and offered ordinary people great opportunities to succeed in life. In his own work, James warranted this practice by giving it the forward-looking and respectable name of pragmatism.

John Dewey (1859–1952)

John Dewey deserves special attention here because, building on concepts fashioned by Peirce and James, he promoted pragmatic ideas to show how science is relevant to political liberalism. Dewey started teaching philosophy at the University of Chicago in 1894, moved to Columbia University in 1904, and retired in 1929, but remained active as an Emeritus Professor at Columbia and the New School for Social Research, which he helped to found.

We may regard Dewey as a "social" rather than "technical" philosopher because he claimed that pragmatism can inform public life and democracy in America. When right-wing and left-wing ideologues mocked liberalism as insipid, feeble, and naïve, and when fascist and communist dictators sent armies to assault democrats in countries like Spain, Czechoslovakia, Poland, Finland, Denmark, Norway, Belgium, and Great Britain, Dewey insisted that liberal ideas are realistic and that democratic institutions can energize and defend a decent society on the basis of pragmatic education, pragmatic research, and pragmatic decision-making.

Science

Like Peirce and James, Dewey started by rejecting philosophies that searched for axioms about nature's eternal character and then recommended that men should live according to those "absolute" truths. He proposed instead to understand the world via "experimentalism," or science, wherein reason and contemplation are useful but should be supplemented by data which we can acquire by inspecting that world in tangible ways.[17]

The pragmatic emphasis on experimentalism had important social implications which could be inferred from what Peirce and James said but which Dewey developed more explicitly. First, experimentalism suggests

---

[17] David Marcell, *Progress and Pragmatism: James, Dewey, Beard, and the American Idea of Progress* (1974), pp. 232–246.

that we need not regard nature as a fixed set of conditions within which people must live. This is because experiments can help us to understand how to reshape the natural order – for example, with immunizations against disease and dikes in Holland – in ways that serve human needs, whatever those may be. Second, the new approach to knowledge does not consist in particular truths that it discovers, such as how to vulcanize rubber or broadcast radio waves. What distinguishes science, instead, is that it is not an enterprise aimed at discovering this or that particular fact or theory but a technique for endlessly revealing more and more about our world.

The Scientific Community

Third, this ongoing collection of information, immensely valuable to society, can be carried on in a systematic way by what would eventually be called "the scientific community." Dewey did not use that term, but he spoke of "organized intelligence," by which he meant that when scientists work together to collect data, generate and test hypotheses, and then check each other's findings, the sum total of knowledge expands beyond any individual's capacity for discovery.[18] Science is thus progressive in that, as research unfolds over time, it presents each human generation with a more advanced starting point of knowledge than that enjoyed by its predecessors.

Democracy

As for Dewey's eventual destination, he linked pragmatism to politics as follows: *Democracy, where citizens choose between partisan platforms and try out various policies, is like science applied to public affairs.*[19] It was a striking analogy, updating previous and often metaphysical concepts of democracy. In effect, democratic voters and their representatives can imitate science – if they are educated to that end – by debating political ideas with an open mind and a willingness to go where the evidence points.

This process is neither simple nor easy because every society hosts a spectrum of groups and interests, some of which regard "evidence" incompatibly and some of which clash intensely with others. Some compromises will emerge, though, and some policy proposals will be enacted

---

[18] John Dewey, *Liberalism and Social Action* (1935, 1963), throughout but especially p. 51.
[19] This is a paraphrase. For some of the links between political and scientific methods, see John Dewey, *The Public and Its Problems: An Essay in Political Inquiry* (1927), pp. 143–219.

into laws. Then, as time passes, the same citizens and their representatives – properly versed in making democratic choices – will consider whether or not those laws produce results that justify leaving the laws in place. If not, the system permits its members – who we may regard as a "political community" analogous to a "scientific community" – to use their civil and electoral rights together to talk things over and decide to replace unsatisfactory laws with others more likely to generate desirable consequences.

The bottom line is that Dewey advocated maintaining America's democratic institutions and practices, from constitutionalism to frequent elections, from the separation of powers to the right of free speech. In his view, those devices enable the nation to deploy "democracy" as a political "method" for testing proposals rather than as a technical "plan" for reaching a particular set of policy results. That is, Dewey envisioned a modern world of constant change and evolution, where new interests – social and economic, secular and religious, industrial and environmental, rural and urban – must continually be weighed and accommodated. Only a democratic society, he insisted, modeled after the scientific consideration of ideas, has the flexibility needed to confront that world successfully. Or, as Dewey proclaimed, "It is not that liberalism creates the need, but that the necessity for adjustment defines the office of liberalism."[20]

Political Lessons

Three vital political lessons emerged from Dewey's version of pragmatism. First, it strongly condemned the many dictatorships which plagued Dewey's world. Marxist, fascist, and Nazi regimes all assumed that in any country there is a fixed truth that can be discovered by parties or leaders and that thereafter should be accepted without question by all citizens. For Dewey, the ideologies that inspired such regimes amounted to modern manifestations of philosophical "absolutism." They placed in power unaccountable strongmen who, believing that they knew what is true for all time (there is the absolutism), would prevent citizens from searching for new truths that might help them to live well in an ever-changing world. For instance, Hitler's racial obsessions exemplified this sort of rigid orthodoxy, as did Stalin's dedication to "historical materialism."

Dewey's second political lesson did not stand out as obviously as the first but was equally important. On both sides of the Atlantic, for an

[20] Dewey, *Liberalism and Social Action*, p. 49.

entire generation, social, economic, and military upheavals shattered people's lives and challenged their beliefs. Under the circumstances, there were men and women even in America who decided that passionate, colorful, and exciting ideologies of the Right or the Left helped them to understand the nature of leaders and ordinary citizens, the rights and duties that those people should possess, the way they should organize the societies in which they live, and the frictions that may arise between such societies as each pursues its vision of a good life, sometimes at the expense of its neighbors.

Dewey and his liberal colleagues felt that, in rhetoric at least, they could not defend liberalism decisively against these attractive new ideas. The challengers offered beguiling visions of national glory, racial triumph, and classless utopia. Against these temptations, liberalism's original faith flowed from a slightly dowdy eighteenth-century notion of natural rights, such as those in the Declaration of Independence, which could not be validated by the scientific testing that liberals admired.[21]

The solution, Dewey suggested, was that Americans should judge the twentieth-century ideas of Left and Right not by how rhetorically persuasive they seemed but by what outcomes they produced in the real world. Like Thomas Paine, Dewey appealed to common sense. Anyone following his prescription would notice, he thought, that authoritarian ideologies on both sides of the aisle – no matter how flashy and inspiring – lead not to peace, order, and prosperity but to war, discrimination, and concentration camps. Here was the logical sequence of thinking that, in the late 1930s, led Americans to increasingly speak of "totalitarianism." This term labeled modern dictatorships not by their competing ideologies of class, race, and nation, but by the shared tactics – such as deploying secret police, imprisoning "enemies" of the state, forbidding opposition parties, censoring newspapers, and more – which they used to oppress their own and conquered populations.[22]

Against Storytelling

The third political lesson which flowed from Dewey's pragmatism related, crucially, to the business of large-scale storytelling. What Dewey recommended was a momentous shift in the grounds of political debate

---

[21] In *Freedom and Culture* (1939), p. 112, Dewey specifically points out that natural law explanations are no longer tenable.

[22] Les Adler and Thomas Paterson, "Red Fascism: The Merger of Nazi Germany and Soviet Russia in the American Image of Totalitarianism, 1930s –1950s," *American Historical Review* (April, 1970), pp. 1046–1064.

whereby Americans would focus less on principles and more on results. This did not mean that they should abandon what they regarded as democratic devices. However, the new focus would take into account, first, that ideologues of the Right and the Left promote large stories – which to some audiences embody powerful images of success and failure, progress and retreat, good and evil, salvation and damnation – and it would recognize, second, that some people do not live by bread alone. Instead, they might hunger emotionally for large stories that explain where we are in time, how we reached this point, and what we should do about going forward together. In truth, many people, perhaps by personality and perhaps by circumstances, need such stories.

But here is where Dewey's final lesson came into play, because it was exactly the rhetorical attractiveness of stories that worried him. Narratives of the Right and Left offered dazzling leaders, torchlight rallies, martial excitement, collective farms, and heroic workers – that is, stirring visions of power, glory, solidarity, and enemies who we can love to hate. Accordingly, Dewey especially feared storytelling because, as we have seen, liberal thinkers could not decisively contest captivating stories told by their adversaries when – in the light of social science research – the liberal ideas they had to offer no longer seemed unquestionably true. Dewey's pragmatic solution to this signature liberal weakness was to insist that stories of the Right and the Left, and anywhere else, must be tested by their consequences rather than by their logical, aesthetic, or emotional elegance. In short, Dewey wanted Americans to consider long and hard not what authoritarians may *promise* but what they are likely to *deliver*.[23]

The bottom line here is that, without anticipating the liberal predicament that was yet to come – namely the storytelling gap that liberals confront today – classical pragmatism leads logically to a succinct and cardinal imperative: *Leave storytelling aside. Don't look at the world via stories. Stories may be attractive. Stories may even be inspiring. But stories are unreliable. Stories are misleading. And they may also be treacherous.*

Here was a powerful moral for people who accepted Dewey's thesis that democracy is like science, that it uses frequent elections, independent judges, and free speech to test policy results, and that it is a necessary and endless process of jockeying between new and old interests, between

---

[23] As Dewey complained, "It is both astonishing and depressing that so much of the energy of mankind has gone into fighting for ... the truth of creeds, religious, moral, and political, as distinct from what has gone into efforts to try creeds by putting them to the test of acting upon them." John Dewey, *The Quest for Certainty: A Study of the Relation of Knowledge and Action* (1929), p. 277.

modern and traditional notions of how to live and prosper together. On behalf of that ideal, to be wary of political stories was – perhaps unexpectedly – a virtue whose merit would seem ever more obvious as Americans increasingly saw dictatorial horrors; first from afar, and then first-hand when Allied ground forces entered Europe during World War II.[24] Later, the Cold War – punctuated by Soviet tanks in Poland, Hungary, and Czechoslovakia – continued to drive home the same lesson.[25] This is the wariness that John F. Kennedy invoked in 1962, when he declared that "The great enemy of the truth is very often not the lie – deliberate, contrived, and dishonest – but the myth – persistent, persuasive, and unrealistic. Too often ... we enjoy the comfort of opinion without the discomfort of thought."[26] Years later, much that we now know and see of radical Islam encourages the same wariness.

Pragmatic Humanism

We should bear in mind that Dewey's popular sort of pragmatism expressed optimism that can be described as flowing from humanism. "Liberalism" is thus linked historically to "humanism," because "disenchantment" arising in the Enlightenment went hand in hand with confidence in "human agency." In effect, humanists rejected Edmund Burke's aristocratic notion that modern people cannot successfully fashion new governmental principles or practices but should instead live according to long-standing habits and inherited inclinations. As Burke proclaimed in his great polemic against the French Revolution:

We know that *we* have made no discoveries, and we think that no discoveries are to be made, in morality, nor many in the great principles of government, nor in the ideas of liberty, which were understood long before we were born.[27]

---

[24] David Ciepley, *Liberalism in the Shadow of Totalitarianism* (2007), recalls how by the late 1930s – and even more during the Cold War – some liberal philosophers feared storytelling because it might, as in Nazi Germany and Soviet Russia, facilitate state sponsored "indoctrination." See this fear in Louis Hartz, "Goals for Political Science: A Discussion," *American Political Science Review* (December, 1951), pp. 1001–1005.

[25] President Truman expressed America's Cold War view along these lines when he asked Congress on March 12, 1947, for $400 million to support democratic forces in Greece and Turkey. As Truman put it, the choice was between a way of life embracing majority rule based on political freedoms or a "second way of life based upon the will of a minority forcibly imposed upon the majority. It relies upon terror, oppression, a controlled press and radio, fixed elections, and the suppression of personal freedom." See "'The Truman Doctrine' speech" (1947).

[26] John Kennedy, "Commencement Address at Yale University" (1962).

[27] Edmund Burke, *Reflections on the Revolution in France* (1790, 1955), pp. 97–99, especially 97. For similar reservations about human agency, see George Will, "Rewriting

Dewey's philosophy spurned Burke's passivity. Instead, by offering a methodical explanation of what people can do to exercise satisfactory agency, pragmatism codified the looser, common-sense humanism of liberals like Thomas Paine who spoke out against Burke. Early humanists like Paine opposed the Old Order's ruling stories, which recommended and validated the political and religious institutions that many Enlightenment thinkers sought to dethrone. Next came pragmatism, a philosophical foray that emerged from Enlightenment skepticism and gathered strength from Darwin's resounding demonstration of the power of the scientific method. Subsequently, by linking that method to democracy, pragmatism updated humanism's preference for understanding the world via science rather than stories. And finally, waves of authoritarian stories after World War I and continuing into the Cold War provided dreadful examples of what sort of rhetoric that liberals should scrupulously avoid.[28] The Islamists who run the Islamic State of Iraq and al-Sham (ISIS) and who aspire to recreate a seventh-century caliphate, teach the latest version of this lesson with their execution videos.

The Rub

Especially in the light of circumstances at the time, the sequence of Dewey's ideas seemed both plausible and commendable. We should note, however, that in the long run it had a serious shortcoming. By challenging the usefulness of stories and warning that they may be dangerous, the pragmatism that Dewey preached contributed to the storytelling gap which now constitutes an electoral disadvantage for the liberal camp. This is a catch-22 to which we will return.

Philosophical Pragmatism

From Peirce, James, and Dewey, we see how pragmatism relates to the world *generally*. As for the way it relates *specifically* to the liberal predicament in recent years, we should return to the question I asked earlier: *If*

History on the Filibuster" *Washington Post* December 22, 2012): "Conservatives believe that 98 percent of good governance consists of stopping bad – meaning most – ideas. So conservatives can tolerate liberal filibusters more easily than liberals, who relish hyperkinetic government, can tolerate conservative filibusters."

[28] Cold War liberals invented the "end of ideology" concept to promote pragmatic social reforms and to demonstrate that large political stories – that is, ideologies – were dangerous and unnecessary. See Daniel Bell, *The End of Ideology: On The Exhaustion of Political Ideas in the Fifties* (1960); Seymour Martin Lipset, *Political Man: The Social Bases of Politics* (1960); and Chaim Waxman (ed.), *The End of Ideology Debate* (1969).

liberals don't tell stories, what do they do politically? The short answer to this question (later we will make it longer) is that liberals "do" pragmatism. Sometimes they recommend doing this, and sometimes they recommend doing that. And sometimes they try this, and sometimes they try that. And then, when circumstances permit, they check to see if what they did works well. If not, they are willing to try something else.

According to historian James Kloppenberg, these facts of modern political life characterize the career of Barack Obama, the titular head of the liberal camp in America today. Writing in Obama's second White House year, Kloppenberg therefore argued that the President should be classified as a "philosophical pragmatist."[29] Kloppenberg traced this outlook back to Pierce, James, and Dewey. Subsequently, he defined Obama's pragmatism as a commitment to "open-endedness and experimentation," rather than to "absolute" principles.[30]

Kloppenberg described the sensibility that underlies Obama's pragmatism as being formally rooted in "antifoundationalism," "particularism," "perspectivalism," and "historicism":

By antifoundationalism and particularism, I mean the denial of universal principles ... By perspectivalism I mean the belief that everything we see is conditioned by where we stand ... By historicism I mean the conviction that all human values and practices are products of historical processes and must be interpreted within historical frameworks.[31]

Academics are more likely than ordinary citizens to dwell on such formal concepts. However, in regard to political practices, Kloppenberg insisted in plainer language that Obama was not wedded to fixed principles. The President had already begun to encounter massive Republican negativism, as expressed in Senator Mitch McConnell's 2010 declaration that his party's main aim should be to assure that Obama would spend only one term in office.[32] However, the Harvard historian concluded that, in principle, Obama aimed to fashion governmental projects by seeking common denominators among conflicting interests and aspirations. Matching Dewey's promotion of one reality check after another, in Kloppenberg's view the President believed that this search for reasonable

---

[29] James Kloppenberg, *Reading Obama: Dreams, Hope, and the American Political Tradition* (2011), pp. xi–xii.

[30] *Ibid.*, pp. xi–xiii. In the same vein, see Dewey, *The Public and Its Problems*, p. 74, p. 202, on judging institutions, events, and policies by their "consequences" rather than by absolute principles such as "individualism" or "collectivism."

[31] Kloppenberg, *Reading Obama*, p. 79.

[32] See Mitch McConnell, "Top GOP Priority: Make Obama a One-Term President," *National Journal* (September 23, 2010).

and effective public policies is best conducted in a public conversation that is always open to new ideas and arguments.[33] As Kloppenberg said, democracy in this mode – as an ongoing method rather than a collection of good results – entails "struggling with differences, then achieving provisional agreements that immediately spark new disagreements."[34]

Other scholars, such as political scientist Stephen Skowronek, agree with Kloppenberg's thesis about Obama.[35] They do so because plentiful evidence supports it. For example, at a vital moment in the President's career, pragmatism clearly inspired his "First Inaugural Address" in 2009. As the President said in that speech:

What the cynics fail to understand is that the ground has shifted beneath them, that the stale political arguments that have consumed us for so long, no longer apply. The question we ask today is not whether government is too big or small, but whether it works, whether it helps families find jobs at a decent wage, care they can afford, a retirement that is dignified.[36]

Liberal Politicians

Pragmatism animated several Democratic presidents before Obama, although Kloppenberg did not dwell on them. We have already cited Franklin Roosevelt's *explicit* pragmatism. But Roosevelt also affirmed pragmatism *implicitly*. For example, when asked if he had a political philosophy, FDR replied: "Philosophy? I am a Christian and a Democrat – that's all."[37] What was left, as when the President tried creatively to overcome hard economic times, was a sort of muddling through that can be called "pragmatism."

---

[33] Kloppenberg, *Reading Obama*, p. 161.

[34] *Ibid.*, p. 83.

[35] See Stephen Skowronek, *Presidential Leadership in Political Time* (2011), p. 186:

[Obama] privileges the pragmatic, rational, problem-solving ethos. He exudes the progressive spirit of post-partisan engagement, of openness to new information, of realism in dealing with friend and foe alike, of steadiness in pursuit of policy solutions to big national challenges, of faith in expertise.

[36] Barack Obama, "First Inaugural Address," January 20, 2009. Obama is also a humanist, although Kloppenberg does not use that term. Thus in the same speech:

[T]here are some who question the scale of our ambitions, who suggest that our system cannot tolerate too many big plans. Their memories are short, for they have forgotten what this country has already done, what free men and women can achieve [human agency] when imagination is joined to common purpose and necessity to courage.

[37] Quoted in Frances Perkins, *The Roosevelt I Knew* (1964), p. 330.

Other pragmatic, but also liberal, presidents included John F. Kennedy, who declared in his Yale Commencement Address in 1962:

What is at stake in our economic decisions ... is not some grand warfare of rival ideologies which will sweep the country with passion, but the practical management of a modern economy. What we need is not labels and clichés but more basic discussion of the sophisticated and technical questions involved in keeping a great economic machinery moving ahead.[38]

Lyndon Johnson sounded much the same note in 1964 at the University of Michigan:

[T]he Great Society is not a safe harbor, a resting place, a final objective, a finished work. It is a challenge constantly renewed, beckoning us toward a destiny where the meaning of our lives matches the marvelous products of our labor.[39]

For the most part, liberal candidates who don't reach the White House are also pragmatic. For example, Governor Michael Dukakis of Massachusetts, accepting the Democratic nomination in 1988, announced that "this election isn't about ideology. It's about competence."[40] And Senator Paul Tsongas (D-MA), who sought the Democratic presidential nomination in 1992, similarly promoted systematic practicality. In *The Road From Here: Liberalism and Realities in the 1980s* (1981), Tsongas praised:

... realism – non-ideological, clear-eyed realism. My interest is in what works, not what should work ... [therefore] the demise of the Democratic Party [in the 1980 national election] was due to one basic fact: reality does not bend to fit [the party's] political theory.[41]

In other words, according to Tsongas, Democrats lost in 1980 and entered the Reagan era because they clung to outdated ideas and did not pragmatically confront the changing facts of social and economic life in America.

[38] But even when he sees JFK as pragmatic, Bruce Miroff, *Pragmatic Illusions: The Presidential Politics of John F. Kennedy* (1979), is less inclined to credit him with being liberal.

[39] See Lyndon B. Johnson, "Remarks at the University of Michigan."

[40] Dukakis, "'A New Era of Greatness for America': Address Accepting the Presidential Nomination at the Democratic National Convention in Atlanta." G. H. W. Bush answered Dukakis's claim when he accepted the Republican presidential nomination in 1988. Competence, said Bush, tells us when the trains are running on time but not where they should go. Therefore, he continued, the election of 1988 was not about competence but about beliefs, values, and principles. As we have seen, for the Right these are conveyed by stories, which Bush then proceeded to tell or allude to. See George Bush, "Address Accepting the Presidential Nomination at the Republican National Convention in New Orleans".

[41] Paul Tsongas, *The Road From Here: Liberalism and Realities in the 1980s*, p. xiii.

Liberal Journalists

Beyond office holders and candidates, pragmatism is likely to inspire liberal journalists. For example, E. J. Dionne argues in *Our Divided Political Heart: the Battle for the American Idea in an Age of Discontent* (2013), that, although conservatives believe otherwise, America's authentic national narrative praises what he calls "the Long Consensus." According to this story, generation after generation of Americans promoted both individualism *and* community, sometimes using government to strengthen the one (say, by abolishing slavery) and sometimes using it to strengthen the other (say, by building dams for the Tennessee Valley Authority). This view of American values is inherently pragmatic because it is not anchored in a particular set of first principles or a political program. Thus Dionne postulates a continual tension between pursuing "the local and the national, the individual and the communal, the economic and the civic," depending on what circumstances, or predictable outcomes, prescribe to us as appropriate and effective public policies.[42]

As if to buttress this point, conservatives regard liberal journalists as pragmatic and criticize them for it. Those journalists tend to see the charge as true. They know, for example, that their own general convictions can be traced philosophically to a late-eighteenth-century insistence on practical fact-gathering. Thus, in a 2004 conversation reported by Ron Suskind and frequently cited afterwards, Suskind quotes an anonymous and presumably conservative Bush II White House aide :

The aide [probably Karl Rove] says that guys like me [Suskind] "were in what we [the White House aides] call the reality-based community," which he [the aide] defined as people who "believe that solutions emerge from your judicious study of discernable reality." I [Suskind] nodded and murmured something about enlightenment principles and empiricism. He [the aide] cut me off. "That's not the way the world really works anymore," he continued. "We're an empire now, and when we act, we create our own reality."[43]

The aide's sense of things here is clear. In his eyes, "reality-based" liberals such as Suskind, by sticking to empiricism, were small-minded pragmatists limited by "the facts," while Bush II's White House rose boldly above circumstances.[44]

[42] *Our Divided Political Heart*, p. 21.
[43] Ron Suskind, "Faith, Certainty and the Presidency of George W. Bush," *New York Times* (2004).
[44] In *The Assault on Reason*, p. 60, Al Gore agrees with Suskind about the Bush White House:

When you boil down precisely what went wrong with the Bush Iraq policy, it's fairly simple. He waged the politics of blind faith ... He adopted an ideologically driven view of Iraq that

The Bottom Line

Liberal politicians, journalists, think-tankers, activists, and voters are more concerned with winning elections and getting things done than they are with explaining philosophically what underlies their liberalism. Therefore most of what they say and write focuses on doing rather than on justifying. Furthermore, whether or not they are philosophical pragmatists cannot be proved by citing a few more or a few less examples of credo statements. This is because liberalism is not a card-carrying enterprise, no one knows exactly who the class of liberals are, the number of liberals is impossible to ascertain, and no one can therefore say for sure how many examples of confluence will prove, statistically speaking, that liberalism and pragmatism are inherently linked.[45]

Nonetheless, it seems clear that in the sweep of American history (and certainly in recent years) liberals have been more committed to citing facts (empiricism) and revising circumstances (reform) than advocating fundamental beliefs (expressed in long-term stories). This is what Kloppenberg means when he postulates philosophical pragmatism as the hallmark of Obama's approach to public life. However, it remains to ask where that pragmatism is headed and to what sorts of circumstances it is directed. We now turn to that question.

was tragically at odds with reality ... When that painful reality began to displace illusion in the public's mind, the President made increasingly strenuous efforts to silence the messengers of truth and create his own version of reality. His seeming contempt for the rule of reason ... apparently tempted him to the ... illusion that reality itself has become a commodity that can be created and sold with clever propaganda and public relations skills.

45 However, for big data enthusiasts, I Googled "liberalism and pragmatism" on January 27, 2016 and received "about" 23,400,000 results.

6

Shklar's Fear

Now I am become Death [Shiva], the destroyer of worlds.

The Bhagavad-Gita, quoted by Robert Oppenheimer after witnessing the world's first nuclear explosion at Alamogordo, New Mexico on July 16, 1945.

Kloppenberg argues that Obama's liberalism is pragmatic. In support of that thesis, he emphasizes the President's philosophical aspirations. These presumably flow from what Obama learned in school, the great writers he studied, the books he read, and how he related to them. Other liberal presidents, politicians, and journalists can be seen as expressing some of the same sentiments.

There is, however, a second scholarly thesis about what liberalism is. It draws our attention to where liberals direct their philosophical pragmatism. That is, it describes the conditions they are likely to address and, if troublesome, seek to improve. According to this thesis, liberalism is driven by what political scientist Judith Shklar called "fear." That is why I opened this chapter with Robert Oppenheimer's anguished warning about the awesome force that modern science has unleashed and that modern people must somehow control.

Fear

In an essay entitled "The Liberalism of Fear," Shklar claimed that liberals are people in modern history who advocate overthrowing various forms of what they regard as tyranny.[1] These might include witch trials, torture,

---

[1] Judith Shklar, " The Liberalism of Fear ," in Nancy Rosenblum (ed.), *Liberalism and the Moral Life* (1989), pp. 21–38.

public executions, *lettres de cachet*, taxation without representation, naval impressments, slavery, and Native American displacement. And they might move on to lynchings, railroad rebates, municipal corruption, child labor, "yellow dog" contracts, concentration camps, female mutilation, ethnic cleansing, crony capitalism, deindustrialization, mandatory prison terms, homophobia, and more. All of these existed either during the Old Order or in other places later.

Shklar did not say so but there is no grand narrative here because, as generations pass, liberalism targets different forms of tyranny according to time and place. That is why – again not noted by Shklar – intellectual historians like Alan Ryan are unable to list which notions, if any, are shared by great exemplars of the liberal persuasion such as John Locke, Adam Smith, Thomas Jefferson, John Stuart Mill, Isaiah Berlin, and John Rawls.[2]

Differences like these aside, from historical examples Shklar regarded liberals as people who do not know what they *do* want together but rally around what they *do not* want. That is, they do not agree on ideal arrangements which citizens should create but on appalling conditions that they should avoid. Shklar makes this point formally when she says that liberalism does not:

offer a *summum bonum* toward which all political agents should strive, but it certainly does ... begin with a *summum malum*, which all of us know and would avoid if only we could. That evil [the liberal target] is cruelty and the fear it inspires, and the very fear of fear itself.[3]

In which case, liberalism – at least since the Enlightenment – exists to criticize the existing order and improve upon it. In Shklar's view, that is what the *philosophes* did,[4] what the Founders did, what Franklin Roosevelt

---

[2] The same pluralism characterizes modern liberalism. See E. J. Dionne, "Foreward," (2007), in Neil Jumonville and Kevin Mattson (eds.), *Liberalism for a New Century* (2007), p. xvi:

There are many brands of liberalism ... Some people are drawn to liberalism because of its commitment to individual rights; others, because of its devotion to economic justice. Some liberals are communitarian. Others mistrust communitarianism. Some liberals define their cause as a defense of the well-being of "working families." Others see any mention of families as hopelessly homophobic and sexist. Some liberals are trade unionists. Others are investment bankers. Some liberals favor free trade and see globalization as inevitable. Others devoutly mistrust free trade and want to put the brakes on globalization.

[3] Shklar, "The Liberalism of Fear," p. 29. By focusing on what all liberals are against rather than what some liberals are for, Shklar avoids the analytical problem of synthesizing multiple liberalisms raised by Alan Ryan, *The Making of Modern Liberalism* (2012).

[4] Thus Voltaire's slogan, "*ecrasez l'infame*" ("let us stamp out infamy.")

did, and what is happening today. As if to prove the point, Richard Rorty cited Shklar's thesis and defined himself as a liberal opposed to cruelty.[5] In the same spirit, law professor Alan Dershowitz, in *Rights From Wrongs: The Origins of Human Rights in the Experience of Injustice* (2005), concludes that even if we do not manage to agree on what are rights, we should at least agree on what are wrongs.

Shklar did not use Kloppenberg's terminology, and therefore did not propose that liberalism expresses "philosophical pragmatism." Nevertheless, she and Kloppenberg were on the same analytical wavelength, because she ascribed a pragmatic approach in social affairs to liberals by claiming that liberal thinkers and doers tend to identify some circumstances as social defects and then campaign to repair them. In effect they thereby behave pragmatically by promoting what they consider to be specific, tangible, and effective ways to eliminate tyranny, exploitation, and discrimination.[6]

The Conservative Alternative

More political than philosophical, and more a matter of describing projects than of delivering justifications, the liberalism that Shklar embraced does not much interest American rightists. Their alternative view of what liberalism is about can be explored in the writings of conservative intellectuals who are more learned and subtle than Ronald Reagan, Grover Norquist, George W. Bush, Rand Paul, Jim Demint, Ted Cruz, Ben Carson, Mike Huckabee, Rush Limbaugh, Michael Savage, Laura Ingraham, and Sean Hannity. Such writings include Alasdair MacIntyre, *After Virtue: A Study in Moral Theory* (1984); Stephen Carter, *The Culture of Disbelief: How American Law and Politics Trivialize Religious Devotion* (1994); Paul Kahn, *Putting Liberalism in Its Place* (2005); Charles Taylor, *A Secular Age* (2007); Michael Gillespie, *The Theological Origins of Modernity* (2008); Steven Smith, *The Disenchantment of Secular Discourse* (2010); Brad Gregory, *The Unintended Reformation: How a Religious Revolution Secularized Society* (2012); George Marsden, *The*

---

[5] Richard Rorty, *Contingency, Irony, and Solidarity* (1989), pp. xv–xi.

[6] Philosopher Charles Frankel, in *The Case for Modern Man* (1956), p. 33, defines liberalism as a passion for social reform. Similarly, historian Arthur Schlesinger, Jr., in "The Liberal Opportunity," *The American Prospect* (March, 1990), pp. 10–18, assumes a commitment to problem-solving when he proposes that "in a democracy politics is about something more than the struggle for power or the manipulation of image. It is above all about the search for remedy."

Twilight of the American Enlightenment (2014); and Larry Siedentop, *Inventing the Individual: The Origins of Western Liberalism* (2014).

In these and similar books, philosophical conservatives start their critique of liberalism by recalling that Western Europe was "Christian" before it became "enlightened." It follows, in their opinion, that important Enlightenment ideas – such as the power of reason, the need for disenchantment, the separation of religion and state, the centrality of individualism, and the importance of human dignity – arose out of Christian concepts and practices such as the papal Two Swords doctrine, which distinguished between spiritual and temporal authorities, and the anti-clericalism of Protestants, who denied that priests possess a mystical power to mediate between God and their parishioners.

From this point of view, Enlightenment writers who together challenged Christian principles and performances, such as Spinoza, Diderot, Voltaire, Rousseau, Hume, and Kant, in doing so undermined a European sense of divine order and purpose that, over time, would have produced human progress without being provoked by more radical ideas.[7] Here was a crucial turning point in Western history according to conservatives, because while Enlightenment thinkers chipped away at Christianity they and their liberal descendants never provided an acceptable replacement for Christianity's ethical narrative, which was advancing satisfactorily without them.

These claims rest on a common denominator, which is the charge that liberals, now on the American Left, have failed to assemble a shared substitute for what we may call Christianity's "alpha story" of how God created the universe and human beings in it, and of how in that universe a loving relationship with God is necessary to provide human beings with meaningful lives and moral guidelines.[8] In more critical moments, conservatives are even likely to argue that not only did liberals undermine Christianity's alpha story, but they also set the philosophical stage – or paved the ideological way – for the rise of terrible regimes such as German Nazism, Soviet Communism, and Chinese Maoism.[9]

---

[7] Anthony Pagden, *The Enlightenment and Why It Still Matters* (2013), especially pp. 406–414, rejects the conservative claim that Christianity would have produced modern progress without outside prodding. In effect, that is also the message of Philipp Blom, *A Wicked Company: The Forgotten Radicalism of the European Enlightenment* (2010), Jonathan Israel, *A Revolution of the Mind: Radical Enlightenment and the Intellectual Origins of Modern Democracy* (2010), and Matthew Stewart, *Nature's God: The Heretical Origins of the American Republic* (2014).

[8] Alasdair MacIntyre, *After Virtue* (1984), 2nd edn., pp. 51–61.

[9] Thus John Gray, in *Enlightenment's Wake: Politics and Culture at the Close of the Modern Age* (1995), pp. 229–231, claims that the Counter-Enlightenment was actually a

The Liberal Project

Shklar rejected this conservative way of looking at liberalism when she insisted that liberals in public life are not in the business of creating new moral systems but seek only to correct obvious and painful sorts of tyranny. To that end, liberalism is "not a philosophy of life such as has been traditionally been provided by various forms of revealed religion and other comprehensive *Weltanshauungen*."[10] In fact, it is not a philosophy at all, she said, because liberals do not regard themselves as responsible for knowing what the moral order should look like in the long run. They only insist that it must stop tolerating patent cases of brutality now.

In sum, according to Shklar, liberalism is not a project designed to create new ethics, with "positive doctrines about how people are to conduct their lives or what personal choices they are to make."[11] Therefore liberalism should refrain from telling people what it means to be happy.[12] In the American context this point carries special weight because, before the Revolution in 1776, it was long assumed that individuals should chiefly pursue salvation as a sort of happiness defined by priests, ministers, metaphysicians, and theologians rather than ordinary citizens. The Declaration of Independence proclaimed instead, in the name of Shklar's liberalism, that everyone is entitled to pursue happiness on his or her own.

The Conservative Sidestep

Conservative philosophers do not directly refute Shklar's view of what liberalism is or is not about. Instead, they sidestep her historical claim by insisting that *all* people – even atheists – seek to understand what Charles Taylor calls the "fullness" of human life beyond "imminent" circumstances,[13] or hope to discover answers to what Brad Gregory calls "life questions" about how we should live and the ethical standards we should maintain.[14]

---

child of the Enlightenment because the latter so emptied society of meaning that people were desperate for a replacement view.

[10] Shklar, "The Liberalism of Fear," p. 21.

[11] *Ibid.*

[12] *Ibid.*, p. 31.

[13] Charles Taylor, *A Secular Age* (2007), pp. 597–617.

[14] Brad Gregory, *The Unintended Reformation: How a Religious Revolution Secularized Society* (2012), pp. 74–82. See also Charles Kesler, *I am the Change: Barack Obama and the Crisis of Liberalism* (2012), p. 229. Kesler notes that, according to Shklar, liberals oppose cruelty. But, he continues, as "relativists" they never explain that "hatred of cruelty is no more moral or rational than love of cruelty." That is, hatred of cruelty is a mere "value judgment, with no ground in truth or science or Being or anything else supposedly 'out there.'"

It follows that conservatives not only impute to all people – including atheists – a constant curiosity about such matters,[15] but they also go on to describe modern society as dominated by a scientific discourse that is "shallow, empty, and pointless."[16] Consequently, they say, even modern people, who are free to choose among many lifestyle "options," are anxious to understand not only how to program their digital gadgets but also what life is for. As Taylor says, "I am taking it as axiomatic that everyone [including liberals], and hence all philosophical positions [such as those of John Rawls and Ronald Dworkin], accept some definition of greatness and fullness in human life."[17]

Philosophy Over Politics

Ergo, rightists bypass Shklar's *political* emphasis by claiming that liberalism has failed as a *philosophical* project. Here is a rhetorical move that changes the subject rather than addresses the charges. Having shifted the grounds of debate, rightists then deny that human beings can use reason to discover conclusive ethical principles, as some Enlightenment *philosophes* had hoped. This is because reason leads to many plausible opinions, in which case modern thinkers cannot agree on the best way to organize society and how to behave in it. Consequently, conservatives say, we must locate some transcendent authority that will override disagreements and prescribe the necessary principles for us. In their view that authority is, and always has been, God.[18]

Of course, according to secular people, scientists such as Galileo, Franklin, Jenner, Darwin, Pasteur, Curie, Einstein, Hubble, Crick, and Salk, have "disproved" the existence of God – or at least have set Him aside as He and His works appear in the Bible. Consequently, there can be no turning back. In reply, conservatives insist that the validity of disproofs

---

[15] Dinesh D'Souza, *What's So Great About Christianity* (2007), p. 198, disagrees with both Taylor and Gregory on this point. D'Souza criticizes both atheists and agnostics because, he says, they are:

> entirely incurious about the most important questions in life: Why are we here? Is this life all there is? What happens when we die? These great mysteries press themselves on all humans who ponder their situation, and yet there are people who refuse even to consider those mysteries.

[16] Steven Smith, *The Disenchantment of Secular Discourse* (2010), p. 219.

[17] Taylor, *A Secular Age*, p. 597.

[18] This argument in theological terms appears in, for example, William Lane Craig, *Reasonable Faith: Christian Truth and Apologetics*, 3rd edn. (2008). Moreover, secular conservatives may stipulate the need for Judeo-Christian "values." For example, Tammy Bruce, *The Death of Right and Wrong: Exposing the Left's Assault on our Culture and Values* (2003), pp. 39–58.

has been greatly exaggerated and that God is still with us. Along these lines, Brad Gregory argues that God is "radically distinct from the universe as a whole ... unimaginable and incomprehensible."[19] It follows that He can "never be shown to be unreal via empirical inquiry," which is the province of science.[20] Presumably, He can instead be approached via theology or metaphysics – neither of which can, epistemologically speaking, be challenged by scientific standards of analysis that pertain only to tangible actors and concrete events.[21]

Other conservatives affirm God and His Kingdom differently, by positing a sort of equivalence between "scientific" and "religious" knowledge. After all, theoretically, if neither is more conclusive than the other, we are entitled to settle on either.[22] To buttress this point, Charles Taylor claims that choosing between religion and disenchantment entails not "proofs" or "obviousness" but "dispositions," "anticipatory confidences," or "leaps of faith."[23] Thus Darwinism did not produce "facts" that falsified a "moral outlook." Instead, when Darwin offered a new hypothesis about the origin of species, "one moral outlook gave way to another."[24] Yet such moral outlooks are inconclusive, says Taylor, because they "function as unchallenged axioms, rather than unshakeable arguments."[25]

---

[19] Gregory, *The Unintended Reformation*, p. 30.

[20] *Ibid.*, p. 32.

[21] D'Souza makes this point in *What's So Great About Christianity*, p. 198:

> [W]hen Christopher Hitchens [author of *God is Not Great: How Religion Poisons Everything* (2009)] routinely dismisses religious claims on the grounds that "what can be asserted without evidence can also be dismissed without evidence," he is making what philosophers like to call a category mistake. He is using empirical criteria to judge things that lie outside the empirical realm. He wants evidence from a domain where the normal rules of evidence do not apply. Beyond the reach of reason and experience the absence of evidence cannot be used as evidence of absence.

> See also David Berlinski, *The Devil's Delusion: Atheism and its Scientific Pretensions* (2009), p. 45: "[T]he question I am asking is not whether he [God] exists but whether science has shown that he does not."

[22] Conservative activists often promote this notion. For example, see Mel Gabler and Norma Gabler, *What Are They Teaching our Children?* (1985), p. 133: "Evolution and creation really are hypotheses, though we shall use the term theory to describe both." See also George W. Bush insisting that schools should teach "the theory" of evolution as well as "the story" of creation. Bush is quoted in Mark Crispin Miller, *The Bush Dyslexicon: Observations on a National Disorder* (2002), p. 141.

[23] Taylor, *A Secular Age*, pp. 551–556.

[24] *Ibid.*, p. 563.

[25] *Ibid.*, p. 590.

Taylor's chain of philosophical reasoning, like that which underlies Zeno's Paradox, seems to me logically plausible.[26] However, exactly what scientists do – such as when they discover the "truth" that penicillin cures many bacterial infections –cannot entirely be explained by philosophical analysis.[27] In which case it seems certain that no modern philosopher – no matter how metaphysically astute – would have voluntarily sat next to the tower at Ground Zero in Alamogordo, New Mexico on July 16, 1945, waiting for scientists to try out the world's first atomic bomb, confident that opinion on how to make it was based on a "moral outlook" no more accurate than any of the others.

Church and State

Unlike Christian-Right activists such as Jerry Falwell,[28] when philosophical conservatives reject liberalism for failing on ethics they rarely advocate an across-the-board return to popular Christian doctrines, such as those endorsed by the Presbyterian General Assembly in 1910 when it deliberately set out to resist the spread of modern liberalism in thought and deed. The Assembly's "Five Fundamentals," which went on to inspire various groups of fundamentalist and evangelical Americans, included the miracles of Christ, the virgin birth, the resurrection, the crucifixion as a symbol of Christ's atonement for Christians' sins, and reverence for the biblical text as inspired by God.

Since at least the 1970s, Christian-Rightists such as those in the Moral Majority and Focus on the Family have often endorsed such principles.[29] But philosophical conservatives, at least in America, do not much admire faith in miracles and biblical inerrancy, and do not admire what Thomas Hobbes called "invisible powers."[30] Such rightists are more likely to

---

[26] In Zeno's Paradox, Achilles can't catch up with a running turtle because every time he travels half of the distance to the turtle, the turtle runs forward a little and therefore will always stay ahead of Achilles, if only very slightly.

[27] This is because we know from experience rather than philosophy that penicillin works. See Jerry Coyne, *Faith vs. Fact: Why Science and Religion Are Incompatible* (2015), p. 206.

[28] For example, Jerry Falwell, *Listen America!* (1980); Tim LaHaye, *Faith of our Founding Fathers: A Comprehensive Study of America's Christian Foundations* (1990); and D. James Kennedy, *What If America Were a Christian Nation Again?* (2003).

[29] Thus D. James Kennedy, "Reclaiming America for Christ," in D. James Kennedy, Gary Bauer, John Ashcroft, *et al.*, *Reclaiming America for Christ* (1996), p. 8, assures us that "[I]f all the Christians in America simply led one person to Christ this year, this nation would once again be overwhelmingly Christian, and most all [sic] of the problems of society would vanish like snow before the rising sun."

[30] *Leviathan* (1651), Part 1, Ch. 6. See Hobbes also on "the Kingdom of Fairies," *Leviathan*, Part 4, Ch. 47.

suggest that society should pay serious respect – which many modern people do not – to theological propositions that some citizens want to promote in public, since, as Paul Kahn says, "Real people ... do not live by reason, but by the faith that fuels imagination."[31]

Without being specific, then, Steven Smith recommends that we should be "more open" than we are today to non-scientific thoughts, ideas, and truths.[32] His point is that secular Americans should welcome public debate over concerns expressed by religious people because those concerns are important to pious citizens.[33] To this end, George Marsden insists that there should be no prejudice, in public discussions, "against religiously based views simply because of their religious nature." Rather, those views should be debated in public life when they are presented "through reasoned arguments that look for a common ground of widely shared concerns."[34]

In fact, without saying so explicitly, Smith and his colleagues want to renegotiate – if not repeal – America's separation of church and state. However, that separation is largely based on bitter experience rather than philosophical analysis. Where that is so, it teaches that religious convictions are so potentially dangerous that they must not be permitted to invest public debate or policy. Smith addresses this fear when he observes that, in one liberal scenario, bypassing separation might lead Christian voters to try to ban abortion "because this is the will of God." But this supposition is a "caricature," says Smith, because "even devout religious believers who are at all thoughtful hardly ever say *that* sort of thing, exactly."[35] In other words, according to Smith, we can safely

---

[31] Paul Kahn, *Putting Liberalism in its Place* (2005), p. 288.

[32] Smith, *The Disenchantment of Secular Discourse*, pp. 211–225.

[33] *Ibid.*, pp. 223–225.

[34] George Marsden, *The Twilight of the American Enlightenment* (2014), p. 175. Marsden probably means that America should maintain severe punishments for murderers because murder is unreasonable, rather than because it is forbidden by biblical commandments.

[35] Smith, *The Disenchantment of Secular Discourse*, p. 220. The qualifications built into this sentence – "thoughtful," "hardly ever," and "exactly" – suggest that some philosophical Christians may feel uncomfortable with their co-religionists who, in Smith's term, may be less than "thoughtful." So much for millions of American Christians who profess allegiance to sectarian axioms expressed in church manifestos such as the (Calvinist) Westminster Catechism or the (Catholic) Apostle's Creed. A philosophical Jew may use the same ploy. Thus Leon Wieseltier, "Crimes Against Humanities" *The New Republic* (September 3, 2013): "Only a small minority of believers in any of the scriptural religions, for example, have ever taken scripture literally." So much for tens of thousands of Israeli Jewish settlers who regard themselves as living not in the West Bank of the Jordan River but in Judea and Samaria.

abolish separation because our neighbors are more likely to resemble Martin Luther King and Albert Schweitzer than Thomas de Torquemada or Osama Bin Laden.

This optimistic respect for what pious voters might promote is characteristic of Stephen Carter's view of how "contemporary liberalism" should interpret the Constitution's First Amendment as it relates to religious freedom. In his "Evolutionism, Creationism, and Treating Religion as a Hobby" (1984), Carter argues that scientific and theological beliefs are, philosophically speaking, roughly equal in validity, the one based on "empiricism" and the other on "hermeneutics." That being so, the latter deserve to be debated openly when public policy is at stake.[36]

Carter apparently believes that America's government will never, or almost never, enforce religious orthodoxy. He therefore promotes much the same benign view of piety at greater length in *The Culture of Disbelief* (1994). George Marsden is similarly optimistic. As he says:

> Although religious people may reasonably be expected to act with a degree of civility in the public domain, showing respect for others and their differing views, it is not reasonable or practical to expect them to act in the public realm without reference to their deeply held, religiously based moral convictions.[37]

Lilla's Gloss

In *The Stillborn God* (2008),[38] historian Mark Lilla doubts that modern piety is benign. We may therefore count him as one of Shklar's fearful liberals. He implicitly rejects Carter's assertion that "What is needed ... is a willingness to *listen,* not because the speaker has *the right voice* [religious] but because the speaker has *the right to speak* [a constitutional right]."[39] In the political world that Lilla admires, citizens of every faith and walk of life are *entitled to speak* in public. Here is the very essence of democracy. Nevertheless, as a matter of common sense, other citizens are not *obliged to listen* when religious principles are promoted in public. This is because we know, from bitter experience, that some of those principles might be enacted into law by majority vote and thereby tyrannize people who hold different beliefs.

---

36 Stephen Carter, "Evolutionism, Creationism, and Treating Religion as a Hobby," *Duke Law Journal* (December, 1987), pp. 977–996.

37 Marsden, *The Twilight of the American Enlightenment*, p. 158.

38 Mark Lilla, *The Stillborn God: Religion, Politics, and the Modern West* (2008).

39 Stephen Carter, *The Culture of Disbelief: How American Law and Politics Trivialize Religious Devotion* (1994), p. 230.

Lilla reminds us that history is instructive on this point. The Enlightenment arose among Europeans who, against a historical backdrop of the Reformation and Counter-Reformation, knew what horrendous wars could emerge from rampaging religious sentiment. As a result, thinkers like Thomas Hobbes and John Locke successfully recommended what Lilla calls "The Great Separation." Their aim was to erect an intellectual barrier between political *theology*, which seeks to serve God's will, and political *thought*, which focuses on citizens rather than God, or on ordinary people's needs rather than His. In many Western countries, driven by fear of future dissonance and violence – which might flow from piety – this recommendation led to longstanding stories of divine works and intents being relegated mostly to private life.[40]

In short, in Western history according to Mark Lilla, an existing ethical system was undermined by Enlightenment thinkers and doers who believed that it had generated warfare and tyranny and that it would continue to do so if it were not checked. In their eyes, and in those of Lilla, overthrowing the Old Regime was necessary. It did not follow, however, that liberals were obliged to replace what they rejected. That is, their brief did not include fashioning new ethical standards for post-Enlightenment societies.

On the contrary. According to Lilla, liberalism is strong to the extent it knows what is patently wrong – politically speaking – with religion. That does not mean, though, that liberalism is qualified to say what is right across the board. Rather, Lilla notes, when liberals have offered such guidance they have usually had little success, such as when thinkers like Thomas Paine and the Unitarians tried to make Christianity more reasonable and progressive than it had been.[41]

As Lilla points out, the problem facing liberals is that, because political moderates are haunted by the religious wars of the Reformation, they feel they must uphold strict prohibitions against public expressions of religion based on an unforgiving political reality. However, it follows that in modern times what remains permissible is practical politicking, which is predominantly secular, full of unsightly compromises, and short on inspiring stories about how God wants people to live.[42] Such politicking does not

---

[40] Lilla, *The Stillborn God*, especially pp. 55–103.

[41] Thus in *The Age of Reason* (1793), Paine advocated deism, according to which reasonable people do not need revelation or organized churches to help them to understand that God wants us to do good works.

[42] For a classic liberal defense of democratic politicking – untidy, banal, infuriating, and uninspiring as it may be – see Bernard Crick, *In Defense of Politics* (1962, 1993).

speak powerfully to men and women who hope for a quest greater than affluence or a calling more meaningful than shopping, regardless of how dangerous it might be politically.

In Lilla's world, Enlightenment thinkers dethroned political theology but also hoped that an open-minded form of religiosity – properly blended into education in a non-partisan way – would inspire people to good citizenship, mutual tolerance, personal courtesies, neighborly generosity, national pride, economic prudence, and even ecumenicalism. Advocacy for this sort of useful decency, which informs teachings by what is called "liberal Christianity" today[43] and which Orthodox Jews might chide gently as *parve*,[44] leads Lilla to observe – perhaps with an eye on American evangelicals – that "the liberal deity turned out to be a stillborn God, unable to inspire genuine conviction among those seeking ultimate truth."[45]

Lilla reminds us that, by banning "higher" intentions from the public square, liberal concepts and practices have forestalled a great deal of violence and oppression. But how to maintain the relatively decent and tolerant order which reigns in Western democracies today will always remain for liberals an open question, a matter of continually weighing costs and benefits. Lilla therefore offers no formula that will guarantee long-term success for the liberal project, but instead concludes by stating his own credo:

We modern liberals] have wagered that it is wiser to beware the forces unleashed by the Bible's messianic promise than to try exploiting them for the public good. We have chosen to keep our politics unilluminated by the light of revelation. If our experiment is to work, we must rely on our own lucidity [reason].[46]

---

[43] On "liberal Christianity," which inspires mostly "mainline" churches rather than evangelicals or fundamentalists, see Christopher Evans, *Liberalism Without Illusions: Renewing an American Christian Tradition* (2010). Criticism of this outlook was summed up by H. Richard Niebuhr, *The Kingdom of God in America* (1937), p. 193, who defined liberal theology as: "A God without wrath brought men without sin into a kingdom without judgment through the ministrations of a Christ without a cross."

[44] *Parve* is a Yiddish word that can be translated as "neutral" and is commonly used, in Jewish slang, to connote "wishy-washy." According to the rules that define a kosher diet, meat and milk products should not be eaten together, whereas *parve* products (such as water-based sherbert rather than ice cream) contain neither milk nor meat and therefore can be eaten with either.

[45] Lilla, *The Stillborn God*, p. 301.

[46] *Ibid.*, p. 309. For examples of the piety that Lilla feared, see David Kertzer, *The Pope Against the Jews: The Vatican's Role in the Rise of Modern Anti-Semitism* (2001), and Papal Encyclicals Online, "Syllabus Condemning the Errors of the Modernists" (1907).

7

Liberal Outrage

The life of the law has not been logic: it has been experience. The felt neces-
sities of the time, the prevalent moral and political theories, intuitions of
public policy, avowed or unconscious, even the prejudices which judges
share with their fellow-men, have had a good deal more to do than the syllogism in determining the rules by which men should be governed.
Oliver Wendell Holmes, Jr., The Common Law (1881)

James Kloppenberg described liberalism as an expression of pragmatism,
while Judith Shklar explained how liberals direct pragmatism against
cruelty and tyranny. Their overlapping insights help us to understand
an obvious but not always noticed fact of contemporary American life,
which is that liberals have generated a great many angry books in fields
like race relations, family life, consumerism, food politics, mass communications, gender status, environmental studies, government secrecy, money
in elections, welfare, globalization, public transportation, unemployment, education, corporate power, and Wall Street manipulations. These
books are, from one realm to another, powerful expressions of what liberals and other Americans are "experiencing," as future Supreme Court
Justice Oliver Wendell Holmes, Jr. might have remarked. Kloppenberg's
thesis predicts that such books, each angry about something in its own
way, will usually call for pragmatic repair of current practices. On this
score, Kloppenberg is correct, because liberals tend to write that *there* is a
problem, *this* is what it costs us, and *here* is how we can fix it. But, angry
liberal books also confirm what Shklar postulates because, in a way, *their
common aim is to expose indecency – including, of course, various forms
of tyranny.*

So Shklar is also correct. Books in the Shklarian vein are written by – among others – journalists, activists, think-tankers, and academics. Wherever they come from, these writers share a powerful sense of dissatisfaction – even outrage – arising from situations that they see as generating inequality, violence, blight, oppression, and waste, and that they therefore view as patently worthy of reform.[1] In this state, while they are unable to derive assurance or equanimity from conservative alpha stories – such as those about benevolent traditions and a benign marketplace – which frame the great complexities of life, liberals are annoyed and sometimes even infuriated by a wide range of situations, one after another and side by side, that seem to them simply intolerable.

So much to do! So little time! Liberal expressions of outrage amount to a latter-day version of the "muckraking" that Progressives generated in America more than a century ago, when they denounced – among other offenses to decency – industrial monopolies, financial concentration, food adulteration, municipal corruption, unhealthy slums, and dangerous workplaces. The same outrage now fuels an outpouring of media writing and broadcasting which journalists call "accountability reporting,"[2] and which directs a stream of urgent facts and moral admonitions to people who historian Richard Hofstadter called "literate citizens."

Humanism Versus Conservative Alpha Stories

In their relation to the liberal predicament, liberal complaints stand on one side of a large ideological divide. The assumption that underlies them all is "humanism." According to that outlook, a critic of social, economic, or political practices defines and exposes indecencies (*a la* Shklar) because he or she believes that ordinary people, via democratic institutions, can fashion and implement political solutions for most of the "problems" – actually "puzzles," as we saw in Chapter 1 – that beset modern America.

Much of this humanism denies alpha stories on the Right, which, as we have seen, recommend the reign of tradition, small government, and "free markets." Such stories propose that difficult circumstances in life, if

---

[1] As in Robert Reich, *Beyond Outrage: What Has Gone Wrong with Our Economy and Our Democracy, and How to Fix It* (2012). Reich is not really beyond outrage but rather driven by it.

[2] On "accountability reporting," see Dean Starkman, *The Watchdog That Didn't Bark: The Financial Crisis and the Disappearance of Investigative Reporting* (2014), pp. 1–15. See also Thomas Paterson, *Informing the News: The Need for Knowledge-Based Journalism* (2013).

they are at all given to repair, can be overcome by lining up with powerful forces that need little or no human supervision. Heed ancestral injunctions; espouse conventional virtues; proceed energetically but privately; compete fiercely yet fairly. These are the watchwords of right-wing storytelling in America today. Abide by them and much of what troubles you will eventually right itself. That is what conservatives like Ronald Reagan, William Bennett, Charles Murray, Newt Gingrich, William Kristol, Bill O'Reilly, George Will, Rand Paul, Ted Cruz, Marco Rubio, Paul Ryan, and Thomas Sowell say.

When this sort of storytelling is set aside by liberal books about, say, race, gender, industry, family, difference, commerce, climate, piety, finance, and defense, it is obvious that liberals are promoting humanism – that is, deliberate and concerted human agency when necessary – because they hope to revise historic social roles and practices according to modern understandings. This project can be traced back at least to the Enlightenment, because to challenge traditions is, by definition, to believe that reasonable people can successfully replace customary guidelines.[3]

The humanistic determination to change many time-worn practices, even while conservatives admire longstanding traditions in principle, is so obvious that we need not spend time explicating it.[4] However, the liberal attack on conservative support for small government and "free enterprise" is more complex, and warrants some consideration here.

To begin with, liberal complaints reject a conservative model of self-correcting markets proposed by Austrian School economists like Ludwig von Mises and Friedrich Hayek, extended by Chicago School economists like Milton Friedman and Gary Becker, and incorporated into governmental practices by politicians like Ronald Reagan and George W. Bush.[5]

---

[3] That is the main theme in Matthew Stewart, *Nature's God: The Heretical Origins of the American Republic* (2014). Stewart shows how Benjamin Franklin, George Washington, Thomas Jefferson, Benjamin Rush, and other Founders, often known as deists, were actually humanists because – inspired by Lucretius, Galileo, Bruno, Hobbes, Spinoza, Locke, and Newton – they believed that men (not so much women) were capable of using their reason to replace principles, practices, and institutions they inherited in societies dominated by Christian traditions, some of which the Founders regarded as tyrannical.

[4] Corey Robin, *The Reactionary Mind: Conservatism from Edmund Burke to Sarah Palin* (2011), p. 7, describes conservatives from one era to the next as clinging to power and privileges to the point where conservatism "is the theoretical voice of ... [an] animus against the agency [humanism] of the subordinate classes." Shklar could have said the opposite about liberals – intellectuals and activists – who have been *for* subordinate classes and *against* tyrants.

[5] The evolution of this idea is explored in Daniel Jones, *Masters of the Universe: Hayek, Friedman, and the Birth of Neoliberal Politics* (2012), and Angus Burgin, *Great Persuasion: Reinventing Free Markets Since the Depression* (2012).

Here, the chief presumption is that only a variable, flexible, adaptable, and unregulated marketplace, *not* shaped by human design and *not* distorted by political interventions, can foster a "price system" that will keep track of all the "information" that people need to pursue their "utility preferences."[6] Here is a model that admires "free markets" and condemns "big government," as when Republicans like Grover Norquist have, for a generation now, advocated cutting government budgets in order "to starve the [governmental] beast."[7]

In the light of conservative disdain for most political activism – for humanism, in short – liberal economist Joseph Stiglitz speaks out against almighty markets and in favor of constructive humanism when he explains that:

What's been happening in America [economic inequality growing] has also been happening in many countries around the world. But it is not inevitable. It is not the inexorable workings of the market economy. There are societies that have managed things far better ... [than] the United States for most of their citizens, measured not just in terms of income but in terms of health, education, security, and many other aspects that are key to determining the quality of life ... Another world is possible. We can achieve a society more in accord with our fundamental values, with more opportunity, a higher total national income, a stronger democracy, and higher living standards for most individuals.[8]

Wants Versus Needs

Books by liberals like Stiglitz evoke a distinction that many conservatives sidestep when they assume that an "invisible hand" in economic affairs will promote human wellbeing. Such conservatives insist that markets produce things that people "want" – and what could be more considerate and democratic than letting citizens buy those things? The alternative – government regulation of economic practices – would constitute,

---

[6] Von Mises first made this argument in "Economic Calculation in the Socialist Commonwealth (1920)," which appeared in Friedrich Hayek (ed.), *Collectivist Economic Planning: Critical Studies on the Possibilities of Socialism* (1935), pp. 87–130. The assumption is that markets work well and need little or no government intervention. Albert Hirschman, *The Rhetoric of Reaction: Perversity, Futility, Jeopardy* (1991), explains how conservatives label most such intervention as perverse, futile, or dangerous in order to challenge liberal assumptions about the ability of human beings to deliberately improve social relations and institutions.

[7] On Norquist, see Jacob Hacker and Paul Pierson, *Off Center: The Republican Revolution and the Erosion of American Democracy* (2005), p. 33.

[8] Joseph Stiglitz, *The Price of Inequality: How Today's Divided Society Endangers Our Future* (2012), p. 266.

in rightist parlance, a "nanny state" that unfairly imposes on ordinary people preferences they do not themselves entertain.[9]

Liberals agree that markets produce many things that people *want*, from home appliances to accounting services, from pizza parlors to World Series baseball. And certainly there is some virtue in markets assuring a considerable measure of choice. At the same time, however, liberals say that markets do not offer all the goods that people *need*. The point here is that prevalent, conventional, and routine getting and spending do not always take into account every good that citizens would choose for themselves if they could consider together what can foster their health and happiness.

Wants as opposed to needs. This dichotomy is at the heart of, for example, Robert Skidelsky and Edward Skidelsky's *How Much is Enough?: Money and the Good Life* (2012). The Skidelskys leave aside models of *rational* markets, which, as a thought experiment, many economists admire. They insist instead that what *real* markets generate – including urban sprawl, destruction of tropical rain forests, pollution, personal anxiety, deindustrialization, temporary work, fast food, climate change, financial crises, Twitter, and more – is not necessarily what is good for us.[10] The same concern inspires books like Paul Wachtel, *The Poverty of Affluence: A Psychological Portrait of the American Way of Life* (1989); Barry Schwartz, *The Costs of Living: How Market Freedom Erodes the Best Things in Life* (1994); Robert Kuttner, *Everything for Sale: The Virtues and Limits of Markets* (1998); David Myers, *The American Paradox: Spiritual Hunger in the Age of Plenty* (2000); Juliet Schor, *Born to Buy: The Commercialized Child and the New Consumer Culture* (2004); and Raj Patel, *The Value of Nothing: Why Everything Costs So Much More Than We Think* (2009). As Michael Sandel says:

the logic of buying and selling no longer applies to material goods alone but increasingly governs the whole of life. It is time to ask whether we want to live this way ... [but] we can't answer this question without deliberating about the meaning and purpose of goods, and the values that should govern them.[11]

---

[9] Richard Nixon told this Republican alpha story about the nature of American life to Nikita Khrushchev, insisting that "'To us [Americans], diversity, the right to choose ... is the most important thing. We don't have one decision made at the top by one government official.'" See Richard Nixon and Nikita Khrushchev, "The Kitchen Debate" (1949).

[10] Robert Skidelsky and Edward Skidelsky, *How Much is Enough? Money and the Good Life* (2012), especially pp. 86–95.

[11] Michael Sandel, *What Money Can't Buy: The Moral Limits of Markets* (2012), p. 6, p. 202. Economists George Akerlof and Robert Shiller, *Phishing for Phools: The Economics of Manipulation and Deception* (2015), miss this point when they describe how capitalists sell commodities that look like they will, but don't, provide what consumers want.

Liberal Books

Humanism versus markets is the overall contest, wherein liberals usually promote human creativity; wants versus needs is a distinction that helps liberals to choose targets, which they often define as problems to be solved by government projects. For the most part, the confrontation does not play out elegantly and abstractly in a duel between intellectual distinctions. Instead contestants crowd into specific policy realms, promoting fierce debates that highlight particular issues, practices, paragons, and miscreants.

We cannot discuss here the full spectrum of liberal complaints regarding what they view as intolerable circumstances which must be fixed. There are too many problems and they change too quickly as circumstances and events evolve. We can, however, review a score of liberal exposés – selected more or less at random – and summarize them in chronological order to gain a sense of their gravity and variety. This is an exercise that shows how, decade after decade, hundreds if not thousands of such books add up to a torrent of liberal discontent, a massive shout against existing conditions, a continual demand for sweeping solutions to endless crises, therefore a constant chorus of: "This is awful! Do something!"

Overkill?

Of course we already know not to expect from these books a shared narrative or bumper sticker – a liberal alpha story – about where we are and how we can build a better society. That is, we already know something about what is *not* there in liberalism, and the books we are about to survey will confirm that absence. This does not mean, however, that there is *nothing* there. On the contrary, in a political sense, there is *too much* there in liberalism.

In that sense, via books expressing outrage, we are about to observe a kaleidoscopic quality of today's left. After that, in Chapter 8, we will move on to consider how the sheer volume of liberal allegations – unilluminated by a shared story but constantly proliferating, constantly evolving, constantly dramatic, and constantly militant – became a point of

---

Thus the conventional vocabulary of economics (Akerlof and Shiller are both winners of the Sveriges Riksbank Prize in Economic Sciences in Memory of Alfred Nobel) eschews philosophy and treats frustrated *wants* as a central problem in capitalism today, whereas Sandel – like Skidelsky and Skidelsky – raises the question of whether or not what we *want* is what we *need*.

repeated contention with far-ranging implications between liberals and conservatives in modern America.

Silent Spring

Let us begin with *Silent Spring* (1962), which Rachel Carson wrote to warn against terrible dangers posed by insecticides, pesticides, and fungicides. The book began with a powerful allegory about a sad and silent spring, which is a season that should generate awesome natural renewal but is marred when chirping birds and their offspring, killed or crippled by man-made poisons, fail to appear. Having caught the attention of readers with that horror story, Carson went on to explain that poisons used in modern agriculture are mostly artificial chemical compounds, which living things cannot fend off because their bodies have evolved to resist only natural materials.

Most importantly, Carson conveyed a foreboding about how birds, bees, fish, crops, trees, mice, deer, foxes, cows, and other living things, wild and domesticated, may unexpectedly acquire dangerous accumulations of poisons not intended for themselves – as, for example, when Dutch Elm leaves were sprayed with DDT (dichlorodiphenyltrichloroethane) and later ingested by earthworms who were then eaten by robins, causing DDT from the worms to pile up in the robins' bodies and eventually kill them. By drawing attention to how living things interact with each other Carson introduced readers to the concept of "ecology," in which a helpful substance in one area can have deadly consequences in another. The solution, she said, was to exploit natural forces – for example, releasing sterilized screw-worms into the environment – so that rates of reproduction for that pest would fall precipitously.

The Feminine Mystique

In *The Feminine Mystique* (1963), Betty Friedan introduced America to "the problem that has no name." She explained that she discovered this problem when many women who she interviewed, especially in middle-class suburbs, said that they felt they were underachieving when they aspired merely to become happy wives, mothers, and housekeepers. These women were often college graduates who yielded to what Friedan called "the feminine mystique" in American life and then wondered why they felt unfulfilled.

According to Friedan, the feminine mystique was a set of powerful assumptions and images which portrayed women as physically and emotionally designed not to pursue careers but to serve as mothers and helpmates to men, who would lead society outside the family. This mystique was buttressed by Freudian misconceptions but also by ubiquitous advertisements which, in effect, encouraged women to stay home and seek happiness by buying the foods, appliances, cleaning materials, children's toys, furniture, and other paraphernalia that attend good housekeeping.

In Friedan's alternative view, the feminine mystique held women back, denied them their right to self-development, prevented them from working at constructive jobs, and kept them away from exciting projects in science, industry, medicine, commerce, and education, which provided men with a sense of great worth. The solution, said Friedan, was for women to choose their own goals in life, resisting axioms of conventional thinking that tried to sell them short.

The Making of a Counterculture

Speaking on behalf of young people in *The Making of a Counterculture: Reflections on the Technocratic Society and the Youthful Opposition* (1969), Theodore Roszak indicts modern society for being ruled by what he calls a "technocracy." These are our highly respected leaders in education, industry, management, government, and more who, on the basis of what is known today as "scientific expertise," set rules of the game and terms of discourse in their respective fields. The rest of us must defer, because most people think that members of the technocracy really "know" what they are talking about whereas everyone else has only "opinions" to guide his or her view of even vital human affairs. For example, the experts tell us that it is sometimes rational – such as in "thinking about the unthinkable" – to consider using nuclear weapons, in which case, according to Roszak, young people are confronted with a society run by people who are willing to risk genocide and universal extinction.

The alternative to a culture of scientific expertise, says Roszak, is a counterculture committed to propositions which we can grasp but not "prove" in the modern fashion. That is, propositions about love, friendship, the good, the true, and the beautiful. Many people, some more and others less learned, used to understand such matters, says Roszak. But they were displaced on center stage in modern life when scientists such as Darwin discovered techniques for discovering how we can know about the world around us. Against such technocrats, Roszak insists that we must leave aside – at least occasionally – the scientific question of "how can we know?" in order to ask the older, philosophical question of "how shall we live?" This is the question that disturbs young people, he says, and they may have to save us all by addressing it with their healthy instincts rather than with laboratory experiments.

The Limits To Growth

The Club of Rome, a private philanthropic organization, commissioned *The Limits To Growth: A Report of the Club of Rome's Project on the Predicament of Mankind (1972)* to analyze trends in population growth, food production, industrialization, pollution, and the consumption of nonrenewable resources. Whereas modern economists, politicians, activists, and citizens tend to promote private enterprise and free trade for their ability to generate economic growth, *The Limits To Growth* insisted that GNP, or any other measure of growth, cannot expand endlessly at current rates. For example, even a 1 percent annual rate of growth will increase production and consumption exponentially and therefore cannot continue indefinitely. The circle here is more vicious than virtuous. A little more population every year requires more industrial activity and food production, which requires more pollution and consumes more nonrenewable resources such as oil, iron, coal, and land.

The *Limits To Growth* argued that if current trends continue, the practice of growth will eventually implode, either from natural causes such as climate change, deforestation, and the exhaustion of arable land, or from social frictions flowing from – for example – crime, famine, racial tensions, urbanization, and war. The goal, then, must be to implement social policies, encouraged by widespread education and fashioned by democratic representatives, designed to prevent implosion before it occurs. Technically speaking, that is possible if modern societies will aim to establish a "stable state" or "equilibrium economy," wherein population size and capital use are held constant and proportionate to each other. In such societies, innovation and technology – such as speedier computer chips – would advance, but only within the existing parameters of capital or resource consumption.

News From Nowhere

According to *News From Nowhere: Television and the News* (1974), Americans learn much of what know they about current events from television broadcasts, which they believe are accurate. But televised news reports do not mirror reality, says Edward Epstein. In fact, such reports are driven less by events than they are by the organizational needs of corporations that create news broadcasts. These include time slots of only a few minutes for each story, even if the event being described is of great importance; pursuit of high ratings to attract a larger audience than competing stations so that advertisements can be sold for more money; the fact that audiences will tune in to see exciting images rather than "talking heads," even though only the latter can accurately explain the significance of whatever events are being reported; the need to present all circumstances – no matter how diffuse and persistent – as if they constitute a story with a beginning, rising action, and some sort of resolution; and the reluctance to unsettle complacent viewers by challenging national myths and conventional wisdom.

Epstein observed that some people believe that distorting imperatives such as these can be neutralized if journalists who present television news will practice "professionalism." That is, if those journalists will be especially knowledgeable about the events they describe, and if they will be faithful to a shared set of ethical standards, their reporting will truly reflect what happens and what it means. Unfortunately, announcers cannot know much about very different events which arise unexpectedly, and journalism in great corporations cannot heed ethical standards when the chief requirement is profitability for the whole enterprise. The bottom line, predicts Epstein, is that newscasts will not improve until the corporate entities that produce them will be redesigned.

The Fate of the Earth

In *The Fate of the Earth* (1982), Jonathan Schell announced to his readers that like it or not there are approximately 50,000 nuclear bombs in the world, and they contain an explosive force 1,600,000 times greater than the bomb dropped on Hiroshima in 1945. Everyone hopes for peace. But if war comes, a Soviet first strike could deliver 7,000 weapons and 17,000 megatons to America. In that event, a single 20-megaton Soviet bomb dropped on New York City would kill – via radiation waves, electromagnetic pulse, thermal pulse, blast wave, and radioactive fallout – up to 20 million people, or 10 percent of the nation's population.

Some Americans might survive a coast-to-coast attack. But their complex economy would vanish, and survivors would probably fail to create even a primitive one to replace it. Add to that the environmental destruction caused by massive radiation and other side effects across the land, and Schell concluded that the United States would be reduced to a republic of insects and hardy grasses. Russia – and, by extension, the rest of the world – would suffer similar damage.

Furthermore, even if governments and statesmen will dismantle and ban nuclear bombs, the nuclear danger will not necessarily recede, according to Schell. That is because once science has demonstrated that such bombs are possible, that knowledge cannot be suppressed or lost. So the long-term danger can be contained only by a new ethical outlook whereby modern people will decide that they are responsible, now and forever, for preserving the human race and all other living things. Only such a conviction, not yet on the political horizon, can save civilization from what Schell implied would be the fate of the earth.

The Predatory Society

Paul Blumberg writes in *The Predatory Society: Deception in the American Markeplace* (1989) about a "propensity to deceive" in profit-seeking firms. He bases his argument on what sociology students at City College in New York told him about their work experiences over fifteen years. Out of 638 students, 455 (71 percent) reported that the firms where they worked practiced consumer deception or fraud. These ploys might include serving chopped halibut instead of crab meat, weighing containers along with food items, marking up items before "sales," selling the wrong sizes of clothing, replacing adequate insurance policies with others more expensive, and "churning" stocks to generate unnecessary brokers' commissions. Such scams work especially well on "dumb" customers such as tourists, on "distracted" customers such as the father of the bride, and on "ignorant" customers such as people who have to get cars or televisions fixed. As Blumberg remarks, in a predatory society paranoia may be a sign of good mental health, because there really are plots afoot against us.

But why do capitalists cheat so often? Recalling the fictional manufacturer described in Arthur Miller's play "All My Sons," Blumberg refers to reported cases of cheating such as selling defective brake systems for American fighter planes, concealing the terrible hazards of asbestos, and exporting to the Third World drugs and chemicals banned in the United States. Such behavior, says Blumberg, is inevitable in organizations where the gain from profit can exceed the gain from other values.

To explain all of this, Blumberg rejects the pro-market theory, which says that when capitalists cheat it is not because of market circumstances but because they suffer from character flaws and behave badly. According to Blumberg, "greed, mendacity, and deception" are structural outcomes of capitalism itself. In that economic system, capitalists know that they may earn more if they will refrain from pursuing their good instincts. Therefore preaching virtue in business school courses cannot repair the situation because those who deceive us know already that what they do is "wrong." But changing rules of the game – for example, increasing government regulation – may encourage good people to behave well.

Satisfaction Guaranteed

After the Civil War, many Americans still made much of their own food and clothing. Then, in the late 1800s, the possibilities for mass production improved immensely. When that happened, Susan Strasser observes in *Satisfaction Guaranteed: The Making of the American Mass Market* (1989), manufacturers sought to persuade people to switch to what modern factories could provide. The technological (and also financial) imperative was to get Americans to buy enough to empty shelves that were constantly replenished by more and newer products. Toothpaste (Colgate), breakfast cereals (Kellogg), safety razors (Gillette), cookies (Nabsico), personal cameras (Kodak), and other now familiar items came into vogue. They were heavily advertised to turn "customers" into "consumers" and conveniently marketed in new forums such as department stores (Macy's, Marshall Field's), mail order houses (Montgomery Ward, Sears Roebuck), and chain stores (Kresge, A&P).

Standard economic theory, says Strasser, misreads the mass market. Formerly, people decided what things they wanted and then bought them. But later, manufacturers saw what factories could produce and persuaded Americans that those things were what they wanted. For example, Crisco (Procter and Gamble) was a vegetable shortening that kosher housewives could use to cook either meat or dairy products, thus the advertising slogan claiming that "the Hebrew Race has been waiting 4,000 years for Crisco."

In these circumstances, the capitalism that modern Americans have inherited is wonderfully productive – but also wasteful (planned obsolescence, disposable "goods," "extravagant packaging," and so on) and destructive (loss of rain forests, pollution of beaches, use of fossil fuels, and so on,) The system encourages people to ignore such downsides by seeing themselves as individual consumers - that is, as miniscule actors who cannot affect what happens at large. But we are actually buying together, says Strasser, in which case the totality of our purchases, which consume more than we need, requires collective decisions – actually political – to rein in a market that too often lets manufacturers rather than citizens decide how we should live together.

Chain Reaction

Thomas and Mary Edsall explain in *Chain Reaction: The Impact of Race, Rights, and Taxes on American Politics* (1992), how electoral strategies and outcomes between Democrats and Republicans in America, after approximately the Goldwater campaign of 1964, can be understood as reflecting the collapse of New Deal alliances. In this story, Republican talk about taxes and "rights" sent coded but persuasive messages to many white Democrats, especially those of modest income and skills.

Generally speaking, Republicans like Ronald Reagan portrayed taxes as designed to take money from hardworking, thrifty whites and use it to provide government services to lazy, improvident blacks. At the same time, conservatives described the "rights revolution" – which sought protection and benefits for blacks, women, gays, students, prisoners, and others – as a disruptive force that would upset traditional patterns of status and influence. On this score, Republicans scorned Democrats as promoting a conglomeration of "special interest groups" with no vision for all Americans but only blatant and unfair pay-offs – discrimination, really – for their members. That was, for example, what Reagan said about Walter Mondale and Geraldine Ferraro in 1984.

Eventually the two vectors of race and rights – both defined as zero-sum games – combined in a "chain reaction" that encouraged New Dealers to leave the Democratic coalition and vote for Republican candidates. All along, Edsall and Edsall insist, the strongest force in the new equation was a deliberate and steady appeal to racism, skillfully camouflaged behind talk of rights and taxes rather than of color. The strategy was similar, they say, to that of white-Southern-planter-textile elites who, from Reconstruction to the Civil Rights era, willfully incited class conflict in America between poor whites and blacks.

The Way We Never Were

America is more prosperous now than it was in the past. But many people are unhappy. Why is that so? Because "the traditional family" has broken down. This conservative syllogism is the target of Stephanie Coontz's *The Way We Never Were: American Families and the Nostalgia Trap* (1992), a historical essay aimed at puncturing the myth that American families in the past were like those portrayed in "Leave It To Beaver" and "Ozzie and Harriet." In fact, most successful families in American history were not virtuous little islands of self-reliance like the heroes of *Little House on the Prairie*. Instead, they were entities requiring constant outside support – such as cheap homesteads, networks of canals, railroads, and highways, agricultural research stations, veterans' benefits, subsidized mortgages via Fannie Mae and Freddie Mac, and prosperity fueled by government research grants in medicine, aviation, computers, agriculture, energy, and more.

For Coontz, family success has always flowed less from "individualism" than from "interdependence," whereby people effectively interact with neighbors and society. Therefore, focusing especially on the nineteenth and twentieth centuries, she explains how consumerism, wars, materialism, globalization, and large cultural trends affect mothers, fathers, and children, sometimes for the worse. For example, mothers are not increasingly choosing to abandon their children by going out to work. Rather, many women are forced into working because, without a second wage earner, average family incomes would plummet in today's market. The bottom line for Coontz, then, is not to blame family members for misbehaving but to instill institutions – banks, workplaces, churches, schools, and more – with continuity, trust, and mutual obligations that will enable families to serve all their members well.

More Liberal Books

Ecological disasters, oppression of women, the tyranny of technocrats, the perils of economic growth, the unreliability of televised news, an impending nuclear catastrophe, the ubiquity of capitalist cheating, an irresponsible producer sovereignty, the coding of political racism, the myths of family independence: in this roll call, we can begin to see the kaleidoscope of liberal complaints. Everywhere one looks, danger, discrimination, persecution, or inequity loom. According to liberals, it is as if the natural and social sciences announce a modern but valid version of Chicken Little's warning that "the sky is falling." Yet that is only half of our list, which itself is only partial.

One World, Ready or Not
People who explain globalization as competition *between* nations are mistaken, says William Greider in *One World, Ready Or Not: The Manic Logic of Global Capitalism* (1997). In fact, the cardinal consequence of globalization is that it evokes conflicts *within* nations – between capitalists and workers, between businessmen and unions, between peasants and townspeople – in which some prosper and other suffer as large international corporations wax and wane. In those

circumstances, statesmen and citizens of the same nation are no longer able to define their nation's public interest, its social contract, or its national bargain. Who should get what? Who deserves what? Politics becomes confused, and economic forces – such as Boeing, Monsanto, Toyota, Fiat, Nestle, Caterpillar, Dow Chemical, the Quantum Fund, Sony, and more – exploit the confusion to entrench themselves strongly and profitably, sometimes via tax havens like the Cayman Islands, Hong Kong, and Lichtenstein.

This latest round – and there were others in history – of economic imbalances started with the invention of the microchip in 1958–1959, which led to computerization, which facilitated automation, which turned capital into the key factor of modern production, and which made money increasingly mobile throughout the world. In fact, capital encouraged what Greider calls "the politics of escape," whereby corporations, banks, and investors pressured their national governments into easing governmental control of private money and financial instruments to the point where capital could easily move across national borders and avoid most taxation.

The result was to enlarge what economists call "creative destruction" whereby, as economic productivity and efficiency go up, social services, ecological decency, and public goods go down. In obvious cases, competing governments entice job-creating corporations with free infrastructure and low taxes, in which case the public money used to pay for those bribes becomes unavailable for amenities such as education, libraries, roads, and hospitals.

In Greider's tale, globalization unfolds in two stages. First, there have been painful years of direct social conflict. In those years, First and Third World workers have been thrust into ferocious competition, with First World people losing millions of good jobs and taking severe pay cuts while Third World workers – say in Malaysia, Vietnam, and China – work in modern sweatshops for as little as $0.25 per hour. The second stage is yet to come, because the marriage of science and technology will inevitably generate overproduction. Eventually the system must collapse because it churns out more and more consumer goods – even while, under globalization rules, it shifts most of the profits from that activity to the relatively few people who control it.

Those people will not buy everything that is available. Therefore, the stuff that is piling up can only be sold if government acts to assure that more people will share in the profits and therefore be able to afford whatever stores will offer them. But that is exactly what will not happen as long as today's economic winners, to protect their current incomes, manage to impose their will and the "free market" narrative on globalization.

The Heat is On

Like Jonathan Schell on nuclear weapons, Ross Gelbspan writes in *The Heat is On: The Climate Crisis, The Cover Up, The Prescription* (1998), about a subject that many people would like to ignore. Thousands of scientists in organizations like the Intergovernmental Panel on Climate Change (IPCC), citing peer-reviewed research findings, estimate that continuing to burn fossil fuels rather than developing renewable energy sources will double atmospheric carbon dioxide by 2050, thereby raising average ground temperatures by around 6 to 8 degrees Fahrenheit. The results – some already visible – will fill a catalogue of horrors, including rising sea levels, destruction of plankton, heatwaves, droughts, forest fires, insect driven plagues, deforestation, desertification, shifting oceans currents, and more.

Opposing such scenarios are a few scientists who insist that there is no proof that global warming is occurring – or, if it is, what its consequences might be. Such scientists are often subsidized by energy corporations and they usually publish their claims in non-peer-reviewed journals, such as *World Climate Report*, which are also funded by energy corporations. Therefore they discount the basic concept of ecology, which notes that in nature everything is connected to many other things, in which case a change in one place is certain to have consequences, perhaps disastrous, somewhere else. For example, a change in Atlantic Ocean temperatures may reroute the Gulf Stream, with incalculable effects on climate all over Europe.

Gelb argues that fossil fuel subsidies should be invested in renewable energy such as wind and solar power, that energy conservation should be stepped up by law, making power plants much more efficient than they are today, and that international currency transfers should be taxed and the proceeds invested in Third World infrastructure for clean energy. What he prescribes, Gelb admits, will be opposed by powerful fuel and transportation corporations and will require a long-term public commitment to government regulating at least part of the marketplace.

Race to Incarcerate

According to Marc Mauer in *Race to Incarcerate* (1999), federal, state, and local prisons housed 326,000 inmates in 1972. By 1997, they housed 1,626,000, which was a five-fold increase. What is peculiar about these figures is that American rates of crime are roughly comparable to those in other industrialized societies, except for a high American murder rate which is fueled by easy access to firearms. In other words, something cultural is driving more Americans – relatively speaking – into prison than citizens of countries like Japan, Norway, Great Britain, Australia, South Korea, and Switzerland.

For the most part, Marc Mauer locates that cultural impulse in racism. Incarceration rates for all American population groups were low until around the mid-twentieth century, while indeterminate sentences were linked to the prospect of rehabilitation. Later, a more punitive outlook was widely adopted, especially by conservatives like Barry Goldwater, Richard Nixon, Ronald Reagan and George H. W. Bush. In their eyes, "law and order" could be achieved if criminals would be "incapacitated" by isolation and punishment. Therefore mandatory sentences became fashionable, inmates piled up with little hope of release, and rehabilitation was scorned as a "liberal" misconception.

The result is that the number of African American inmates rose to more than 50 percent of all people imprisoned in America by the mid-1990s, even though African Americans were only 13 percent of the population. Many of these were convicted of drug crimes, because poor black families could not afford private medical help and counselling for their wayward children, and because the penalties for possession of crack cocaine –common in black ghettoes – were much more severe than those for powder cocaine – the white drug of choice. Furthermore – and conveniently for some white politicians – in places like Florida where former felons are not permitted to vote, Republican state officials banned more than 200,000 African American citizens (mostly Democrats) from choosing between Al Gore and George W. Bush in the 2000 presidential election.[12]

The McDonaldization Of Society

By *The McDonaldization Of Society: An Investigation into the Changing Character of Contemporary Social Life* (2000), George Ritzer means the process by which principles that animate McDonald's restaurants (24,800 restaurants worldwide in 1998) have increasingly come to

---

[12] Bush won the popular vote in Florida by 537 votes out of a total of 5,825,023 ballots cast. As a result, he received Florida's 25 electoral votes and gained a 271 vs. 266 vote victory in the Electoral College. See Jack Rakove (ed.), *The Unfinished Election of 2000: Leading Scholars Examine America's Strangest Election* (2001).

dominate other organizations engaged in dining, manufacturing, marketing, health, entertainment, and more. He sees four such principles: efficiency, including simplifying the product and streamlining the process; calculability, including standardizing the size of hamburgers, French fries, and drinks; predictability, including providing steady service and cleanliness; and control, including dumbing down work so that cheap and unskilled "associates" can easily be hired and fired, and luring customers into expanding profits by doing some of the restaurant's work themselves, such as clearing tables.

These principles support what Max Weber called "formal rationality" – the hallmark of modern society – in the sense of fitting means effectively to ends. By using examples, Ritzer shows that the same principles underlie much activity in modern institutions ranging from factories to supermarkets, airlines to universities, hotels to hospitals. The problem, he says, is that organizations which seek profit – or at least solvency – tend to maximize formal rationality to gain those ends, even though in the process they promote irrationality by enforcing standards, rules, and procedures which may prevent employees or customers from living up to their human potential. Ending on a pessimistic note, Ritzer concludes by expecting McDonaldization to continue. Therefore he offers no suggestions for taking collective action to promote decency in the circumstances.

Off Center

In *Off Center: The Republican Revolution and the Erosion of American Democracy* (2005), Jacob Hacker and Paul Pierson discuss what they call "off-center" government. They observe that standard democratic theory assumes that ideologically some people are on the Right, some are on the Left, and many are in the center, mainly undecided and fairly moderate. The theory also assumes that candidates will tack to the center. That is, they will aim at enlisting whichever side of the spectrum – left or right – is closest to them plus voters from the center to make a majority and win elections. In short, elected officials will govern mainly from or near the center.

Hacker and Pierson point out, however, that American politics since Ronald Reagan have contradicted this conventional wisdom, because Republicans have moved very far right and have proposed or enacted policies that the center opposes. These policies, especially benefitting wealthy people, included Ronald Reagan's and George Bush II's tax cuts – "their size, their structure, their distribution" – which led to severe national budget deficits. They also included efforts to impeach Bill Clinton and later privatize Social Security. In such cases, polls showed repeatedly that more than half of all citizens wanted something else, yet Republican officials stayed far on the Right and in most cases managed to get re-elected.

Off Center discusses various techniques that recent Republicans have employed to pursue their sharply conservative, rather than moderate, agenda. These include preventing roll calls on popular measures, such as on the option of censuring Bill Clinton rather than impeaching him in the House of Representatives; mislabeling new laws, as in the drug subsidy plan for Medicare beneficiaries that guaranteed enormous profits for drug and insurance companies; withholding information, such as about the unequal effects of tax cuts that conservatives sponsor; permitting the expiration of widely endorsed laws, like the Federal ban on assault weapons; keeping moderate Republican officials in line by threatening to support or actually supporting far-right candidates in primary elections; discouraging high rates of moderate voting by opposing same-day voter registration; suppressing socially minded unions, as when Ronald Reagan discharged thousands of federal air controllers; and gaming the mass media by repeating there, again and again, exciting but misleading "talking points" ironed out in advance by party strategists.

After explaining why liberals have been largely overwhelmed by relentless "power brokers" like Tom DeLay, Grover Norquist, and Karl Rove, Hacker and Pierson eventually make some suggestions – such as strengthening unions and encouraging voting – for "empowering the center" and "meeting the challenge." The most feasible of these suggestions is that, in the future, Democrats should intensively use the Internet to strengthen their base and reach out to moderate people.

Gun Show Nation

Joan Burbick observes in *Gun Show Nation: Gun Culture and American Democracy* (2006), that there are an estimated 200,000,000 private guns in America, that there have been 500,000 gun-related murders since 1965, and that a similar number of gun-related suicides have occurred in the same time. Nevertheless, guns are easy to obtain. The question is, what does all this signify?

Gun enthusiasts say they support private gun ownership because it is benign. People rather than guns kill people, they say. Burbick insists instead, that the presence of 200,000,000 guns in America is not benign and that the pro-gun lobby actually represents an American subculture, promoted mainly by and for white men. She traces this ideology back to traditional stories of ordinary Americans bravely resisting governmental tyranny. Such stories are endlessly elaborated in magazines of the National Rifle Association and in publications sponsored by gun manufacturers. They also live in popular imagination via folk heroes such as the Texas Rangers and Buffalo Bill, and in films starring "he-men" like John Wayne, Clint Eastwood, Sylvester Stallone, and Arnold Schwarzenegger.

The modern version of these stories praises the Constitution's Second Amendment. Gun advocates say that it guarantees to hardy and upstanding individuals a right to own guns, and they argue that those guns protect their virtuous owners from overweening government and violent criminals who might assault them or their homes. Burbick describes this view as especially reassuring for certain white people – including "the blue collar demographic" – who were once more admired and influential than they are now in America, and especially congenial to those who fear the rise of minorities such as African Americans, Hispanics, women, and gays.

Her bottom line, then, is that gun enthusiasts are natural allies of other Americans who feel displaced or marginalized, such as those who oppose abortion or the teaching of evolution in public schools. The problem, in Burbick's view, is that instead of applying moral fervor and political energy to repairing discrimination, poverty, dilapidated housing, dysfunctional schools, outsourcing, and so forth, pro-gun activists promote the idea that such conditions can be addressed by arming the citizenry to resist their spillover effects.

Washington Rules

In *Washington Rules: America's Path to Permanent War* (2011), Colonel Andrew Bacevich (ret.) scathingly describes what he calls "Washington rules," which are based on a "credo" of America leading, saving, liberating, and transforming the world and on a "sacred trinity" whereby America, to serve the credo, should maintain "a global military presence" capable of projecting "global power" that will, when ordered into combat, practice "global interventionism." These principles and axioms were first expressed by, among others, the Central Intelligence Agency led by Allen Dulles, which overthrew governments around the world, and the Strategic Air Command led by Curtis LeMay, which eventually listed for nuclear destruction more than 10,000 targets in the Soviet Union. They are also commitments that have, for half a century, justified what Dwight Eisenhower called a "military–industrial complex" which – under John Kennedy, Lyndon Johnson, and Richard Nixon – fought a disastrous war in Vietnam and which – under George Bush II – started two limited wars in Afghanistan and Ira, and one endless, worldwide war against "Terror."

Bacevich argues that American citizens and politicians have not challenged Washington's rules, but should do so because they are disastrous. First of all, the rules don't work. America gets into wars it cannot win because its credo misleads Washington into thinking that people in countries it invades, like Vietnam, yearn for American tutelage. Second, administering the rules has placed the country on a permanent war footing, which is precisely what the Founders – who abhorred standing armies – tried to avoid. Third, while not winning wars, constantly losing them has changed the Army's honorable goal of defending America into a mission for "winning hearts and minds," as in Iraq, even though the Army has no talent for such persuasion. And fourth, following the rules uses up – annually and unnecessarily – hundreds of billions of dollars that are needed elsewhere. They might be invested, for example, in repairing the nation's infrastructure and reviving cities like Detroit.

13 Bankers

In *13 Bankers: The Wall Street Takeover and the Next Financial Meltdown* (2011), Simon Johnson and James Kwak explain how American banks came to control assets worth $36 trillion in 2007 and derivatives worth $33 trillion in 2008. The tale unfolds mostly via deregulation from the 1970s until the Crash of 2008, from permitting variable brokerage commissions to canceling state laws against usury, from introducing mathematical evaluation of assets and risks to fashioning the ideology known as the Efficient Market Hypothesis, from allowing adjustable mortgage rates to securitizing mortgages, from creating junk bonds to fashioning derivatives, from initiating interest rate swaps to inventing credit default swaps, from lifting limits on interstate banking to permitting commercial banks to engage in investment banking, from placing derivatives beyond government supervision to getting a policy mandate from Washington to offer mortgages to low-income people who were likely to default.

In these circumstances there were several immense problems. One was that although new financial instruments such as derivatives were very profitable for financiers, they were so complicated that most clients could not understand their ramifications and therefore had to rely on explanations coming from brokers, who were not always serving them properly. Another was that banks and brokers concentrated on assessing "credit risk" and therefore took little account of "liquidity risk." That being the case they did almost nothing to prevent the liquidity crunch that precipitated the Crash, when housing prices stalled, lenders pulled back, brokers could not find cash to cover mortgage defaults, and millions of people lost their jobs and homes.

There was also a philosophical question. Did the power and income of the financial industry, before and after the Crash, serve a useful social function? That is, were those actors supplying money necessary for economic enterprise or were they buying and selling mainly sterile paper, earning fees and commissions on every move, but skimming from rather than contributing to the "real" economy – and therefore, for Johnson and Kwak, demonstrating a need for stringent government regulation?

The Shallows

Nicholas Carr tells us, in *The Shallows: What the Internet is Doing to our Brains* (2011), that to collect his thoughts and write this book he moved from a Boston suburb to pastoral Colorado and disconnected from his cell phone, the Web, email, and social media. In other words, he realized that he was a casualty of the digital revolution and could only write about it at length by resisting its ability to shorten his attention span, its tendency to flood his mind with distractions, and its physiological effect on his neurological wiring to the point where the "deep" thinking characteristic of the "age of print" had become difficult if not impossible for him.

Carr assumes that "intellectual technologies" – such as alphabets, clocks, printing, broadcasting, and computers – shape the way we regard ourselves and the world around us. Then he turns to neuroscience to explain how our brains are to some extent "plastic," which means that their neurons are not "hard-wired" irrevocably but can "adapt," sometimes usefully, to physical and mental stimuli. The downside to this plasticity is that intellectual technology may force some "adaptations" upon us at the expense of old but valuable skills and capacities. This is where serious reading can become difficult or even impossible for people who spend too much time responding to snippets of data via the World Wide Web, smartphones, and social media.

Some enthusiasts believe that technology is neutral, that we can use our instruments without permitting them to change us. Carr shows that this is not so, that something always gets lost. An email, for example, does not contain the same information as a letter written in Victorian England. And reading an e-book while constantly tempted to check into one's Internet connections is not like reading a printed book privately, quietly, and deeply. Surely there are gains in this new age. But one trade-off is a flattening of perception, a shallow view of life.

The Price of Inequality

In *The Price of Inequality: How Today's Divided Society Endangers our Future* (2012), Joseph Stiglitz considers the implications of greatly skewed incomes and wealth – the top 1 percent owns 35 percent of the nation's wealth – in modern America. On the one hand, much of the gap arises because some people benefit from "rents." These are present in income that is unearned in the sense that it flows from "market imperfections" rather than from the size of a person's contribution to social wellbeing. Examples include agricultural subsidies (Archer Midlands), low taxes on capital gains (Wall Street), military service contracts (Halliburton in Iraq), network externalities (Microsoft's operating system), market size (gigantic banks), the privately priced Medicare drug benefit program (Big Pharma), protective tariffs, and more. Most of these arise from a combination of lobbying power (buying influence) and "framing" (ideological persuasion), both of which wealthy people especially can afford.

On the other hand, today's inequality is greater than that needed to stimulate creativity and thereby prosperity. On this score Stiglitz argues, against market fundamentalists, that the American economy is treading water because of weak aggregate demand rather than because of government meddling. In pointedly Keynesian terms, he insists that Milton Friedman's monetarism is unrealistic and that only government intervention in the economy can reduce rents, redistribute incomes, and thereby revive economic growth so that millions of American will find new jobs and save their over-mortgaged houses.

The bottom line for Stiglitz, who rejects the panacea of laissez-faire based on market models rather than the real thing, is that "no one succeeds on his own." Hardworking and creative people do well if the economy works as it should, in which case everyone needs the ways and means that only government can create in and around the economy. These include public goods such as a healthy environment, educational opportunity, scientific and technological research, and physical infrastructure. Accordingly, Stiglitz recommends that government should cut the national deficit by raising taxes on the rich, eliminating corporate subsidies, charging pollution fees, and reducing military waste, and that politicians should redistribute income by using budget savings to stimulate growth, improve schools, overhaul the health care system, and maintain full employment.

Coming Apart

The list grows: the perils of climate change, the costs of globalization, racist incarceration, industrial rationality as pioneered by McDonald's, ruthless politics practiced by radical Republicans since Ronald Reagan, America's unique passion for private guns, unnecessary burdens imposed by a military–industrial complex, the financial swindles that drove America into the Crash of 2008, the digital drain on human intelligence and competence, and how inequality undermines the economy that supports us all.

These are the charges – in which case, in the world according to liberal thinkers, the overall impression based on vigorous research and passionate advocacy is that once again the sky is falling. There is no single explanation for such an outpouring of apprehension. But to be anxious is perhaps inevitable for people who have no alpha story for public affairs, that is, no comforting narrative that will infuse their lives, lay down priorities, and say with great confidence where we are today and where we need to go tomorrow.

8

The List Syndrome

I came to think that [President Jimmy] Carter believes fifty things, but no one thing. He holds explicit, thorough positions on every issue under the sun, but he has no large view of the relations between them … Carter thinks in lists, not arguments; as long as the items are there, their order does not matter, nor does the hierarchy among them.

James Fallows, "The Passionless Presidency" (1979)

In sum, liberals don't tell inspiring stories to the public or themselves. More exactly, they don't tell the same inspiring stories that other liberals tell. Instead, says Kloppenberg, they approach their circumstances pragmatically. Consequently, as Shklar observes, they tend to fume when – in their view – social institutions and practices work poorly or not at all. We can see this in the books that they write. Yet since, to liberals, social failures occur frequently, it follows that people on the Left spend much of their time complaining about what should be fixed.[1]

The result of the Left's constant complaining in one form or another is that liberal intellectuals, activists, and politicians tend to promote lists of proposals for new or improved government programs and policies. This is the reason for James Fallows's comment above on Jimmy Carter, for whom he worked as a speechwriter.[2] But before we explore what I call

[1] Many professors display this syndrome. Therefore Robert Wuthnow, "The Culture of Discontent," in Neil Smelser and Jeffrey Alexander (eds.), *Diversity and Its Discontents: Cultural Conflict and Common Ground in Contemporary Society* (1999), p. 31, claims that in "academic and popular social science … [t]he few writers who emphasize what is right with America are regarded by fellow academicians as being hopelessly naïve."

[2] This comment appears in James Fallows, "The Passionless Presidency: The Trouble with Jimmy Carter's Administration," *The Atlantic Monthly* (May, 1979).

"the list syndrome" and some of its consequences, let us stipulate that if Kloppenberg and Shklar are on target, we should regard pragmatism, culminating in grumbling, as the default setting for liberalism. The syndrome is straightforward: *modern life isn't easy; let's check out the facts; in many cases, they testify to urgent problems; here's what we must do to relieve or solve those; if nothing is done, terrible consequences will follow.*

Although neither Kloppenberg nor Shklar say so, to the extent that liberals are at heart pragmatists rather than raconteurs, they are politically vulnerable during modern campaigning. This point underlies our original concern. Alpha stories, which liberals lack, do not guarantee electoral success. But when voters seek assurance and meaning – say, via the categorical heuristic of supporting candidates who promote familiar expectations and aspirations – stories that weave together those sentiments may help to produce both.

The Original Questions

Let us briefly backtrack. I posed two questions in Chapter 1. The first was: *Why don't liberals tell stories (in the sense of narratives?).* I eventually answered that question by showing how, from starting points in disenchantment and humanism, liberals came to embrace pragmatism rather than narratives. Kloppenberg and Shklar agreed on this sequence, although using different terms.

Of course, as we observed in Chapter 4, liberals are not politically retarded and therefore many of them know that their camp lacks powerful stories. For example, even President Obama knows that he has a problem with stories. Thus when reporter Ron Suskind interviewed him in 2011, the President said that he won the 2008 election because he told a persuasive story of "a diverse and forward-looking nation" but later lost "the narrative thread" of that story, which told "the American people about where we are and where we are going."[3] Moreover, when he later appeared on "CBS This Morning" in 2012, the President remarked that his first term narrative was weak:

[The] mistake of my first term was thinking that this job was just about getting the policy right ... But the nature of this office is also to tell a story to the

[3] Ron Suskind, *Confidence Men: Wall Street, Washington, and the Education of a President* (2011), p. 479.

American people that gives them a sense of unity and purpose and optimism, especially during tough times.[4]

Yet if that was the case, let us proceed now to ask my second question: *if liberals don't tell stories (again in the sense of narratives), what do they do instead?* That is, if even the President loses track of his story, how – in a pragmatic fashion – do leaders on the left invite voters to support liberal projects?

Obama As Exemplar

To answer that question, let us regard Barack Obama as a liberal exemplar of our time. As such, most of what he writes and says, in books and speeches, is *typically* liberal. Therefore, in a sense, what he publicly promotes as a liberal is, by definition, pragmatism.

Well, yes, but not exactly. Most of what Obama does is *pragmatic*. But that does not mean that everything he does is *liberal*, because what the President could accomplish since taking office in 2009 has been severely limited by massive conservative resistance to any initiative coming from people on the Left. Democratic President Lyndon Johnson led the Congress to enact extraordinary civil rights acts in 1964 and 1965. But he received support to that end from moderate Republicans such as Robert McCulloch (R-OH) in the House of Representatives and Everett Dirksen (R-IL) the Senate.[5] By the time Democratic president Bill Clinton took office, fierce partisanship had so embittered national politics that neoconservative William Kristol was advising Republicans, and Speaker of the House Newt Gingrich was leading them, to reject almost automatically any Democratic policy initiative.[6] Under the circumstances, intense Republican opposition to Clinton's health care proposal prevented the Senate from even voting on the bill. Then, by the time Obama proposed a watered down "Patient Protection and Care Act," which Republicans scorned as "Obamacare," it passed in both houses of Congress in 2010 without receiving a single Republican vote.[7] And this despite the fact that the bill contained compromises, such as the absence of a single-payer

---

[4] The president was interviewed by "CBS This Morning" on July 12, 2012. Linda Boerma, "Obama Reflects on His Biggest Mistake as President" (2012).

[5] In the House of Representatives, 153 Democrats and 136 Republicans voted for the Act. In the Senate, 46 Democrats and 27 Republicans voted for the Act.

[6] See William Kristol, "The 1993 Kristol Memo on Defeating Health Care Reform" (2013).

[7] For vote totals on this bill, see HealthReformVotes.org, "How Members of Congress Voted on Health Reform: Roll Call Votes on Significant Health Reform Legislation" (2016).

option, designed to help Obama to avoid a Republican filibuster in the Senate.

Obama's Pragmatism

So liberalism and pragmatism – what the liberal president did and did not do, what he said and did not say, what he wanted and what he settled for – are important, related, and impossible to analyze systematically. In which case a qualification is in order. In the following pages, I cannot summarize seven tumultuous years of the Obama presidency. I can, however, justify refraining from blow-by-blow descriptions of political friction – who won, who lost, on what issue, and why – between the White House and Capitol Hill by assuming that there are two kinds of political pragmatism that bear on liberalism. The first attaches to "promotions." The second attaches to "projections." And the second is more important for our purposes.

Promoting Pragmatism

Via the term "promotions," we may begin by setting aside the behavior popularly called "pragmatic." To this end, I will use the term "promotions" to refer to "effective political maneuvering" – that is, to what a politician does "pragmatically" to advance his or her objectives, and to how he or she deals "pragmatically" with situations that deserve to be confronted or ignored. Such maneuvering, or promoting, can be difficult to fathom, especially when those who practice it conceal their aims at least partly. Furthermore, lack of transparency appears often because politicians of every persuasion, whichever ends they pursue, often obfuscate to get something rather than nothing. In this sense, they do what they think they must to achieve half a loaf rather than none.

Accordingly, getting half a loaf is one way to define everyday pragmatism. But since aiming at half a loaf frequently motivates conservatives *and* liberals, the exercise tells us nothing about pragmatism in principle, as a matter of philosophical preferences.[8] Thus Obama favored bailing out American financial giants (via the Troubled Asset Relief Program, enacted in 2008 but administered mostly during 2009–2010) and

---

[8] This is why James Kloppenberg, *Reading Obama: Dreams, Hope, and the American Political Tradition* (2011), pp. xi–xii, draws a distinction between "philosophical" and "vulgar" pragmatism, where the later focuses on compromise and is mainly "an instinctive hankering for what is possible in the short term."

supported providing stimulus money (via the American Recovery and Investment Act of 2009) for infrastructure repair and other projects. To do either or both required the federal government to increase enormously the national debt, therefore many proposed expenditures were denounced, say by the nascent Tea Party, and some were blocked, say by Republican senators. This raises a question: exactly what aspects of what was done or not done did Obama actually want?

As a case in point, after the bailout and stimulus were enacted, and while hundreds of billions of dollars were being distributed more to Wall Street than to Main Street, critics noticed that millions of desperate homeowners – ordinary citizens – got very little mortgage relief.[9] Many of those people subsequently lost their homes. Does that mean that Obama did not care, philosophically, about their plight? Or does it mean that he did less than what he wanted to do for homeowners because, in a zero-sum climate of decision-making in the capital, bankers and their lobbyists greatly influenced the direction of subsidies and handouts emerging from Washington?[10] These, after all, were mainly allocated according to the "too-big-to-fail" pro-business thinking of presidential advisors like Secretary of the Treasury Timothy Geithner and Chairman of the National Economic Council Larry Summers.[11]

Furthermore, Obama wanted to regulate some aspects of health care. He therefore led Congress – or at least most of the Democrats in it – to approve the Patient Protection and Affordable Care Act 2010, commonly known as "Obamacare." While on his way to that coup, the President did not propose that the Act would include a "single-payer option." Yet, by leaving out government health insurance as a possibility for people not covered by Medicare, the Act awarded private insurance companies the business of selling new health care policies to tens of millions of uninsured Americans. Is that what Obama wanted in principle? Or was he just maneuvering efficiently – for example, surrendering to the opinion of his advisors such as White House chief of staff Rahm Emanuel, who insisted that a single-payer option would be rejected even by the Democratic majority in Congress?[12]

---

[9] See Neil Barofsky, *Bailout: How Washington Abandoned Main Street While Rescuing Wall Street* (2013).

[10] In 2009, the "financial sector" (finance, insurance, real estate) spent $473 million on lobbying. See OpenSecrets.org, "Ranked Sectors" (2016).

[11] On the influence of pro-business advisors, see Suskind, *Confidence Men.*

[12] See Paul Starr, *Remedy and Reaction: The Peculiar American Struggle Over Health Care Reform* (2011), and Rosemary Gibson and Janardan Singh, *The Battle Over Health Care: What Obama's Reform Means for America's Future* (2012).

And what about foreign policy? James Mann argues that Obama and his security aides approached defense decisions "pragmatically" as members of a post-Vietnam War generation committed to realism in world affairs.[13] This means that – from Afghanistan to Iraq, from North Korea to Iran, from Libya to Egypt, from Syria to the Islamic State to the Ukraine – they located themselves somewhere between human rights enthusiasts (incipient interventionists abroad) in the Democratic Party and regime change advocates (incipient interventionists abroad) in the Republican Party.

The problem here was that being "somewhere" between this and that stance on security issues – for example, on what do about Egyptian democracy and how to treat private data collection by the National Security Agency – constitutes a form of everyday pragmatism, of the President proceeding unpredictably rather than acting consistently according to values embodied in a powerful theory or narrative, such as the Cold War policy of "containment." Indeed, in a way the serial positioning of Obamians on this score repeats the flexibility of President Richard Nixon, who – inspired by National Security Advisor Henry Kissinger – decided that the Soviet Union and the Republic of China were no longer Cold War adversaries united against America by their scorn of capitalism and democracy. As such, Washington need not confront them together unswervingly in a spirit of "containment" but could instead apply to them separately, and even differentially, a vague concept of "détente" which no one knew exactly how to define, measure, deploy, or justify.[14]

To sum up, pragmatic "promotions" are of little account in my project because they arise from a non-partisan talent for playing power games that might include bargaining behind the scenes or exerting pressure on colleagues by "going public."[15] Accordingly, the ability to promote political ends is a neutral skill that all politicians start with or acquire over time. Therefore Republicans and Democrats, conservatives and liberals, rightists and leftists, storytellers and pragmatists, personally have more or less of it.

To be sure, some liberal commentators feel that Obama has failed to produce the changes he promised and they complain that he displays little talent for what I am here calling "promotion." They say he should have at

---

[13] James Mann, *The Obamians: The Struggle Inside the White House to Redefine American Power* (2012), pp. 45–55.

[14] On détente, see Robert Dallek, *Nixon and Kissinger: Partners in Power* (2007), pp. 285–368.

[15] Samuel Kernell, *Going Public: New Strategies of Presidential Leadership* (2006), 4th edn.

least managed, for example, to close the Guantanamo prison.[16] They may forget, though, that other liberal presidents, sometimes regarded as political virtuosos, often achieved less than what they wanted. Thus Franklin Roosevelt led Congress to pass the Social Security Act of 1935 only after he placated white, racist, Southern politicians by excluding from the Act's pension system farm workers and maids, who in the former Confederacy were most likely to be black Americans.[17]

Projecting Pragmatism

Commentators have argued endlessly over Obama's promotional failures. Let us leave such matters to historians and consider instead what characterizes the President's "projections." I use the term "projections" to refer to what the President tells voters that he wants to do. Accordingly, Obama's projections constitute a statement of what – to the public, at least – he stands for, or what this typical liberal hopes to achieve for America.

I will consider such projections here in the framework of a previous observation. This is because Obama's projections, as we shall see, usually appear in the form of his describing various "problems" and then saying what he proposes to do about them. Therefore, with regard to what he thinks is not working in America or abroad, and to what he hopes to do about that, Obama's projections represent, more or less, the outlook which Kloppenberg called "philosophical pragmatism."

The First Obama

In the realm of projections, there are two Obamas. First, there is the Illinois senator, already considering a run for the Presidency, who published an inspirational book called *The Audacity of Hope: Thoughts on Reclaiming the American Dream* (2006). In it, he suggested a liberal interpretation of America and the Democratic Party. The book promoted a warm and fuzzy understanding of American public life, with poignant reminders of how the country had on occasion pulled together during, say, World War II. In *The Audacity of Hope*, Obama recommended to readers a new and admirable kind of politics in which ordinary people

---

[16] For the liberal case against Guantanamo, see American Civil Liberties Union, "Close Guantanamo" (2016).
[17] Ira Katznelson, *Fear Itself: The New Deal and the Origins of Our Time* (2013), pp. 133–222.

could – and should – engage in grassroots activism to counteract the sometimes baleful influence of professional politicians, their campaign consultants, and lobbyists.

The Audacity of Hope discussed topics such as opportunity in America, values in America, education in America, politics in America, family life in America, and race relations in America. The discussion was lucid; the tone was cool; the narrator was modest; partisanship was dismissed as querulous; and Obama repeatedly claimed that Americans on the whole are more reasonable and compassionate than what President George W. Bush was doing in their names.

The Senator from Illinois did not say, however, exactly how he would resolve great issues if elected President. In fact, *The Audacity of Hope* did not prescribe remedies beyond calling on voters to behave more soberly and considerately than in the past. Still, it assumed that large public problems could not be solved solely by reliance on "free markets" or dedication to longstanding traditions. Here was an implicit commitment to reason, humanism, and practicality, with roots in the Enlightenment. These sentiments would hopefully be rounded out in campaign speeches with recommendations for tangible, specific, and practical governmental policies and programs.

The Second Obama

The second Obama collected some of his campaign speeches and amplified them with several chapters of policy talk in *Change We Can Believe In: Barack Obama's Plan to Renew America's Promise* (2008). This book displays a "liberal list syndrome," the likes of which we saw in books by Senator Charles Schumer and Congressman Rahm Emanuel.[18] In effect, such lists flow from liberal complaints that are described in endless books – and articles, blogs, speeches, talk shows, think tank reports, documentary films, and more – some of which we summarized in Chapter 7. The bottom line is that this or that problem, among many which vex us, urgently requires repair. In the case of Obama – and very significantly so – his speeches included promises for action, unlinked by any alpha story, aimed at problems troubling every minority, interest group, demographic,

---

[18] For additional and typical lists, see Peter Levine, *The New Progressive Era: Toward a Fair and Deliberative Democracy* (2000); Thom Hartmann, *Screwed: The Undeclared War Against the Middle Class* (2007); and Hedrick Smith, *Who Stole the American Dream?* (2012), pp. 379–409.

and market segment whose electoral support candidate Obama hoped to enlist.

Domestic Proposals

Here, then, are some of the domestic policy promises appearing in *Change We Can Believe In*, all designed to relieve or resolve some problem defined by candidate Obama. The list should be read quickly. Its significance lies not in specific proposals but in their totality, in that they wash over us like a tsunami of advice from the current affairs shelves at Barnes and Noble. It is as if Obama – an erudite and up-to-date liberal – proposed to use public policy constantly, widely, and relentlessly to mend the defects in modern society which fuel liberal outrage.

Therefore: send rebate checks of $1,000 to American families. Save 1 million jobs. Increase fuel efficiency standards. Create 5 million new green jobs. Require 10 percent of electricity to come from renewable resources by 2012. Invest in a digital smart grid. Help local communities through tough times. Eliminate income taxes for seniors making less than $50,000. Make polluters pay. Invest in early childhood education. Recruit, prepare, retain, and reward America's teachers. Reduce the high-school dropout rate. Deploy next-generation broadband. Double federal funding for basic scientific research. Create a national infrastructure reinvestment bank. Support Amtrak funding and the development of high-speed rail. Support rural economic development. End tax breaks for companies that send jobs overseas. Shine a bright light on Washington lobbying. Expand AmeriCorps. Support parents with young children. Close the pay gap for women. Support a woman's right to choose. Crack down on employers that hire undocumented immigrants.

Restore wetlands. Ease the burden of high gas prices and make oil companies share in the sacrifice. Help workers displaced by trade and globalization. Expand the earned income tax credit. Raise the minimum wage. Protect workers and their right to organize. Establish a credit card bill of rights. Cap exorbitant interest rates and improve disclosure. Restore fairness to bankruptcy rules. Give family farmers the stability they need to thrive. Lower health care costs by $2,500 per family and improve quality. Guarantee health coverage for every American. Bring down the cost of prescription drugs. Ensure that every child gets a world-class education. Make college affordable for everyone. Create automatic workplace pensions. Preserve social security. Secure homeownership for American families. Make it easier to balance work and family. Bring opportunity to areas of concentrated poverty. Pay for all proposals by cutting deficit spending and reducing government waste. Give tax relief to the 98 percent of households making less than $250,000 a year. Eliminate special tax breaks for corporations. Simplify tax filings for middle-class Americans. Create a special fund for emergencies and deficit reduction.

Foreign Policy

On foreign policy, a similar collection of promises appeared. Here are some of them from just one chapter in *Change We Can Believe In*.[19] Again, the list should be read quickly, so that it will fall upon the inner ear as an avalanche, no less, of suggestions.

Ergo: Begin a responsible, phased withdrawal from Iraq. Launch a diplomatic surge concerning Iraq. Prevent a humanitarian crisis in Iraq. Focus on Afghanistan and Pakistan. Redeploy American troops to Afghanistan. Strengthen NATO's hand in Afghanistan. Train and equip the Afghan army and police. Increase nonmilitary aid to Afghanistan by $1 billion. Demand more from the Pakistani government. Stand with the Pakistani people. Work with our allies to fight terrorism. Prevent bioterrorist attacks. Harden our cyber infrastructure. Strengthen homeland security. Increase the size of our ground forces. Fully equip our troops for the missions they face. Reconfigure the military to handle new threats. Preserve America's global reach in the air. Maintain American naval dominance. Improve our intelligence estimates. Fully fund veterans' medical care. Improve veterans' mental health care. Improve transition services for returning veterans. Combat homelessness among the nation's veterans. Expand family medical leave to cover families facing reserve military deployment.

Prevent Iran from becoming a nuclear power. Phase out highly enriched uranium from the civil sector. Help other nations prevent theft, diversion, or spread of nuclear materials. Eliminate North Korea's nuclear weapons programs. Set the goal of a world without nuclear weapons. End our long-term dependence on foreign oil. Practice tough diplomacy. Strengthen America's partnerships and alliances. Rally the world to stop global warming. Double foreign assistance to $50 billion. Eliminate the global education deficit. Lead the effort to combat HIV/AIDS, tuberculosis, and malaria. Provide sustainable debt relief to developing countries. Achieve a world of capable, democratic states.

[19] Barack Obama, *Change We Can Believe In: Barack Obama's Plan to Renew America's Promise* (2008), pp. 101–142.

The Second Term

Obviously, the list syndrome is a campaign device designed to offer something to many disparate voters.[20] But there is more to the matter than that, because the practice of making one policy promise after another continued into the White House even after Obama was elected President and empowered as the country's chief executive. For example, in the President's "Second Inaugural Address" (January 21, 2013) he promised – among other things – to support railroads and roadbuilding and scientific research laboratories, to train more math and science teachers, to make federal tax codes more fair, to reform schools to provide better job skills, to encourage the creation of sustainable energy sources, to foster better wages for working women and equal rights for gay people, to improve voting procedures for all citizens, and to resolve immigration difficulties.[21]

Less than a month later, in his fifth "State of the Union Address," (February 12, 2013), Obama reiterated some of, and added to, his most recent proposals.[22] Accordingly, he promised to improve the Affordable Care Act by reducing subsidies to drug companies and raising charges for wealthy seniors, to simplify the federal tax code, to close its loopholes and deductions for well-off and well-connected people, to speed up issuing new permits for oil and gas exploration, to encourage the construction of more energy-efficient homes and business facilities, to create a "Fix-It-First" program of repairing national infrastructure such as 70,000 decaying bridges, to save "responsible homeowners" money by helping them to refinance their mortgages, to make pre-schooling available to every child in America, to redesign high schools to better equip them to help teenagers acquire job skills, to strengthen border security against illegal immigration, to establish "a responsible pathway to earned citizenship," to raise the minimum wage to $9.00 an hour, to provide tax credits to businesses that "hire and invest," to bring home 34,000 American soldiers from Afghanistan within a year, to wind down America's war in Afghanistan by the end of 2014, and to make the War on Terror "more transparent" and "consistent with our laws and system of checks and balances."

---

[20] It may also be judged a symptom of liberal fecklessness. That is a main theme in Karen Paget, "Citizen Organizing: Many Movements, No Majority," *The American Prospect* (Summer, 1990), pp. 115–128.

[21] See Barack Obama, "Second Inaugural Address."

[22] See Barack Obama, "State of the Union Address."

The 2012 Campaign

The interim deduction here, reflecting philosophical pragmatism, is that these proposals, made before and after campaigns, are what liberalism stands for. But the bottom line is that the same proposals don't hang together, because they are not framed by a powerful alpha story. Keeping this latter point in mind, we can understand why, when Jonathan Alter tracked the 2012 Obama campaign in *The Center Holds: Obama and His Enemies*, (2013), he described no storyline. On the contrary, as he said, "A pragmatic absence of ideology [liberal stories] was no shield against the other side's passionate ideology [conservative stories]."[23] A liberal story also fails to appear in Richard Wolffe in *The Message: The Reselling of President Obama* (2013), in which Obama's campaign "message" changed from day to day as he strove mainly to demonstrate that he was not Mitt Romney.

Similarly, Dan Baltz in *Collision 2012: Obama vs. Romney and the Future of Elections in America* (2013), saw no Obama campaign narrative. Instead, he argued that during 2012 there was "little noticeable competition" between the candidates in "the battle for ideas." In other words, short-term tactics and personal attacks dominated the contest between Obama and Romney. This was, (although Baltz did not say so) to Romney's benefit because – although he did not win – Republicans already lived emotionally within their alpha stories, even if Romney did not retell those tales every day.

The Liberal Mood

In sum, the pragmatic sort of thinking which underlies "projecting," which defines problems and calls for activism dedicated to solving them, inspires and justifies what Obama says in public. Unfortunately for liberalism and Democrats, the President does not project a consistent narrative to draw his promises together. We can bring some order to this potpourri, though, by saying that his policy proposals "resonate" with a general historical backdrop of liberal talk.[24]

---

[23] Jonathan Alter, *The Center Holds* (2013), p. 4.

[24] Many liberals – politicians, activists, pundits, and scholars – insist that the elite and wealthy exploit the commoners and poor, and those liberals say that they favor what we might call *truly* "equal rights and opportunities." (This is why conservatives often complain that liberals promote not "equal rights" but equal "results.") In that sense, in various chapters of this book, Galbraith, Frank, Ehrenreich, Postman, Kuttner, Lasch, Reich, Wolfe, Sandel, and more, are on the same page. But does that mean that what they say adds up to an alpha story? The analytical problem here is in deciding where a story starts

For example, the President's economic suggestions flow from a liberal rather than conservative understanding of how people behave economically. Thus – along with John Maynard Keynes and Paul Krugman – Obama assumes that good times depend on maintaining economic demand rather than, as recommended by Milton Friedman, Ronald Reagan, and George W. Bush, stimulating supply. Moreover, his domestic policy proposals resemble what Obama regards as New Deal achievements, for example in the realm of public works and infrastructure. Furthermore, his health care program extends what Obama regards as America's post-World War II "social contract."[25]

Old and New Individualism

And finally, Obama recommends that American "individualism" will take into account the growing "interdependence" in American life. Here is a central tenet of philosophical pragmatism, which John Dewey promoted in his *Individualism Old and New* (1929–1930).[26] Dewey had in mind first the "old" and traditional individualism commended by earlier generations, who conquered a natural frontier, praised self-reliance, promoted personal initiatives, admired individual competence, idealized rational economic men, and inspired Herbert Hoover's concept of "rugged individualism."[27] Against all this, Dewey described a latter-day, "new" individualism of modern people living on a settled continent, confronting a social rather than natural frontier, challenged by complex relationships based on nationwide rather than local forces, and dependent on scientific

and ends, or where one exists at all. In my view, conservatives are advantaged on this score because they can take a specific right-wing book, article, or candidate's speech, and compare its details to the three conservative alpha stories that are promoted, faithfully and repeatedly, by other right-wing books and activists. But in the liberal writings that I have cited, which are focused on a range of targets, Americans are unlikely to discern a liberal alpha story because they don't see it expressed elsewhere – wholly, powerfully, and repeatedly. And that, of course, is part of the liberal predicament, because if liberals don't tell alpha stories, the other stories that they do tell – sometimes vividly and incisively – don't obviously hang together.

25 On the social contract, see Lawrence Jacobs and Theda Skocpol, *Health Care Reform and American Politics* (2012), p. 45. Thinking about what was long called the "social contract" is not always accompanied nowadays by use of the same term. For example, Joseph Stiglitz, *The Price of Inequality: How Today's Divided Society Endangers our Future* (2012), p. xvi, says that growing inequality undermines a mutually beneficial "deal" that was struck after World War II between higher- and lower-income Americans.

26 John Dewey, *Individualism Old and New* (1930, 1999).

27 For example, on October 22, 1928, Hoover recommended "rugged individualism" in a major campaign speech. See Hoover, "Principles and Ideals of the United States Government."

and technological achievements capable of controlling nature and shaping it to human needs.

In these circumstances, said Dewey, "material prosperity" does not flow from the old, or "pecuniary," individualism. That individualism, he continued, "has been the cause of some great fortunes, but not of national wealth; it counts in the process of distribution, but not in ultimate creation."[28] Personal initiative is, of course, important. But society moves forward, said Dewey, on the basis of science, which he described as a joint endeavor rooted in "the experimental method" whose work is performed by many people and whose discoveries accumulate over many generations.

Franklin D. Roosevelt, writing soon after Dewey, recognized the new individualism in his "First Inaugural Address" (1933) when he insisted that the government programs he would propose to Congress were based, "as a first consideration, upon the interdependence of the various elements in all parts of the United States – a recognition of the old and permanently important manifestation of the American spirit of the pioneer."[29] Obama evoked the same principle when he claimed on July 13, 2012 in Roanoke, Virginia that successful Americans "didn't get there" by themselves. Instead, other people helped them by creating a supportive environment with schools, bridges, roads, the Internet, the GI Bill, the Hoover Dam, and so forth. As Obama said, "You're not on your own, we're in this together."[30]

Interdependence as described by Dewey was the basis for a potential alpha story linked to the notion that American government – as the Constitution's Preamble says – should work to advance quality of life goods such as justice, domestic tranquility, the common defense, the general welfare, and the blessings of liberty. As if Dewey's promotion of interdependence were not enough, the promise had been renewed by FDR's twelfth "State of the Union Address" (1944) – sometimes called "The Second Bill of Rights" speech. In that speech, Roosevelt reminded listeners that no one can prosper without the aid and support of goods that only government can assure, in which case everyone has a right to employment, food, clothing, shelter, education, health care, and retirement security, which government should provide or guarantee.

---

[28] Dewey, *Individualism Old and New*, p. 47.
[29] See Franklin D. Roosevelt, "First Inaugural Address."
[30] See Barack Obama, "Remarks by the President at a Campaign Event in Roanoke, Virginia."

So there already existed a liberal concept of interdependence, and Obama kept it alive by writing and speaking about it from time to time. But he did not expand his talk about the new individualism into a fully-fledged story, repeated again and again, because he is not a storyteller.[31] Nevertheless, Republicans saw the potential electoral danger. Therefore, on behalf of conservative notions of self-reliance, the free market, and small government, "interdependence" was strongly attacked by Obama's Republican adversary Mitt Romney.[32]

Thus on July 17, 2012, in Irwin, Pennsylvania, Romney countered the president's Roanoke speech delivered four days earlier by praising individuals rather than government. He conceded that there are government workers "who make a difference in our lives, our schoolteachers, fire fighters, [and] people who build roads." But Americans pay taxes, according to Romney, so that such people – rather than "the government" – can provide the infrastructure within which individual initiative and commerce can prosper. At that point, it is not all of us together but specifically entrepreneurs who build businesses, such as Ford, McDonald's,

---

[31] But see Cass Sunstein, *The Second Bill of Rights: FDR's Unfinished Revolution and Why We Need it More Than Ever* (2004), and Harvey Kaye, *The Fight for The Four Freedoms: What Made FDR and the Greatest Generation Truly Great* (2014).

[32] Throughout his 2012 campaign, Romney promoted an economic model according to which various actors play roles that complement one another and together produce economic growth. In that model – championed by Milton Friedman, his disciples, and innumerable capitalists – people who succeed financially, such as CEOs of large corporations, hedge fund managers, internet tycoons, and real estate, have no social responsibilities except those that voluntarily take upon themselves outside the office and at home. When applied to the business community, this model is sometimes called "the shareholder theory" of corporate responsibility, as if the proper role of business leaders is to make as much legal profit as is possible for the people who own stock (shares) in their companies. According to the model, one recognizes only *shareholders* and not *stakeholders* in the business – that is, CEOs should serve investors, but not children who live next door to chemical plants, not bulldozer operators who repair the nation's highways, not teachers who educate American workers, not workers who staff assembly lines, not scientists who do basic research, not doctors and nurses who labor to keep citizens healthy, not soldiers who defend the country, and not judges who peacefully settle fierce disputes. In favor of the shareholder theory, see Milton Friedman, "The Social Responsibility of Business is to Increase its Profits," *New York Times* (September 13, 1970). The shareholders approach has been severely criticized by Joel Bakan, *The Corporation: The Pathological Pursuit of Profit and Power* (2005). It is also rejected by Barry Lynn, *Cornered: The New Monopoly Capitalism and the Economics of Destruction* (2010), especially pp. 228–237, where Lynn describes how – on behalf of manufacturing quick cash rather than long-term goods – financiers displaced state officials, professional managers, workers, and small investors as "owners" who together, in a context of New Deal regulations, used to guide and control great and productive corporations.

Microsoft, Papa John's Pizza, and Apple. That is, America is great because of its "free people" rather than because of government activism.[33]

Conservative Responses

To restate the matter, it is characteristic of liberals to complain that many American practices and institutions need fixing. On this score, liberals constitute what John Stuart Mill called "the party of change" as opposed to "the party of order."[34] In America, government officials may respond to liberal complaints with formal legislation, such as during the New Deal and the Great Society but not only then. And sometimes in society rather than in government, public opinion evolves in liberal directions, as in the growing enthusiasm of many Americans for making racial and gender relations more equitable.

It follows that the record of liberal gains and losses is too long and complex for us to describe here. Let us note, though, that the totality of liberal complaints – and there really are a great many – has annoyed conservatives immensely, and that they have interpreted those complaints in ways that powerfully affect the lineup of political forces in America. This happens when incessant complaining makes liberalism look – to people on the Right – so raucous, intrusive, and troublesome as to help conservatives to define themselves in contrast to liberals.[35]

The Counterculture
First of all, conservative determination to reject liberal complaints took off in the 1960s and early 1970s, when innumerable demonstrations and occasional riots were accompanied by angry talk and writing about how politicians, from the President to the Congress to the Defense Department, and large organizations, from the Democratic Party to universities to

---

[33] See Mitt Romney, "Romney's Speech in Pennsylvania Today." For liberals, Peter Singer, *The President of Good and Evil: Taking George W. Bush Seriously* (2004), pp. 10–17, argues that Bush II endorsed a concept of "the ownership society" based on the myth that property is created, acquired, and maintained by private individuals rather than framed, shaped, and preserved by social institutions.

[34] John Stuart Mill, *On Liberty* (1859, 1956), pp. 57–58.

[35] For example, see William Gairdner, *The Great Divide: Why Liberals and Conservatives Will Never, Ever Agree* (2015), p. 35, who argues that "The liberal ... tends to be a malcontent, rarely happy with things as they are, very happy with things as he thinks they ought to be." Therefore Neil Gross, *Why Are Professors Liberal and Why Do Conservatives Care?* (2013), pp. 252–300, points out that liberal professors – constantly complaining, constantly doubting – are a perfect foil for conservative politicians and activists seeking to enlist populist sentiments in America.

corporations such as Dow Chemical, were failing to adequately confront acute problems such as racism, poverty, and the Vietnam War.[36]

Hundreds of thousands of Americans took to streets and campuses – some repeatedly – while neighborhoods burned, "hippies" defied traditional ethics, the Tet Offensive dominated network news, assassins murdered Martin Luther King and Robert Kennedy, pot and acid proliferated, veterans denounced the war, and police riots at the Democratic National Convention turned Chicago into a symbol of official repression. Paul Goodman, Herbert Marcuse, Theodore Roszak, Robert Pirsig, and Charles Reich became household names, at least for ardent liberals.[37] In every realm of private and public life, angry people challenged clichés and traditional practices.

Consequently conservatives began to dwell on what – following Roszak – they regarded as a "counterculture" born in an age of upheaval, which they sometimes called the Age of Woodstock after the music festival attended by 400,000 young fans that took place on an upstate New York farm in August 1969. Sharp criticism came from the Right. For example, according to William Donohue, counterculture people expressed "a raging desire to trample, mutilate, and destroy the norms, values, beliefs, and sentiments of the established culture."[38] Gertrude Himmelfarb added that, in their disdain for America's fighting the Vietnam War, and in their demand for recognizing what they regarded as minority rights, the demonstrators and their radical mentors "liberated" many Americans from some of the longstanding virtues – such as self-restraint, hard work, and patriotism – which sustain decency and prosperity.[39]

Most important, to people on the Right, was the overall thrust of counterculture criticism. There was a sense, they thought, in which insurgents

---

[36] For what happened, see William O'Neill, *Coming Apart: An Informal History of America in the 1960s* (1971); Milton Viorst, *Fire in the Streets: America in the 1960s* (1979); James Miller, *Democracy is in the Street: From Port Huron to the Siege of Chicago* (1988); Todd Gitlin, *The Sixties: Years of Hope, Days of Rage* (1993); and Maurice Isserman and Michael Kazin, *America Divided: The Civil War of the 1960s* (1999).

[37] For example, Paul Goodman, *Growing Up Absurd* (1960); Herbert Marcuse, *One Dimensional Man: Studies in the Ideology of Advanced Industrial Society* (1964); Theodore Roszak, *The Making of a Counter Culture: Reflections on the Technocratic Society and Its Youthful Opposition* (1969); Charles Reich, *The Greening of America* (New York: Random House, 1970); and Robert Pirsig, *Zen and the Art of Motorcycle Maintenance: An Inquiry into Values* (1975).

[38] Donohue, *The New Freedom: Individualism and Collectivism in the Social Lives of Americans* (1990), p. 40.

[39] Gertrude Himmelfarb, *One Nation, Two Cultures* (1999), p. 18. See also Roger Kimball, *The Long March: How the Cultural Revolution of the 1960s Changed America* (2000), p. 248.

aimed not just at specific policy errors such as segregation or the war, but at "the system" itself. The point here, for conservatives, was that social order requires faith and confidence in the major institutions of society – be they courts or legislatures, universities or shopping malls, corporations or professions, marriage or religion. Thus Congressman Newt Gingrich (R-GA) avowed that he thought Watergate was "disgraceful." But he also maintained that holding such a belief did not justify concluding that the system of principles and practices which protects and preserves us all should be scrapped.[40]

Multiculturalism

Second, liberal complaints targeting conformity – which supported "the system" – arose in the 1960s, and morphed into what conservatives strongly criticized as "multiculturalism." Here is an outlook that celebrates the diverse contributions which ethnic, gender, and religious groups make to the mosaic of American life.[41] Some liberals believe that this multiculturalism should be promoted instead of the more conventional "melting pot" theory of immigrant absorption, whereby newcomers should become good Americans by adopting outlooks fashioned mainly by earlier, white, mostly north-European immigrants. Conservative criticism therefore focuses on multiculturalism as a dangerous state of mind[42] – almost a form of anti-Americanism – rather than as what various groups innocently do when, for example, they eat tacos or pray facing Mecca.

To conservatives, multiculturalists do not so much recognize diversity as reject longstanding and widely shared values which have knit together a free and prosperous America for generations.[43] In other words,

---

[40] Newt Gingrich, *Window of Opportunity: A Blueprint for the Future* (1984), pp. 56–57. On liberals undermining the authority of vital institutions, see also Samuel Huntington, *American Politics: The Promise of Disharmony* (1981).

[41] Thus the formal definition, that multiculturalism is "a philosophy of education that stresses the unique contributions of different cultures to the history of the world," which appears in Francis Beckworth and Michael Bauman (eds.), *Are You Politically Correct? Debating America's Cultural Standards* (1993), p. 11.

[42] Thus books like Alvin Schmidt, *The Menace of Multiculturalism: Trojan Horse in America* (1997).

[43] A classic argument to this effect comes from *National Review* editor Richard Brookhiser, *The Way of the WASP: How It Made America, and How It Can Save It, So to Speak* (1991). More recently, Jeb Bush and Clint Bolick, *Immigration Wars: Forging an American Solution* (2014), recommends that immigrants should practice "assimilation" rather than "multiculturalism." See also Jeb Bush promoting "pluralism" over "multiculturalism" in Ed O'Keefe, "What Jeb Bush Meant When He Said the US Should Not Have a Multicultural Society."

multiculturalists promote philosophical "relativism" by arguing that entertaining multiple points of view, pursuing many different ends, and encouraging a variety of acts, are practices worth taking seriously. On this score, rightists accuse liberals of praising too much the corrosive virtues of identity, difference, and gender, and for talking too little about the interlocking principles and convictions – such as the Ten Commandments and love of country – which according to conservatives made first the West and then America great.[44]

In this view, American universities should teach their students about what is American and only after that – if at all – invite them to consider foreign writers and ideas.[45] In the process, says Roger Kimball, teachers should emphasize that immigrants came and continue to come to America precisely in order to escape from multiculturalism, knowing that the real choice "is not between a 'repressive' Western culture and a multicultural paradise, but between culture and barbarism."[46]

A certain symmetry is achieved here when, at the highest level of generality, the debate over multiculturalism reflects the storytelling gap between liberals and conservatives. This happens because, in conservative eyes, there is a sense in which liberals dazzled by multiculturalism promote not a few complementary tales but many separate stories about various groups. Consequently, they leave Americans without an overall and inspiring narrative which makes sense of principles and practices that belong to the entire nation.

In these circumstances, conservatives insist that their own alpha stories are not intended to generate partisan gain but are designed to express and recommend healthy and shared sentiments that can enable the country as a whole to make its way in a sometimes hostile world. Thus William Bennett complained that, after 9/11, liberal American professors failed to convey to their students a firm sense of universal principles – such as

---

[44] For example, Dinesh D'Souza, *The Enemy at Home: The Cultural Left and Its Responsibility for 9/11* (2007). In the same vein, see Ann Coulter, *Treason: Liberal Treachery From the Cold War to the War on Terrorism* (2003), and Sean Hannity, *Deliver Us From Evil: Defeating Terrorism, Despotism, and Liberalism* (2004).

[45] That is not exactly accurate. Some conservatives are enthusiastic about a "canon" of mostly European authors who contributed to what many Americans now regard as their own institutions and principles. These are the sort of thinkers praised by Allen Bloom in *The Closing of the American Mind: How Higher Education Has Failed Democracy and Impoverished the Souls of Today's Students* (1987). A multicultural response to Bloom is provided in Lawrence Levine, *The Opening of the American Mind: Canons, Culture, and History* (1996).

[46] Roger Kimball, *Tenured Radicals: How Politics Has Corrupted Our Higher Education* (1990), p. 206.

the natural human longing for "freedom" – which can justify America's "War on Terror."[47]

A Common Enemy

Third, liberal complaining encourages economic libertarians and social traditionalists to regard counterculturalists and multiculturalists together as a common enemy. Right-wingers need such an enemy because their story of magnificent markets recommends practices which contradict those recommended by their story of excellent customs. That liberals are strident and visible thus makes them a handy target for conservatives who seek to unite their own ranks by focusing on "the other."[48] To attack that other excuses people on the Right – like Ronald Reagan – from having to show exactly how unregulated exchange, traditional values, and small government are all compatible with one another. In many respects, of course, they are not. For example, the Protestant ethic promotes thrift and moderation, whereas admiration for markets and economic growth demands that consumers, via credit cards and second mortgages, will spend more than they earn.[49] Thus the iconic ad of Pan American Airlines years ago: "Fly now, pay later."

In the long run, American conservatives are fated to continue attacking a shared enemy to draw public attention away from clashes between their alpha stories. But because political vocabularies change over time, right-wing talk about a common foe is not the same from one generation to another. For example, during the 1970s and 1980s, but less so today, the culprits were described as members of a "New Class." These were the people – liberals, in short – who, according to conservatives, espoused countercultural and multicultural "values" and therefore deserved condemnation for opposing right-wing principles and projects. They were to be found in occupations including – according to Irving Kristol – "scientists, teachers and educational administrators, journalists and others in the communication industries, psychologists, social workers, those lawyers and doctors who make their careers in the expanding public sector, city planners, the staffs of large foundations, the upper levels of the government bureaucracy, and so on."[50]

---

[47] William Bennett, *Why We Fight: Moral Clarity and the War on Terrorism* (2002), especially pp. 44–70.

[48] I discuss this inconsistency and also the right-wing focus on a common enemy in David Ricci, *Why Conservatives Tell Stories and Liberals Don't: Rhetoric, Faith, and Vision on the American Right* (2011), pp. 81–104.

[49] Daniel Bell, *The Cultural Contradictions of Capitalism* (1976), especially pp. 66–72.

[50] Irving Kristol, "Business and the New Class [1975]," in Irving Kristol (ed.), *Neoconservatism: The Autobiography of an Idea* (1999), p. 207.

Charles Murray had a similar collection of liberals in mind when he indicted "the upper levels of ... academia, journalism, publishing, and the vast network of foundations, institutes, and research centers that has been woven into partnership with government during the last thirty years."[51] A related put-down for leftists in this compendium appeared when conservatives scorned professors as exemplars of liberal carping, arrogance, moral relativism, and situational ethics. Thus Congressman Henry Hyde (R-IL), playing the populist card, declared: "I'm a great believer in the people and their wisdom ... I would much rather be ruled by the first two hundred names in the DuPage County phone book than by the faculty of the University of Chicago, intelligent as they may be."[52]

A New Conservative Story

Conservative talk about the counterculture, multiculturalism, and a common leftist enemy focuses more on liberal *people* than on liberal *politics*. Recently, however, conservative scholars have zeroed in on leftist politicking and suggested a powerful interpretation of what emerges from liberal complaining. They have not actually created a new story but – in line with what we observed earlier – they have in effect updated the old right-wing alpha story that favors limited government. To this end, they argue that liberals of the New Deal, and their successors in the Great Society, deliberately created Washington agencies and programs as a quid pro quo to serve liberal client groups.

Serious disdain for one of liberalism's signature eras appears, for example, in Amity Shlaes's *The Forgotten Man: A New History of the Great Depression* (2007).[53] Shlaes first stipulates that "much of the New Deal hurt the economy." Assuming that to be so, she asks rhetorically how Franklin Roosevelt managed to win large electoral majorities. The answer, she says, lay in his fostering "a new kind of interest-group politics." In fact, "The president made groups [of senior citizens, farmers,

---

[51] Charles Murray, *Losing Ground: American Social Policy, 1950–1980* (1984), p. 42.

[52] Henry Hyde, "The Importance of Transcendent Moral Values," in Michael Deaver (ed.), *Why I am a Reagan Conservative* (2005), p. 59.

[53] In *The Forgotten Man*, pp. 12–14, Shlaes uses the expression "forgotten man" to describe taxpayers who did not benefit from New Deal programs but had to pay for them anyway. She recalls that the unjustly burdened man in this sense was identified first by William Graham Sumner [see William Graham Sumner, *What Social Classes Owe to Each Other* (1961), pp. 107–131], and she claims that FDR used the term "forgotten man" to refer to "the poor, the old man, labor, or any other recipient of government help." This is not quite what FDR said. In fact, he spoke of "the forgotten man at the bottom of the economic pyramid." See FDR's 1932 campaign speech, "The Forgotten Man."

and union workers] where only individual citizens or isolated cranks had stood before, ministered to those groups, and was rewarded with votes."[54] Here is a serious charge against what many Democrats proudly remember as a New Deal coalition dedicated to creating public goods and amenities.

Writing more philosophically, Charles Kesler in *I Am The Change: Barrack Obama and the Crisis of Liberalism* (2012), condemns liberal complaining and decries "the list syndrome" even though he does not use that term. Specifically, he argues that Obama's liberalism can be traced to the progressive outlook embodied in Woodrow Wilson's "New Freedom," Franklin Roosevelt's "New Deal," and Lyndon Johnson's "Great Society." This sort of liberalism is in the spirit described by Judith Shklar, although Kesler does not mention her in this context. It offered a new sort of politics which promised to dedicate government to an endless series of "reform" projects – that is, a list – rather than solutions to one or two specific problems such as segregation or the denial of political rights to women.[55]

Here is what happened, according to Kesler. In effect, the new philosophy – which Kesler calls "progressivism," but which we have called "pragmatism" – abandoned dedication to constitutional, limited rule in favor of an unlimited commitment to beget new Washington agencies, enlarge old ones, and issue endless government regulations. Along the way, new rights were conceived and guaranteed by law,[56] and various groups became beneficiaries of governmental largess. This situation encouraged citizens to engage in interest group politics, with some gaining from New Deal handouts and others losing.[57]

It is a story that clearly scorns the way Democrats talk about government and its proper functions. This is because Shlaes and Kesler together imply that electoral support for a large, active, liberal state does not arise righteously from new and virtuous sensibilities. Rather, it emerges from a sort of high-level political corruption whereby, as a consequence of governmental activism, some citizens enjoy benefits that they don't deserve.[58]

---

[54] Shlaes, *The Forgotten Man*, pp. 10–11.

[55] Charles Kesler, *I am the Change: Barack Obama and the Crisis of Liberalism* (2012), pp. 18–19.

[56] *Ibid.*, pp. 122–145. See the rights posited in, for example, Roosevelt's "Four Freedoms Speech" (1941), and his "State of the Union Message" to Congress, which announced in 1944 a Second Bill of Rights.

[57] Kesler, *I Am The Change*, pp. 144–145.

[58] For example, those groups are described as "special interests" and include "young people, ethnic and racial minorities, radical feminists, gays, environmentalists, [and] public employee unions," according to conservative Kate Obenshain, *Divider-in-Chief: The Fraud of Hope and Change* (2012), pp. 2–3.

The Current Impasse

So here is a final consequence of liberal complaining. In America today, the story we have just seen – about unending avarice in the "welfare state," about one government program following another without end, and about the determination of liberals to give away public money to enlarge their partisan "base" – expresses current sentiments that conservative intellectuals elaborate for conservative activists.[59] As such, it helps us to understand the origins of Mitt Romney's notion, aired in 2012, that 47 percent of Americans are "takers" rather than "makers" – in which case, tempted by government hand-outs, such people remain selfishly in the liberal camp of voters.[60] It also provides a historical backdrop for the contemporary Republican fear that health care regulation and subsidies, whether proposed by Bill Clinton or enacted by Barack Obama, will eventually cement a new and large group of voters into the Democratic Party.[61] Spurred by this fear and led by a Republican majority, on February 2, 2016 the House of Representatives voted for the sixty-third time (but to no avail) to repeal Obamacare.[62]

---

[59] Here is a signature confrontation between conservatives and liberals because, while conservatives regard liberals as committed to enlarging and multiplying government programs, conservatives (reflecting their admiration for "small government") do not intend to use electoral victories for any substantial purpose – except to make war abroad and to roll back the New Deal and other Democratic social projects at home. That Republicans and Democrats differ in this sense is a central thesis in Geoffrey Kabaservice, *Rule and Ruin: The Downfall of Moderation and the Destruction of the Republican Party, From Eisenhower to the Tea Party* (2012). The conservative principle in this equation was stated authoritatively by Barry Goldwater when he wrote:

> I do not undertake to promote welfare, for I propose to extend freedom. My aim is not to pass laws, but to repeal them. It is not to inaugurate new programs, but to cancel old ones that do violence to the Constitution, or that have failed in their purpose, or that impose on the people an unwarranted financial burden.

See Barry Goldwater, *The Conscience of a Conservative* (1960), p. 23.

[60] See Mitt Romney, "Full Transcript of the Mitt Romney Video."

[61] For an example of this fear, see William Kristol, "The 1993 Kristol Memo on Defeating Health Care Reform," addressed to "Republican Leaders" on the subject of "President Clinton's health care reform proposal" and warning that Clinton's plan, if enacted, would persuade many voters that the Democratic Party is "the generous protector of middle class interests."

[62] See Associated Press, "House Unable to Override Veto of Obamacare Repeal."

9

The Great Retreat

And we are here as on a darkling plain
Swept with confused alarms of struggle and flight,
Where ignorant armies clash by night.
Matthew Arnold, "Dover Beach" (1867)

Liberals probably don't know much about Amity Shlaes or Charles Kesler. And when they know something about what those scholars write, they probably aren't much impressed.[1] On the other hand, if they are inclined to fine arts they might read Matthew Arnold's "Dover Beach," with its exquisite rendering of the poet's frustration at not being able to understand why people behave as badly as they sometimes do.

Arnold expressed a certain pessimism that would eventually plague many modern liberals, and that is a mood we should try to understand. Liberal pessimism is so pervasive today, and so relentlessly enlarged by leftist muckraking, that dealing with it adequately would require a shelf of books. Space here is limited, however, therefore the following reflections are brief.

Obama

We should first recall the President's background notions: that Keynes rather than Friedman is the best guide to how government should oversee

---

[1] For example, in 2012 Mark Lilla reviewed Kesler's *I Am the Change* and wrote, in effect, that the book was not worth reading. See Mark Lilla, "The Great Disconnect."

the economy,[2] that government's proper role in America grew out of the New Deal, that the general welfare of Americans should be fostered by a "social contract" between government and citizens, and that "interdependence" is a fact of life which public policy should take into account. Convictions such as these justify a liberal thesis to the effect that after the New Deal – and partly because of it – ordinary Americans (retirees, farmers, veterans, clerks, industrial workers, small businessmen, students, professionals, and more) flourished until about 1970. Then the "middle class" began to lose income and influence, especially after 1980, to the point where restoring prosperity to people in that class became an avowed Democratic policy aim.[3]

These notions appeared during the 2012 campaign,[4] but they were not adopted by leading Democrats as a collective, ubiquitous, drumbeat sort of narrative. That is, they did not drive the Democratic 2012 election campaign as a set of distinct understandings that could function as an alpha story. Instead, some of them showed up in, for example, Jacob Hacker and Paul Pierson, *Winner-Take-All Politics: How Washington Made the Rich Richer – and Turned Its Back on the Middle Class* (2011);[5] Joseph Stiglitz's *The Price of Inequality: How Today's Divided Society Endangers our Future* (2012);[6] Michael Lind's *The Land of Promise: An Economic History of the United States* (2012);[7] Timothy Noah's *The Great Divergence: America's Growing Inequality Crisis and What We Can Do About It* (2012);[8] and Jeff Faux's *The Servant Economy: Where America's Elite is Sending the Middle Class* (2012).[9] When set against the Crash of 2008, talk in this vein condemned government policies based on the conservative narrative of trickle-down or supply-side economics,

[2] By contrast, the Washington-based Cato Institute awards a biennial Milton Friedman Prize of $250,000 "to an individual who has made a significant contribution to the advancement of human freedom." See The Cato Institute, "The Milton Friedman Prize for Advancing Liberty."

[3] Politicians don't clearly define "the middle class" that they talk about so much. When people are asked to describe their own status, 87 percent describe themselves as lower-middle, middle-middle, or upper-middle class. See Pew Research Center, "Most Say Government Policies Since Recession Have Done Little to Help Middle Class, Poor" (2015). The exaggeration here is analogous to parents in the town of Lake Wobegan thinking that all their children are "above average."

[4] Most prominently, they appeared in Elizabeth Warren's speech at the Democratic National Convention in 2012. See Elizabeth Warren, "Elizabeth Warren Speech Text."

[5] Especially pp. 73–91.

[6] Especially pp. 1–27.

[7] Especially pp. 329–362.

[8] Especially pp. 10–27.

[9] Especially pp. 21–45.

which insisted that markets will more or less automatically generate prosperity and wellbeing for whoever works hard and deserves them.[10]

The Move to Growth

Underneath all that, however, there lay an element of retreat, which gathered strength while early twentieth-century "Progressives" – following the lead of Franklin Delano Roosevelt – came to be called "liberals" during the 1930s and 1940s.[11] In 1932, Roosevelt pledged to the American people a "new deal,"[12] which he described as an updated "social contract" that would enable everyone to work, to earn a "comfortable living," and to pursue liberty and happiness.[13] To that end, his governmental activism was designed to thwart the sinister influence of people who the President called "economic royalists"[14] and whose greedy behavior, he argued, generated economic injustice and stunted social progress.[15]

Here was not just a plain recital of annoying facts but the outline of a militant New Deal story. Like many other good stories, from Cinderella to Macbeth, it had heroes and villains. And for some time, buttressed by the New Deal's faith in human agency – here was the "humanism" we have seen all along[16] – it justified liberal projects such as Washington hiring the unemployed and building across the country all sorts of

---

[10] Against this conservative narrative, see Jonathan Chait, *The Big Con: The True Story of How Washington Got Hoodwinked and Hijacked by Crackpot Economics* (2007), pp. 13–44. Trickle-down economic ideas were criticized from Obama's side of the second Romney-Obama debate on October 16, 2013. See Federal News Service, "Transcript of the Second Debate Between President Obama and Republican Nominee Mitt Romney." For a conservative rejection of the trickle-down accusation, see Thomas Sowell, *"Trickle Down" Theory and "Tax Cuts for the Rich"* (2012).

[11] Eric Foner, *The Story of American Freedom* (1998), pp. 201–202, explains that:

> [Roosevelt] consciously abandoned the term 'progressive' and chose instead to employ 'liberal' to describe himself and his administration. In doing so, he transformed 'liberalism' from a shorthand for weak government and laissez-faire economics into belief in an activist, socially conscious state, an alternative both to socialism and to unregulated capitalism.

[12] Franklin D. Roosevelt, "Address at Oglethorpe University in Atlanta Georgia."

[13] Franklin D. Roosevelt, "The Commonwealth Club Address."

[14] Franklin D. Roosevelt, "Acceptance Speech for the Renomination for the Presidency." He also called the culprits "money changers" (in the Temple): see Franklin D. Roosevelt "First Inaugural Address."

[15] For examples of Roosevelt's rhetoric against large corporations and big business, see Franklin D. Roosevelt, "Speech at Madison Square Garden" (1936) and "Second Inaugural Address" (1937).

[16] William Leuchtenburg, *Franklin Roosevelt and the New Deal: 1932–1940* (1962), p. 345: "Heirs of the Enlightenment, they [the New Dealers] felt themselves [to be] part of a broadly humanistic movement to make man's life on earth more tolerable."

infrastructure: parks, dams, libraries, courthouses, airports, schools, hospitals, roads, bridges, and more.[17]

So where did Roosevelt's story go? Democrats did not tell it much after World War II, and they certainly did not promote it much after, say, 1970. But why not? Because on the way to 1970, encouraged by mainstream economists,[18] Democrats switched from raising employment *directly* by creating public works to fostering employment *indirectly* by using the federal budget to stimulate economic growth.[19] This meant that, mostly via what economists call "compensatory finance" or "commercial Keynesianism,"[20] they would press government to generate prosperity so that, hopefully, everyone who wanted a job could get one and earn a living.

The enthusiasm for growth, which rarely asks who gains more or less from it[21] and which regards its side effects as manageable, has by today seized both Democrats *and* Republicans.[22] It therefore became a national consensus value in what Louis Hartz called the "Liberal Tradition." In *The Affluent Society* (1957), John Kenneth Galbraith criticized shortcomings of growth such as waste and pollution. But growth remained attractive, and therefore even when some latter-day liberals extended the economic royalists story they mainly praised growth and regarded as culprits those who, in various ways, selfishly hold it back. This sort of appraisal appears in, for example, Thomas Palley, *Plenty of Nothing: The Downsizing of the American Dream and the Case for Structural Keynesianism* (1998); Thom Hartmann, *Screwed: The Undeclared War Against the Middle Class* (2007); Donald Barlett and James Steele, *The Betrayal of the American Dream* (2012); Thomas Frank, *Pity the*

---

[17] See Jason Scott Smith, *Building New Deal Liberalism: The Political Economy of Public Works, 1933–1956* (2009).

[18] Both Keynesians and monetarists committed themselves to encouraging economic growth. See David Noble, *Debating the End of History: The Marketplace, Utopia, and the Fragmentation of Intellectual Life* (2012), pp. 55–87.

[19] The shift to promoting economic growth is summed up in Alan Brinkley, *The End of Reform: New Deal Liberalism in Recession and War* (1996), pp. 265–271.

[20] Robert Lekachman, *The Age of Keynes* (1968), pp. 285–287.

[21] Who gains or loses, and how much, is a question of distributive justice. Tony Judt criticizes "intellectuals" for not asking that question in modern America. See Tony Judt, *Thinking the Twentieth Century* (2013), p. 361: "Intellectuals ... have come to assume ... that the point of economic policy is to generate resources. Until you've generated resources, goes the refrain, there's no point having a conversation about distributing them."

[22] See Lorenzo Fioramonti, *Gross Domestic Problem: The Politics Behind the World's Most Powerful Number* (2013), pp. 17–81. Fioramonti explains how economists invented the concept of GDP – "the most powerful paradigm of all times" (p. 150) – and how politicians embraced it.

Billionaire: The Hard-Times Swindle and the Unlikely Comeback of the Right (2012); Robert Reich, *Beyond Outrage: What Has Gone Wrong With Our Economy and Our Democracy, and How to Fix It* (2012); and Charles Ferguson, *Predator Nation: Corporate Criminals, Political Corruption, and the Hijacking of America* (2012).

Reasons For the Retreat

This micro-analysis of how Democratic Party leaders and intellectuals moved away from FDR's story is informative and correct. However, it is also narrow-gauge, because accompanying the partisan retreat from enthusiasm for plainly confronting a former foe were events, trends, and dilemmas, evolving over a century and affecting many Americans, which sapped the enthusiasm that liberals once had for promoting a full-bore Progressivism.[23] The factors that came to bear heavily on liberal thinking started in the world of events – both before and after World War II – but were defined and amplified as dangerous, frustrating, and depressing by innumerable liberal expressions of outrage, some of which we have noted.

Thus a certain loss of faith, assurance, and even exuberance stands out when one compares the earlier optimism of Progressives like Herbert Croly, John Dewey, and Walter Rauschenbush with the later pessimism of counterculturalists like Paul Goodman, Herbert Marcuse, and Theodore Roszak. The latter inhabit a world plagued by skepticism in almost every realm of knowledge and practice. Alan Wolfe had this skepticism in mind when, in 2010, he declared that:

The challenge facing liberalism in the future ... is not to beat out its rivals ... Its biggest challenge is to get liberals to once again *believe* in liberalism. Once upon a time they did, and it was in those days that they made such great gains in overcoming economic catastrophe [the Depression], building up society's infrastructure [the New Deal], advancing equality of incomes, gender, and race [after World War II], and confronting with confidence the enemies they faced [during the Cold War].[24]

---

[23] In the Introduction, I left the influence of political money to be explored by other writers. On that score, one could argue that many nominally liberal politicians and many professionals who work in formally liberal think tanks and research institutes are less radical than FDR – who was financially independent – because, without funding, those people might lose their jobs. That is, part of the partisan retreat that I am about to describe may not be an intellectual response to events, trends, and dilemmas but rather an expression of financial timidity. If so, it is a vast subject – and one full of potential ad hominem accusations – best left to other forums.

[24] Alan Wolfe, *The Future of Liberalism* (2010), p. 287.

Social Science

One cause of liberal foreboding was the rise of social science. Before
and after 1900, Progressives such as John Dewey, Albion Small, Simon
Patten, and Louis Brandeis assumed that social science knowledge would
lead to improving economic and political practices by generating shared
understandings of how to make America a more just society. In important respects, the country moved ahead along these lines during the
Progressive Era and the New Deal. That was the meaning of legislation
to break up monopolies, to forbid child labor, to protect unions, to widen
the franchise to women, to impose food and drug regulations, to introduce primary elections, to create bank deposit insurance, to install crop
subsidies, to finance public works, and more.

But social science also showed – for example in works by Sigmund
Freud,[25] Edward Bernays,[26] Harold Lasswell,[27] and Joseph Schumpeter[28] –
that most people are less reasonable and politically competent than popular democratic theories long assumed. In which case, even if modern
thinkers could devise, via empirical research, sober and feasible plans for
improving the quality of American life – for example, plans concerning
race, gender, and gun ownership – there were serious doubts that voters
and their representatives would be sensible enough to endorse and implement those plans.[29] The bottom line here was that democratic politics,
although preferable to authoritarian regimes, looked more and more like
a complicated business that would at best produce ups and downs rather
than a steadily rising line sort of progress.[30]

Physical Science

Apart from losing some of their confidence in democracy, some
Progressives and their heirs came to doubt what we now regard as the
liberal project because they increasingly suspected that human reason,

[25] Sigmund Freud, *Group Psychology and the Analysis of the Ego* (1922), and *The Ego and the Id* (1927).

[26] Edward Bernays, *Propaganda* (1928).

[27] Harold Laswell, *Psychopathology and Politics* (1930).

[28] Joseph Schumpeter, *Capitalism, Socialism and Democracy*, 3rd edn. (1950), "Another Theory of Democracy," pp. 269–283.

[29] Thus Walter Lippmann, *Public Opinion* (1922, 1965), pioneered in using the word "ste-
reotypes" (pp. 53–68) to describe the public as animated by simple-minded images that
do not (p. 19) "automatically correspond to the world outside [their heads]."

[30] For a discussion of some of the complications discovered by social scientists, concerning
how voters derive their preferences and express support for them, see Martin Gilens,
Affluence and Influence: Economic Inequality and Political Power in America (2012), on
"citizen competence," pp. 12–40.

operating through science, was in some respects counterproductive. That is, science, which liberals had long regarded as facilitating or even assuring progress to modern people in their Weberian mode, was no longer seen as a reliable ally.

We can generalize this point. Faith in science as a spur to continual progress – think of vaccinations, steam engines, lightning rods, the telegraph, sewing machines, pasteurized milk, electric lights, cars, televisions, frozen foods, and more – had long generated optimism for many Americans. Even if not always expressed openly, this optimism was constantly present. Thus it served into the mid-twentieth century as a reassuring context for a good deal of Democratic (and Republican) politicking. Then times changed, at least for liberals, to encourage a darker view of human affairs.

The problems on this score are so obvious today that they need little description here. Of course, science produces refrigerators, polio vaccines, the Green Revolution, Boeing jetliners, CorningWare, computers, and more. But it also produces atomic bombs, which threatened to undermine basic morality and destroy humanity. Furthermore, science fuels the technology, such as fracking, that drives economic growth. But technology and growth produce ecological imbalances and environmental destruction, from climate change to species extinction.

Religion

Along with science, theology became problematic. Religious faith inspired a spirit of social amelioration in the thinking of Progressives like John Dewey, Simon Patten, Walter Rauschenbush, Jane Adams, and Wesley Mitchell.[31] But that spirit was not shared by all Americans, or even all Protestants, and this became apparent especially when, in 1925, a state court in Dayton, Tennessee convicted John Scopes of violating a Tennessee law that forbade teaching about evolution to high-school biology students. Radio and newspaper reports of the trial went out to millions of Americans, highlighting powerful fundamentalist sentiments which challenged science and modernity, and which animated the law in Tennessee that justified Scopes's conviction.

Mainline churches including Presbyterians and Episcopalians, inspired by ministers like Reinhold Niebuhr, continued to promote social and economic progress according to Rauschenbusch's concept of "the Social

---

[31] For example, E. A. Ross, *Sin and Society: An Analysis of Latter-Day Iniquity* (1907), defined dangerous and larcenous political and commercial practices as sins.

Gospel."[32] Those churches therefore participated in great reform projects such as the civil rights movement in the 1950s and 1960. But the same denominations steadily declined in membership relative to fast-growing fundamentalist congregations in, say, the Southern Baptist Convention and the Assemblies of God.[33] Meanwhile, left-leaning Americans, such as those who made and staffed the New Deal, increasingly tended to project their enthusiasm for reform in secular rather than theological terms.[34] In short, the piety driving Progressivism's original passion lost much of its power.

Consumerism

Another spur to liberal pessimism was the rise of "Consumerism," which got underway in the decades leading up to World War I.[35] Technically speaking, modern factories and assembly lines, such as those of Ford and Nabisco, changed the contours of American life by generating enormous quantities of commodities that had to be sold. Marketed in new venues like mail-order houses, department stores, and supermarkets, these "goods" were bought by Americans who were tempted out of traditional frugality by sophisticated schemes of advertising and high-powered credit buying.[36] Slowly but steadily, products and acquisitions improved health and living conditions for millions of rural and urban Americans.

The upshot of ever-rising consumption, however, was that in some respects commitment to Progressive reform as expressed in the Social Gospel was overshadowed by a growing faith, almost spiritual, in an economic vision of shopping that called on Americans to buy what they wanted rather than what they needed.[37] This vision was seemingly

---

[32] Walter Rauschenbusch, *A Theology for the Social Gospel* (1917).

[33] Shrinking mainline churches, the growth of fundamentalist and evangelical denominations, and the political activities of both – especially in recent decades – are sketched briefly by Robert Wuthnow, "The Moral Minority," *The American Prospect* (December 19, 2001).

[34] Religious values are not highlighted as an inspiration to New Dealers in Harvey Kaye, *The Fight for the Four Freedoms: What Made FDR and the Greatest Generation Truly Great* (2014). The same is true of Cass Sunstein, *The Second Bill of Rights: FDR's Unfinished Revolution and Why We Need It More Than Ever* (2004).

[35] Consumerism is many things. See the many views of it collected in Neva Goodwin, Frank Ackerman, and David Kiron (eds.), *The Consumer Society* (1997). For a political science perspective, see Benjamin Barber, *Consumed: How Markets Corrupt Children, Infantilize Adults, and Swallow Citizens Whole* (2008).

[36] Susan Strasser, *Satisfaction Guaranteed: The Making of the American Mass Market* (1989).

[37] See William Leach, *Land of Desire: Merchants, Power, and the Rise of a New American Culture* (1993).

scientific, promoted via plausible graphs, charts, and curves, and focused on personal satisfactions. It encouraged citizens to believe that private markets, expanding first in America and then through globalization, will automatically provide so many desired commodities for society[38] that collective action on behalf of public goods is unnecessary – and perhaps even counterproductive.[39]

Economic Growth

No longer citing the Social Gospel, some scholars (such as Galbraith) unsuccessfully railed against this view, which emphasizes benefits rather than costs.[40] After World War II, highways, suburbs, televisions, fast foods, supermarkets, washing machines, garbage disposals, air conditioners, passenger planes, shopping malls, computers, and mobile phones proliferated. Partly this was because acquiring and enjoying more rather than less was popular, in which case material progress was sought by voters and promoted by politicians.[41] And partly this was because many economists, like Walt Rostow in *The Stages of Economic Growth: A Non-Communist Manifesto* (1960), advocated growth passionately, first as a democratic alternative to Communist five-year plans during the Cold

---

[38] The practice of talking about private commodities as if they are "goods" is part of this worldview. It leads to GNP (or GDP) calculations that equally praise the sale of Halloween chocolates and the cost of dental care required after eating them. Liberal politicians occasionally point this out. See Robert Kennedy, "Remarks at the University of Kansas":

> Gross National Product counts air pollution and cigarette advertising, and ambulances to clear our highways of carnage. It counts special locks for our doors and the jails for the people who break them. It counts the destruction of the redwood and the loss of our natural wonder in chaotic sprawl. It counts napalm and counts nuclear warheads and armored cars for the police to fight the riots in our cities ... It does not include the beauty of our poetry or the strength of our marriages, the intelligence of our public debate or the integrity of our public officials.

[39] On encouraging Americans to foster and revere markets, see Jay Richards, *Money, Greed, and God: Why Capitalism is the Solution and Not the Problem* (2009); Angus Burgin, *The Great Persuasion: Reinventing Free Markets since the Depression* (2012); and John Allison, *The Financial Crisis and the Free Market Cure: Why Pure Capitalism is the World Economy's Only Hope* (2013).

[40] See Jules Henry, *Culture Against Man* (1965); Tibor Scitovsky, *The Joyless Economy: An Inquiry into Human Satisfaction and Consumer Dissatisfaction* (1976); and Paul Wachtel, *The Poverty of Affluence: A Psychological Portrait of the American Way of Life* (1989).

[41] Lizabeth Cohen, *A Consumers' Republic: The Politics of Mass Consumption in Postwar America* (2003).

War, and later as the commendable outcome of market-based practices known today as neoliberalism.

The problem, however, was that many Americans – including liberals – became increasingly aware that an ever-rising Gross National Product (or its companion Gross Domestic Product), fueled by science and technology, cause considerable economic, environmental, and psychological damage. These effects overlap in real life but we can single out some of them analytically, starting with drawbacks in the modern economy of growth.

Mobile Capital

A prime economic resource nowadays is "mobile capital." Workers cannot easily leave their friends, homes, neighborhoods, schools, relatives, churches, and familiar routines in order to relocate to places far away. But at the click of a mouse, capital can move to places where doing business entails fewer costs and larger profits; say, from New Jersey to South Carolina or from Los Angeles to Singapore. This mobility eventually fostered the age of "globalization"[42] wherein, for example, clothing and sport shoes came to be manufactured and then purchased by companies like Wal-Mart and Target, mainly in places like Indonesia, Guatemala, Bangladesh, and China.

Deindustrialization

With capital free to relocate, a process of "deindustrialization" set in, whereby a considerable fraction of America's traditional industry – making shoes, tires, flatware, automobiles, household appliances, machine tools, chemicals, televisions, clothing, and more – moved overseas, or to Central America. In the worst cases, this created a rust-belt wasteland of cities like Youngstown, Ohio and Detroit, Michigan.[43] Moreover, even where industry remained it became leaner and meaner, so that some workers were discharged in the name of "downsizing" and others were turned away in the name of "outsourcing." Furthermore, those who still worked – many in the growing service sector that included fast-food chains such as McDonald's and retail giants such as Home Depot – were

---

[42] On globalization, see William Greider, *One World, Ready or Not: The Manic Logic of Global Capitalism* (1997).

[43] Barry Bluestone and Bennett Harrison, *The Deindustrialization of America: Plant Closings, Community Abandonment, and the Dismantling of Basic Industry* (1982), and Judith Stein, *Pivotal Decade: How the United States Traded Factories for Finance in the Seventies* (2010).

increasingly stuck in part-time jobs, unprotected by unions, without retirement and health benefits, and in the category of "contingent labor."[44]

Creative Destruction

All this reflected what Schumpeter called "creative destruction,"[45] whereby some people – like Bill Gates and the Walton family, the Koch brothers and Sheldon Adelson, Steve Jobs and Jeff Bezos, Warren Buffet and Ralph Lauren, Thomas Frist and the Pritzkers, Bernard Marcus and Steven Spielberg, Oprah Winfrey and Michael Bloomberg – did very well by riding the crest of innovation, while others – like coachmen, chimney sweeps, elevator operators, powder monkeys, and linotypists – were set aside as their skills and practices became obsolete. At worst, those at the top in every realm drew away financially from those at the bottom to create what looked like a "winner-take-all" society.[46]

Constant Choice

In this economy of constant growth, consumerism encouraged Americans to buy all that the country produced and imported, and advertisements fostered an individualism which praised everyone's right to make his or her selection among whatever things were available. However, various difficulties flowed from the choices that people made. One was that conflicting "lifestyles" emerged, to the point where many Americans had difficulty identifying with "core values" that had long united friends and neighbors.[47] Another was that money, to buy things and live comfortably, became an implicit standard for judging what people are morally "worth." Here was where Neil Postman remarked that, in modern life, "whoever dies with the most toys, wins."[48] A third was that the multiplicity of choices overwhelmed people's sense of order, community,

---

44 On downsizing, outsourcing, and contingent labor, see Katherine Newman, *Falling from Grace: The Experience of Downward Mobility in the American Middle Class* (1988); Robert Parker, *Flesh Peddlers and Warm Bodies: The Temporary Help Industry and Its Workers* (1994); and Steven Greenhouse, *The Big Squeeze: Tough Times for the American Worker* (2008).

45 Schumpeter, *Capitalism, Socialism and Democracy*, pp. 81–86.

46 Robert Frank, *The Winner-Take-All Society: Why the Few at the Top Get So Much More Than the Rest of Us* (1996).

47 Using different terms, this dilemma is explored in Robert Bellah, Richard Madsen, William Sullivan, Ann Swidler, and Steven Tipton, *Habits of the Heart: Individualism and Commitment in American Life* (1986). See also David Myers, *The American Paradox: Spiritual Hunger in an Age of Plenty* (2000).

48 Neil Postman, *The End of Education: Redefining the Value of School* (1996), p. 33.

continuity, and competence.[49] And above all there was the occasional reminder that, while everyone was straining to keep up with the Joneses, happiness was a constantly receding goal that many people could not attain because the Joneses never stopped working hard to leave everyone else behind by purchasing bigger houses, fancier cars, and more luxurious vacations.[50]

Ecology

Whatever its personal effects, some Americans began to notice that, across the board, perpetual growth might destroy the world which sustains us all. Here, "ecology" was a key concept for drawing attention to vital but not always obvious relationships in nature. Rachel Carson led the way in 1962 with *Silent Spring*, which showed how pesticides could destroy not just insects but also animals such as birds and fish. Garrett Hardin followed Carson in 1968 with his allegory about a "tragedy of the commons," showing how natural assets, such as pasture land that had once been shared in small communities, were being privatized and exploited ruthlessly with no regard for sustainability.[51]

Then came *The Limits To Growth* (1972), which observed that industry and agriculture were not only depleting the environment by using up resources such as rainforests and fertile lands, but were also dangerously polluting the world and therefore destroying some of the natural balances upon which civilization rests. Eventually, air pollution became so serious that the "greenhouse effect" was discovered, which later spurred interest in what is now called "global warming" or "climate change."[52]

Politics I

Political thought entered into the retreat from pre-war Progressivism to post-war liberalism via what political scientist David Ciepley calls the "encounter" with totalitarianism.[53] According to Ciepley, the Great Depression

---

[49] Barry Schwartz, *The Paradox of Choice: Why More is Less* (2004), and Kent Greenfeld, *The Myth of Choice: Personal Responsibility in a World of Limits* (2011).

[50] Fred Hirsch, *Social Limits to Growth* (1976). In addition, stable happiness is not achieved because advertisements encourage people to feel bad about themselves so that, even after they buy something, they will want to buy more. See Naomi Wolf, *The Beauty Myth: How Images of Women are Used Against Women* (1991).

[51] Garrett Hardin, "The Tragedy of the Commons," *Science* (December 13, 1968), pp. 1243–1248.

[52] See S. George Philander, *Is the Temperature Rising? The Uncertain Science of Global Warming* (1998).

[53] David Ciepley, *Liberalism in the Shadow of Totalitarianism* (2006).

challenged the American ideal of "individualism" so severely that the conservative interpretation of that ideal,[54] in an alpha story praising small government and laissez-faire, was widely regarded as either causing the Crash or impeding efforts to overcome it. Later, however, the force of that lesson faded and Americans increasingly saw their society as philosophically and practically competing against autocratic regimes, especially in Nazi Germany and the Soviet Union, which were eventually called totalitarian.

Consequently, in government circles the efforts of latter-day Progressives to deal with the Depression – via government spending, employment, construction, and regulation – faltered. Southern Democrats and other social conservatives, for reasons including racism, had always opposed many New Deal programs.[55] Then, as the 1930s and 1940s wore on, America's encounter with totalitarianism – especially in Nazi Germany – provided a vocabulary strengthening conservative rhetoric against such programs because domestic government activity could now be described as tantamount to dictatorial intervention and state-wide planning. After which, of course, during the Cold War, Soviet and Chinese totalitarianism stepped in to seize America's attention.[56]

The new vocabulary, highly visible in the post-war hysteria of McCarthyism, encouraged a growing national reluctance to use government to promote social and economic reform. One result was widespread support for the fiscal Keynesianism that we have noted, whereby government would manipulate the money supply so that private expenditures rather than public projects would foster economic growth and prosperity. Another result was a renewed national commitment to "consumerism" whereby, after poverty in the 1930s and austerity during the war years, Americans after 1945 competed against the challenge of Communism by increasingly adopting the idea that life is about consumption, that the best sort of consumption is driven by individual preferences, that "free enterprise" serves this impulse efficiently, and that the totality of what individuals choose to consume represents an ever-growing quantity

---

[54] For the conservative story, see Herbert Hoover, *American Individualism* (1922).

[55] On Southern resistance to New Deal social programs that might have challenged white supremacy, see Ira Katznelson, *Fear Itself: The New Deal and the Origins of Our Time* (2013), pp. 133–222.

[56] The triumph of this shift appeared in Dwight Eisenhower, "First Inaugural Address," January 20, 1953, which predicted a "century of trial" during which, "to meet the challenge of our time, destiny has laid upon our country the responsibility for the free world's leadership." Accordingly, "We wish our friends the world over to know this above all: we face the threat – not with dread and confusion – but with confidence and conviction."

of national happiness.[57] In that vision, government projects were rarely needed because even collective needs could be supplied by what is now called "privatization." To little avail, many liberal thinkers, but fewer liberal politicians, criticized various aspects of consumerism.[58]

Politics II

In post-war universities, the rejuvenated prestige of old-style individualism produced what scholars called a "pluralistic" view of American society. According to pluralism, citizens form groups with like-minded individuals, after which democratic outcomes reflect group bargaining and compromises rather than the expression of a national will.[59] In this view, government is morally obliged to regard groups neutrally and therefore refrain, as totalitarian governments did not, from seeking to impose on them society-wide goals and principles.[60]

Political scientist Theodore Lowi highlighted pluralism in *The End of Liberalism: Ideology, Policy, and the Crisis of Public Authority* (1969). At stake was a paradigm shift that undercut the old, Progressive vision of thinkers like Herbert Croley, Richard Ely, Wesley Mitchell, Woodrow Wilson, Walter Lippmann, and more. Such men endorsed the notion that social improvement can be promoted by experts and administrators who know the public interest and seek to advance it. But, as Lowi pointed out, if individuals and their groups have different ideas of what the public interest is, or if they are self-centered, then an overall vision, and support for it, will not emerge. Mainline economists after the war affirmed something similar to this observation, partly because they sought to portray themselves as engaging in hardnosed "science" rather than softheaded "social justice," in which case, according to much economic theory, only individuals and collections of them, rather than experts, were entitled to define "utility" for themselves.[61]

---

[57] For classic accounts, see Susan Strasser, *Satisfaction Guaranteed: The Making of the American Mass Market* (1989); William Leach, *Land of Desire: Merchants, Power, and the Rise of a New American Culture* (1993); and Cohen, *A Consumers' Republic* (2003).

[58] For example, Robert Kuttner, *Everything for Sale: The Virtues and Limits of Markets* (1998); Tim Kassner, *The High Price of Materialism* (2002); Schwartz, *The Paradox of Choice: Why More is Less* (2004); and Michael Sandel, *What Money Can't Buy: The Moral Limits of Markets* (2012).

[59] See sociologist Willliam Kornhauser, *The Politics of Mass Society* (1959).

[60] The shift away from a New Deal emphasis on public interests is described in Ira Katznelson, *Fear Itself*, pp. 477–479.

[61] This acceptance of individual judgment is now being challenged by the nudge syndrome, as in Richard Thaler and Cass Sunstein, *Nudge: Improving Decisions About Health, Wealth, and Happiness* (2008).

Nuclear Weapons

In the post-war world, the existence of nuclear arsenals encouraged liberal foreboding. At Hiroshima, a frightful power appeared suddenly. Its force was measured by, say, Ground Zero, *Nuclear War: What's In It for You?* (1982), which explained in excruciating detail the horrific damage that would be caused by one-megaton bombs, which were fifty times as powerful as the Nagasaki device, falling simultaneously on cities like New York, Detroit, Los Angeles, and Atlanta, instantly killing and injuring millions of people and leaving the living to envy the dead. That strategists like Herman Kahn, who recommended wielding such bombs, were moral delinquents was obvious to, say, Anatol Rapoport, *Strategy and Conscience* (1964) and Philip Green, *Deadly Logic: The Theory of Nuclear Deterrence* (1968). That its spread was inevitable was the message of, say, Jonathan Schell, *The Fate of the Earth* (1982). That politicians could not be trusted with all of science's fruits was pointed out by, say, Friedrich Durrenmatt, *The Physicists* (1962). And that the whole business of producing thousands of nuclear devices was quite mad seemed clear to, say, Eric Fromm, *The Sane Society* (1955).

Faced with competition in which a traditional "victory" of military capitulation between nuclear powers could not be achieved because it risked destroying both sides, former Ambassador to Moscow, George Kennan, recommended the policy of "containment" in 1947. In his plan, direct wars between the United States and the Soviet Union would be avoided while smaller campaigns to contain hostile Russian and Chinese aspirations would be waged by America and its allies around the periphery of the Communist world.[62] When America pursued this strategy, it managed to avoid nuclear war. But the "small" hot wars promoted by containment in Korea and Vietnam were terrible bloodbaths with disappointing results, and the effort to hold back Russia and China created the specter of perpetual war.

Perpetual War

One premise of the Enlightenment was that if people will organize public life reasonably – according to humanism – they can overthrow the culture of monarchical and princely government, which is promoted by stories, and thereby end that culture's practice of constant warfare. As Thomas

---

[62] George Kennan, "The Sources of Soviet Conduct," *Foreign Affairs* (July, 1947), pp. 53–63. In this article, published anonymously, Kennan did not explicitly call for small wars. As a diplomat, he insisted that: "The main thing is that there should always be pressure, unceasing constant pressure, toward the desired goal ... patient but firm and vigilant containment of Russian expansive tendencies."

Paine made this point, who needs kings? They do nothing but "make war and give away places."[63] Along the same lines, the Declaration of Independence justified rebelling against a British "tyranny" imposed on the colonies by force, and the Founders fashioned the Constitution to check power and ambition so thoroughly that, hopefully, American government would serve its people rather than exploit and oppress them.

Now, if peace rather than war is the default setting for public life, government money can be spent on schools, hospitals, parks, libraries, beaches, roads, conservation, public health, scientific research, and other civilized projects. Regardless of how desirable it is to fund such amenities, however, during the Cold War America poured endless billions of dollars into creating a massive military machine to confront its enemies even during peacetime. Doing so seemed necessary because being ready to wage a large modern war, not today but tomorrow, fought with nuclear or conventional weapons, requires training in advance, strike units on constant alert, production of new weapons long before fighting breaks out, multiple delivery systems, early warning installations, constant upgrading of planes, warships, tanks, and ammunition, positioning of forces overseas, and more.

The result - for the first time in American history - was to establish an enormous peacetime army, which between wars warranted huge annual budgets needed elsewhere and which resisted downsizing because defense projects were strikingly profitable in states where defense money was spent.[64] Eventually, President Dwight Eisenhower warned the nation in his Farewell Address in 1961 that this "military–industrial complex" might exercise unwarranted power over a democratic society.

Notwithstanding Ike's warning, the rationale for extraordinary military spending became normal and reigned in Washington until the Soviet Union collapsed in 1989. At that point, conservatives – and especially "neo-conservatives" – began to speak of new enemies who were supposedly dangerous enough to necessitate high defense expenditures.[65] An

---

[63] Paine, "Common Sense (1776)," in Howard Fast (ed.), *The Selected Work of Tom Paine and Citizen Tom Paine* (1945), p. 18.

[64] See Nick Kotz, *Wild Blue Yonder: Money, Politics, and the B-1 Bomber* (1988), on how dispersing the production of B-1 bomber parts to factories all over America earned in Congress the political support of representatives from more than 20 American states. Spin-offs from this sort of military production helped America to increase its foreign arms sales in 2014 to $36.2 billion which was then roughly 50 percent of the world's total arms trafficking. See Nicholas Fandos, "US Foreign Arms Deals Increased Nearly $10 Billion In 2014."

[65] For example, Samuel Huntington, *The Clash of Civilizations and the Remaking of World Order* (1996), and Robert Kagan and William Kristol (eds.), *Present Dangers: Crisis and Opportunity in American Foreign and Defense Policy* (2000). Andrew Bacevich, *Breach*

apparent justification for such fears appeared on September 11, 2001, when Muslim fanatics hijacked four American passenger planes and flew two of them into the World Trade Center in New York City and another into the Pentagon in Arlington.

President George W. Bush promptly declared an endless "War on Terror" and then attacked Afghanistan and Iraq.[66] Obama continued with bombing and drone strikes in places as far flung as Libya and Pakistan. As a result, America's annual military spending went up to about $600 billion, where it remains today roughly equal to that of the next ten major military powers in the world combined.[67] Estimated American costs for the Iraq War have reached $3 trillion,[68] and those do not include severe impairment of America's self-image from moral corruption (greedy and irresponsible contractors), emotional strain (families of soldiers suffering from Post-Traumatic Stress Disorder), and indecent behavior (torture sponsored by the Pentagon and the CIA at places like Guantanamo Bay and Abu Ghraib).[69]

The Standoff

These were some of the events and trends that liberals noticed as the twentieth century wore on. It followed that liberals tended to conclude – helped along by costly wars, persistent racism, political assassinations, urban riots, gender discrimination, stagflation, nuclear accidents, anti-choice legislation, environmental degradation, economic concentration, financial meltdowns, smartphone addiction, fast food obesity, and more – that the sky was falling on modern society. As one liberal remarked in 1981, "Western life seems to be drifting toward increasing entropy, economic and technological chaos, ecological disaster, and ultimately, psychic dismemberment and disintegration."[70] As another observed less

---

of Trust: How Americans Failed Their Soldiers and Their Country (2013), pp. 80–102, describes the post-USSR invention of justifications for new military projects as "searching for dragons to slay."

[66] See George W. Bush, "Address to the Nation on the Terrorist Attacks." In this 2001 speech, the President portrayed "terrorists" as "heirs of the murderous ideologies" that America had confronted in the twentieth century.

[67] See GlobalFirePower.com, "Defense Budget By Country." The Center for Defense Analysis in Washington priced "national security" spending – which includes current forces, military pensions, homeland security, veterans' hospitals, and more – at $989.7 billion in 2015.

[68] Linda Bilmes and Joseph Stiglitz, *The Three Trillion Dollar War: The True Cost of the Iraq War* (2008).

[69] James Risen, *Pay Any Price: Greed, Power, and Endless War* (2014), discusses these costs.

[70] Marshall Berman, *The Reenchantment of the World* (1981), p. 15.

apocalyptically in 2000, liberals still talk about fixing this or that, but they expect few great changes and rarely dream of a future society that will be radically different and better than what they have today.[71]

The situation really was puzzling. As Charles Dickens described the French Revolution in *A Tale of Two Cities* (1859), it was the best of times and the worst of times, it was the age of wisdom and the age of foolishness, and it was the spring of hope and the winter of despair. Similarly, in modern America, great progress was being made by, say, some minorities, feminists, shoppers, television fans, heart patients, sports enthusiasts, hedge fund managers, social media participants, and so forth. But every step forward seemed likely to foster a step backward. One banking crisis after another, one plant closing after another, one tropical storm after another, one police killing after another, one privacy loss after another, one oil spill after another, one hacking disaster after another, one geostrategic conflict after another: the causes for frustration and even outrage were endless.

From all of this, liberals wound up going in many directions, for example following Jimmy Carter, or Bill Clinton, or Barack Obama, or John Rawls, or Michael Walzer, or Richard Rorty, or Robert Reich, or Naomi Klein, or Garrett Hardin, or Andrew Bacevich, or Jonathan Schell, or Robert Kuttner, or others, who together focused on a great number of problems and proposed a wide variety of solutions. Such people offered powerful and persuasive insights. But these did not emerge from common and confident stories, embracing shared proposals backed up by unambiguous convictions. Even worse, political liberals sometimes compromised on what seemed to other liberals to be signature principles – such as New Deal support for organized labor and commercial bank regulation – without even putting up a fight, such as when Bill Clinton adopted a fuzzy re-election strategy of "triangulating" between left-wing and right-wing aims. Here was an open retreat from what now seems like earlier Progressive consistency and confidence.

The Vital Center

In truth, there were so many troubling events, and there were so many frustrated liberals along the way, and there are so many demoralized liberals today, that we cannot know for sure exactly why the liberal retreat evolved as it did. But one path to the present may be said to derive from a sense that the dangers which liberals saw all around them were not just

---

[71] Russell Jacoby, *The End of Utopia: Politics and Culture in an Age of Apathy* (1999).

serious, but also impossible to repair. We can trace this apprehension to at least some liberals postulating a centrist and moderate strategy that, over time, did not succeed.

On this score, soon after World War II, the quintessential liberal historian Arthur Schlesinger talked about occupying the "vital center" in American politics.[72] As an early Cold War warrior, Schlesinger wanted especially to steer the country away from the principles of fascism – or Congressman J. Parnell Thomas (R-N.J.) – on the Right, and the precepts of communism – or former Vice President Henry Wallace – on the Left.[73] Here was the recipe for a sort of "third way which liberals came to promote repeatedly under different names.

For example, think-tanker David Callahan contends that – in realms including family matters, crime and punishment, poverty, and work – some Americans promote "collective responsibility" very strongly while others depend mainly on "personal responsibility." He then insists that the country needs both, and that "the political party that recognizes this has the potential to dominate elections for decades to come."[74] Here is a recipe for a little of this and a little of that.

Similarly, English and journalism professor Eric Alterman observes that it is difficult to say exactly what liberals believe, because times and issues change constantly. In his opinion, however, they are committed to both the individualism of John Rawls and the communitarianism of Michael Sandel, with an addition of classic Western virtues such as temperance, fortitude, tolerance, generosity, forbearance, patience, kindness, and charity. In short, for Alterman, liberals are determined to strike a balance somewhere between idealism and realism.[75]

In truth, the recommendation for operating in "the center" is a default setting for people who – with very good intentions – don't know exactly where to stand. Its virtue is that it steers us away from extremism. Its downside is that, in real-world politics rather than in political philosophy, there may be no vital center. This became clear to liberals when, along with terrible failures in Vietnam which were accompanied by

---

[72] Arthur Schlesinger Jr., *The Vital Center: Our Purposes and Perils on the Tightrope of American Liberalism* (1949).

[73] Thomas became Chairman of the House Un-American Activities Committee in 1947, and Wallace ran for President as the Progressive Party candidate in 1948.

[74] David Callahan, *The Moral Center: How We Can Reclaim Our Country from Die-Hard Extremists, Rogue Corporations, Hollywood Hacks, and Pretend Patriots* (2006), especially pp. 18–19.

[75] Eric Alterman, *Why We're Liberals: A Handbook for Restoring America's Most Important Ideals* (2009), pp. 56–61.

assassinations and riots at home, Theodore Lowi explained that America had become a society dominated not by centrist thinking and policies but by what he called "interest group liberalism."

According to Lowi, many interests arise in modern society, in which case the groups that they form constitute a pluralism of power and influence over government and unorganized citizens. From this institutional reality, said Lowi, there arose a public philosophy that justified running the country according to laws and policies emerging from a moving balance of group interests. This sort of constant maneuvering may produce stability. But it sometimes has the disadvantage – such as that which Keynes said characterized economic equilibrium in capitalist societies – of representing less than optimal public welfare.[76]

Lowi's thesis was academic. But two trends in the 1970s and 1980s seemed to confirm it. First, the New Deal coalition lost much of its cohesion when many Southern and urban whites abandoned the Democratic Party and starting to vote Republican. Here was a demonstration of centripetal forces driving groups apart. Second, a wave of "identity" politics struck the country and encouraged the formation of voting sectors composed of women, young people, African Americans, Hispanics, and others. As a result, even when those sectors tended to lean leftwards, observers increasingly regarded Democrats as a medley of groups rather than a broad-based, like-minded, and stable alliance.[77]

Seeing such trends unfold, political scientists Jacob Hacker and Paul Pierson eventually observed that liberals are "often motivated primarily by one issue – the environment, say, or abortion, or minority rights." Against that sort of pluralism, Hacker and Pierson noted that conservatives still manage to maintain "a broad effort to protect a way of life."[78] In other words, conservatives have not succumbed entirely to the disunity of groups.

Hacker and Pierson did not remark, as we have, that unity on the Right is fostered by large stories, which liberals lack. The two were focused more on the practical interlocking of right-wing groups than on their shared emotional universe. However, sociologist Todd Gitlin – who surveyed the rise of Democratic "movements" against the Democratic

[76] Theodore Lowi, *The End of Liberalism: Ideology, Policy, and the Crisis of Public Authority* (1969), throughout but especially pp. 29–97.

[77] The erosion of the New Deal alliance is described in Thomas Edsall and Mary Edsall, *Chain Reaction: The Impact of Race, Rights, and Taxes on American Politics* (1992).

[78] Jacob Hacker and Paul Pierson, "No Cost for Extremism: Why the GOP Hasn't (Yet) Paid for Its March to the Right," *The American Prospect* (Spring, 2015).

"party" after World War II – explained how single interest groups had undermined that party's sense of common purpose. Therefore he called upon liberals to fashion for themselves a "Big Tent" tale, precisely to overcome their increasing pluralism and fragmentation.[79]

Post-Truth Politics

Group politics encouraged liberals to believe that governmental institutions – including legislatures, parties, elections, and voters – would not enact better public policies even if liberal thinkers might agree, more or less, on what had to be done. But there was also a procedural barrier. The point here is that a liberal worldview assumes that truth will overcome tyranny and light our way to progress, that we can achieve this truth via science, and that we can pass truth on to other people by exercising our right of free speech in newspapers, books, scientific reports, speeches, judicial decisions, legislative debates, and more.[80]

Against all this, America has maintained for decades a maze of social and economic sectors in which groups are entitled to defend their interests. That is to say – unlike in societies more orthodox and rigid, like the eighteenth century's Old Order – everyone in America whose ideas are attacked has a right to fight back, and that is exactly what American groups now do, many with great skill and panache. The result is that policy arguments – saying yes or no to Obamacare, to vaccinations, to voter I.D., to amnesty for illegal immigrants, or to drone strikes in Pakistan and Yemen – never cease, and even facts confirmed by science are contested endlessly. In these confrontations "closure" of debate is prevented because, driven by unquenchable enthusiasm, antagonists will raise money to hire additional "experts" and market their additional testimonies.[81]

Paul Krugman calls this situation "post-truth politics" because he is convinced that scientists, pragmatists, and scholars occasionally discover things about modern society that really are true.[82] He is particularly

---

[79] Todd Gitlin, *The Bulldozer and the Big Tent: Blind Republicans, Lame Democrats, and the Recovery of American Ideals* (2007), pp. 134–153.

[80] On truth and liberalism, see Bernard Williams, *Truth and Truthfulness* (2002), pp. 206–232.

[81] Heclo explains why "closure" rarely occurs today in "Issue Networks and the Executive Establishment," p. 121.

[82] See Paul Krugman, "Imaginary Health Care Horrors" (March 30, 2015). The same notion appears in Paul Krugman, "Hating Good Government" (January 19, 2015) and Paul Krugman, "Zombies of 2016" (April 24, 2015).

annoyed when what he considers to be economically true is denied by groups committed unswervingly to small government and public austerity – both of which, in Krugman's view, sometimes make bad times worse. Other liberals are equally irritated by groups that ignore scientific research on global warming and deny that climate change is a problem or is caused by human activity.[83] Against those groups, some environmentalists have even suggested that, as temperatures rise, our brains naturally respond by screening out relevant evidence.[84]

The standoff among and between groups constitutes a sort of intellectual gridlock – or, as Stephen Miller says, an "ersatz conversation" – in which many people are content to talk past one another rather than with one another.[85] In the largest sense, it flows from a process whereby people get organized and exercise influence on behalf of their own interests rather than public ends.[86] But in another sense, the standoff arises because conservatives understood long before liberals did that they could game the marketplace for ideas by financing a wide array of think tanks, study groups, legal institutes, media watchdogs, newspapers, talk shows, publishers, and other outlets for promoting their view of the world.[87] These heralds powerfully marketed conservative ideas against modern expectations that were likely to arise more spontaneously among ordinary citizens, journalists, academics, and activists.[88]

[83] See, for example, Ross Gelbspan, *Boiling Point: How Politicians, Big Oil and Coal, Journalists, and Activists Have Fueled a Climate Crisis – and What We Can Do to Avert Disaster* (2005); Stephen Schneider and Tim Flannery, *Science as a Contact Sport: Inside the Battle to Save the Earth's Climate* (2009); James Hoggan and Richard Littlemore, *Climate Cover-Up: The Crusade to Deny Global Warming* (2009); Clive Hamilton, *Requiem for a Species: Why We Resist the Truth About Climate Change* (2010); Naomi Oreskes, *Merchants of Doubt: How a Handful of Scientists Obscured the Truth on Issues from Tobacco Smoke to Global Warming* (2011); and Chris Mooney, *The Republican Brain: The Science of Why They Deny Science – and Reality* (2012).

[84] George Marshall, *Don't Even Think About It: Why Our Brains are Wired to Ignore Climate Change* (2014).

[85] Stephen Miller, *Conversation: A History of a Declining Art* (2007), pp. 269–281.

[86] Mancur Olson, *The Rise and Decline of Nations: Economic Growth, Stagflation, and Social Rigidities* (1982), offers a systematic explanation of how groups multiply and clog up the world's public policy arena.

[87] The rise of the conservative "counter-establishment" is discussed in Ricci, *Why Conservatives Tell Stories and Liberals Don't: Rhetoric, Faith, and Vision on the American Right* (2011), pp. 149–156. See also Jacob Hacker and Paul Pierson, *Off Center: The Republican Revolution and the Erosion of American Democracy* (2005), pp. 135–162.

[88] In *On Liberty* (1859), Mills says nothing about how deliberately, intensively, and widely promoting ideas might cripple his marketplace for ideas. Thus he did not foresee the powerful and expensive gaming of that marketplace described in Jane Mayer, *Dark*

In 1998, Hillary Clinton fought back against criticism of her husband by calling these organized forces "a vast right-wing conspiracy."[89] The phrase was widely reported. But conspiracy in this realm wasn't really necessary because, once conservative spokespeople were in place (mostly openly and transparently), some of their ideas would triumph in the marketplace not because they were surely correct but because they were massively funded and everywhere proclaimed. The result was that, on issues ranging from sex education to climate change, free trade to Social Security, there could be no consensus on truth.

Liberal Realism

Confronted by a world in which liberal principles, expectations, and aspirations seemed increasingly utopian, and having no alpha stories to justify pressing on regardless, some liberals decided that their Enlightenment faith in human agency was overrated. Consequently, liberalism became more "realistic" than before. For example, while speaking to the nation in his fifth State of the Union message, President Barack Obama could find no more inspiring justification for investing in education – which certainly is a consummation devoutly to be wished – than that well-trained and highly educated workers contribute to economic growth and increase American competitiveness in the world.[90] Absent was any moral, philosophical, or visionary reference to education as a vital and intrinsic good that can help people to enjoy life and live well.[91]

To recap: I have described the liberal retreat by noting bits and pieces of what happened in many realms and what was, I think, noticed by many liberal thinkers. Such a view of the retreat seems to me plausible, and it may appear especially so in the light of four typical liberal books about America today. These represent the thinking of distinguished liberal

---

Money: The Hidden History of the Billionaires Behind the Rise of the Radical Right (2016).

[89] See David Maraniss, "First Lady Launches Counterattack."

[90] See Obama, "State of the Union Address" (2016).

[91] For example, John Adams in 1780:

> I must study Politicks and War that my sons may have liberty to study Mathematicks and Philosophy. My sons ought to study Mathematicks and Philosophy ... Commerce and Agriculture, in order to give their children a right to study Painting, Poetry, Musick, Architecture, Statuary, Tapestry and Porcelaine.
>
> See Adams' letter to Abigail Adams at www.masshist.org/digitaladams/archive/doc?id=L17800512jasecond.

authors, and they all display the syndrome of diminished expectations. Four books are not enough to constitute a statistical trend. But they do indicate something of the background to President Obama's thinking, assuming that he has time to read books.

The Poverty of Progressivism

A summary of various reasons for retreating from Progressivism after World War II appears in Jeffrey Isaac, *The Poverty of Progressivism: The Future of American Democracy in a Time of Liberal Decline* (2003). As a political scientist, Isaac argues (while utilizing much relevant evidence) that important trends in American life no longer support the kind of thinking and confidence that made Progressive reformism both attractive and possible a century ago.

Thus, according to Isaac, the liberal Protestantism that Social Gospelers expressed confidently has been marginalized by a non-humanistic fundamentalism promoted by the New Christian Right. Moreover, modern scholars in leading social sciences – such as political science, economics, and sociology – increasingly promote "abstract empiricism" and "rational choice" theories, thereby offering no overall vision of social welfare for America at large. Furthermore, class identities along with unionized workers have all but disappeared in the age of downsizing and outsourcing, so that "value" discussions rather than debates over "economic justice" have come to dominate electoral campaigns.

Liberalism eventually imploded, especially in the 1960s and 1970s, because liberals focused too strongly on particular and specific issues such as gender, sexuality, race, and ecology. The problem here was that they never managed to explain persuasively to potential constituents how these are related and can drive a common electoral agenda. Finally, voters were increasingly unable to understand the nation's circumstances and respond to liberal reform proposals because "tabloid television" and "infotainment" offered mainly large-scale diversion befitting an age of consumerism, flitting from one thing to another while neither was interested in, or capable of, seeking truth or educating American citizens about the nature of public life.

In sum, Isaac insists that liberalism "crashed in the manner of Humpty Dumpty" and that no one knows how to put the pieces back together again. He also intimates, even more gloomily, that those pieces cannot be rejoined, because "the vision of a revitalized Progressivism is an anachronism" fashioned for a "modernizing" country, whereas "we live in a postmodern age."

The Age of Fracture

Isaac's sentiment, of things falling apart, is echoed by historian Daniel Rodgers in *Age of Fracture* (2011). Rodgers explores leading theories, not necessarily right or left, promoted at universities and think tanks. Therefore his book is populated by scholars such as economists Milton Friedman and Ronald Coase, law professors Bruce Ackerman and Richard Posner, political scientists William Riker and James Buchanan, historian Eugene Genovese, anthropologist Clifford Geertz, and philosophers John Rawls and Alan Bloom, and by public intellectuals such as Michael Novak, Gertrude Himmelfarb, Charles Murray, Dinesh D'Souza, John Rawls, Noam Chomsky, Robert Nozick, and Michael Walzer. In the last several decades, says Rogers, such thinkers have fashioned theories of human behavior that, in their totality, undermine the constellation of concepts by which Americans long understood themselves to be a viable and admirable community.

Overall, the new theories abandoned notions of contemporary Americans interacting together fruitfully, say in social classes or via a national commitment to oppose Communism. Instead, recent thinkers decided that American life is mainly about individuals – be they ordinary citizens or elected officials, businessmen or hired hands – operating in economic or political markets where they are animated by a hope of personal gain rather than inspired by the pursuit of collective virtues.[92] On this score, American scholars postulated assumptions about rational behavior, the complexities of social choice, the uncertainties of a prisoner's dilemma, abstract philosophical justice, differences and identities, and so forth, where all conditions and events unfold within a limited discourse created and maintained by diffuse cultural power – *a la* Antonio Gramsci and Michel Foucault – which no one seems to control.[93]

[92] For example, Daniel Rogers, *Age of Fracture* (2011), p. 64. According to Rodgers, all of these theories commit "the fallacy of composition" (pp. 66–68), whereby collective behavior is deemed to consist of mundane and independent acts. If that is true, there is no room in economic and political thought for a traditional conception of the public interest as something standing above personal preferences and discernable to citizens motivated by reason, sympathy, and solidarity.

[93] The problem here is that "rational" means *effective* in the new lexicon, whereas "rational" in traditional terms means *reasonable*, or *appropriate* to the circumstances. In which case, a sadist could be regarded by modern theorists as "rational" for pursuing his utility preferences efficiently, whereas John Stuart Mill or Sigmund Freud would have considered a sadist to be vicious, depraved, perhaps psychotic, and certainly immoral.

The bottom line for Rodgers is that modern intellectuals, and politicians such as Ronald Reagan who promote hyper-individualism,[94] have left America with no persuasive vocabulary for talking about common sentiments, collective institutions, national solidarity, shared problems, and reasonable solutions. Too often, scholars and think-tankers analyze specific groups rather than the whole, praise charter academies rather than public schools, admire private charities rather than public assistance, extol paid volunteers rather than draftees, and promote the enlargement of business rather than government provision of public goods. Not surprisingly, then, when a national crisis erupted on September 11, 2001, President George W. Bush called not for shared sacrifices – say, emergency taxes – but for shopping as usual.[95] In the light of which Rodgers, like Isaac, sees no solution to the fracturing he sees.

Who Stole the American Dream?

In *Who Stole the American Dream?*, Pulitzer Prize winning journalist Hedrick Smith explains the collapse of what I described early in this chapter as Obama's "background notions." Smith shows how since the rise of Barry Goldwater and Ronald Reagan a hard-working and politically active middle class has been overwhelmed. To this end, its achievements, such as the post-World War II social contract, have been dismantled by conservatives and corporations determined to increase profits without oversight and without limit.

As Smith tells the story, middle-class people in the 1960s and 1970s promoted the prosperity and rights of all Americans via the civil rights movement, the feminist movement, the environmental movement, the consumer protection movement, the trade union movement, and the

---

[94] Reagan's role in American public life was paradoxical. On the one hand we might assume that Reagan, who used powerful rhetoric to praise Main Street traditions in America, thereby promoted a vocabulary of togetherness – in which case he had nothing to do with America falling apart. On the other hand, in *Age of Fracture*, p. 36, Rodgers argues that even while Reagan talked about "we the people," he rarely described them as "working together, their energy and talent joined in a common action." So there was little in Reagan's talk about a sense of the whole. Instead, by promoting individualism – say in the marketplace – he contributed to fracturing America.

[95] For example, soon after the World Trade Center disaster, President George W. Bush, in his "Address to the Nation on the Terrorist Attacks," September 20, 2001, said:

> Americans are asking: What is expected of us? I ask you to live your lives, and hug your children ... I ask you to be calm and resolute ... I ask you to uphold the values of America ... I ask you to continue to support the victims of this tragedy with your contributions ... I ask your continued participation and confidence in the American economy.

peace movement. Then, in the 1980s and 1990s, businessmen, their organizations, and their lobbyists began to practice what Smith calls "wedge economics," whereby the interests of Wall Street were split off from those of Main Street.[96] Consequently, profits and CEO incomes rose drastically and the American Dream of moderate success as a reward for constructive effort began unravelling for millions of ordinary citizens.

Some of these economic moves had to do with globalization, as tens of thousands of American plants closed and millions of well-paid middle-class jobs moved abroad. But achieving the American Dream also became increasingly unlikely due to less visible and highly complex legal arrangements generated by powerful lobbying on behalf of financial institutions. In this realm, some of the landmarks along the way included:

1. The Supreme Court decision in *Marquette National Bank of Minneapolis vs. First of Omaha Service Corporation* (1978), which deregulated credit card interest rates, thereby enabling banks to saddle ordinary Americans with large and long-term debts.

2. The Revenue Act of 1978, which in its clause 401(k) authorized voluntary, tax-free personal retirement accounts that enabled employers to cancel previous, contractual, and lifetime retirement plans for which their companies were responsible.

3. The Depository Institutions Deregulation and Monetary Control Act of 1980, which abolished limits on interest rates for first mortgages and encouraged sub-prime lending.

4. The Garn-St. Germain Depository Institutions Act of 1982, which allowed state banks to issue adjustable rate and no-deposit mortgage loans, both of which enticed many people into borrowing on terms that they did not understand.

5. The Secondary Mortgage Market Enhancement Act of 1984, which authorized "securitization" of mortgages and therefore enabled banks to sell mortgages several times over, in what amounted to a Ponzi scheme that exploded in the Crash of 2008.

6. The Gramm-Leach-Bliley Act of 1999, which repealed the part of the Glass-Steagall Act of 1933 that prevented conflicts of interest by forbidding national and state banks to engage in brokerage and insurance.

7. The Bankruptcy Abuse Prevention and Consumer Protection Act of 2005, which made filing for personal bankruptcy difficult – if

---

[96] Smith, *Who Stole the American Dream?*, pp. 47–64.

not impossible – for ordinary Americans trapped by debt in student loans, credit cards and mortgages.

To reclaim the American Dream in such difficult times, Smith suggests creating a new Marshall Plan, this time focused on domestic needs rather than those of foreign allies and clients.[97] Presently, according to Smith, massive spending on misconceived wars and overseas bases has drained away many of the resources needed to pay for public goods, and relentless laissez-faire economics at home has shifted wealth and income from the nation at large to the top 1 percent of its taxpayers. What the country needs, therefore, is an "industrial policy" – including government funding for infrastructure and research – promoting American manufacturing and the support that it can provide for a large, strong, and vibrant middle class.[98] Here, as Smith says, is a "virtuous circle" that can be embodied in a "social contract" worked out by politicians and representatives of commerce, labor, and other stakeholders in the country's productive institutions.

That contract must reform the tax code so as to equalize taxes on earned and unearned income and to encourage industrial investment at home. It must enforce fair trade practices on low-wage mercantilist countries like China, and it must cut military expenditures as President Eisenhower did after Korea and as President Nixon did after Vietnam. It must revise building and lending practices so as to create affordable housing; it must avoid privatizing Social Security and Medicare so as to assure a decent safety net for all citizens regardless of wealth and income; and it must mobilize the middle class to spur a populist uprising that will raise voting rates, encourage moderate candidates to run for office, and roll back the corrupt influence of unlimited campaign contributions[99] – perhaps by enacting a constitutional amendment to that effect.

Undoing the Demos

Undoing the Demos: Neoliberalism's Stealth Revolution (2015), by political theorist Wendy Brown, is a fitting capstone to our survey of the liberal

---

[97] *Ibid.*, pp. 379–426.
[98] *Ibid.*, p. 393. From 2001 to 2011, the number of Americans employed in manufacturing declined from 17.2 million to 11.7 million, and more than 59,000 factories closed down.
[99] *Ibid.*, pp. 417–420. One of Smith's targets here is the Supreme Court decision in *Citizens United vs. Federal Elections Commission* (2010), which ruled that non-profit corporations should be regarded as equal to natural persons, with a right of free speech that includes the freedom to express their opinions via almost unlimited political contributions.

retreat because she attacks the public philosophy of "neoliberalism" that today challenges liberalism in principle and in practice. According to Brown, the ideology of neoliberalism, now spreading around the world, includes market-based laws and regulations, a mode of making governmental decisions, and an "order of reasoning" about human nature and citizenship. Most important is how, in all of these realms, neoliberal concepts, expectations, and aspirations place "economic man" (*homo oeconomicus*) rather than "political man" (*homo politicus*) at the center of thinking about how to organize and run a modern society and our individual lives.

The problem, says Brown, originates in an outlook promulgated in various ways and in different situations by scholars, politicians, and bureaucrats such as Friedrich Hayek, Milton Friedman, Gary Becker, Ronald Reagan, Margaret Thatcher, Bill Clinton, Angela Merkel, George Bush, Tony Blair, the International Monetary Fund, the World Bank, and the World Trade Organization. These people, she says, endorse the notion that all of us act, and should act, as "economic men," dedicating ourselves to succeeding in the global marketplace and validating ourselves there on the basis of competing successfully and possessing a strong credit rating. It is as if aspirations going back to Aristotle, Mill, and Marx, of citizens seeking a good life for themselves in the polity, are irrelevant to modern life and must be set aside in lieu of individual and collective goals that only markets can define. Technically speaking, those markets want us to fill up on skills and constitute "repositories of human capital." But where that can happen only within parameters set by markets, Brown notes that individuals will no longer enjoy "moral autonomy, freedom, or equality." And that means, essentially, that to endorse neoliberalism is to abandon "humanism."[100]

At the center of this paradigm shift is a denigration of citizenship and education for good citizenship. Competent and happy citizens – that is, "political men" rather than producers or consumers – were democracy's membership ideal for centuries,[101] and it has long been understood that, for citizens to function effectively and rule themselves, they need to understand the world around them. Here is the commitment to truth which liberals endorse. However, Brown observes that, in recent years, American budgets for public education –especially in state universities – have been continually reduced. In this project, liberal arts courses are no longer seen

[100] Wendy Brown, *Undoing the Demos: Neoliberalism's Stealth Revolution* (2015), p. 42.
[101] This is a central theme in David Ricci, *Good Citizenship in America* (2004), *passim*.

as constituting "a social and public good," while other courses – from business administration to communications, from dentistry to electrical engineering – are designed to foster "a personal investment in individual futures ... construed mainly in terms of earning capacity."[102] Overall, more citizens are trained than are educated, with the result that fewer and fewer Americans understand "the powers and problems they are engaging."[103]

Summing up, Brown more or less throws in the towel. In her terms, the "Euro-Atlantic Left," which is today confronted by brutal modern societies, seems unable to "articulate a road out [of the present disaster] or a viable global alternative."[104] Or, in terms of what I have been calling "the liberal predicament," at storytelling time the Left is out to lunch. Instead, says Brown, neoliberalism – which seems scientific, and claims accuracy – tempts people of the Right *and* the Left.[105] Therefore, those people enforce ruthless market solutions, such as recently compelling austerity on innocent Greeks,[106] to the point of sinking into "human impotence, unknowingness, failure, and irresponsibility." In short – and

---

[102] Brown, *Undoing the Demos*, p. 181.

[103] *Ibid.*, p. 175.

[104] *Ibid.*, p. 220.

[105] Consider, for example, that behavioral psychologists tend to encourage us to believe, on the basis of laboratory experiments, that everyone is mentally wired to err. They are less likely to dedicate their research to figuring out how, with adequate education, many people can be taught to make better decisions than they would otherwise. For example, Daniel Kahneman, *Thinking, Fast and Slow* (2012), is 418 pages long. Only on p. 417 does psychologist Kahneman get around to asking, "What can be done about biases?" He does not, in a fit of liberal outrage, demand that government will multiply its expenditures on childhood education and teaching Statistics 101 by a factor of, say, four or five. That's not his job. But he does call for more research:

> Much like medicine, the identification of judgment errors is a diagnostic task, which requires a precise vocabulary. The name of a disease is a hook to which all that is known about the disease is attached, including vulnerabilities, environmental factors, symptoms, prognosis, and care. Similarly, labels such as "anchoring effects," "narrow framing," or "excessive coherence" bring together in memory everything we know about a bias, its causes, its effects, and what can be done about it.

The problem here, as Rodgers says in *Age of Fracture* (although not specifically citing Kahneman), is that social scientists as a class of modern intellectuals are heavily invested in demonstrating systemic failures, which leaves someone else – no one knows exactly who – responsible for running the system that maintains us all.

[106] Regarding oppressing innocent Greeks, whose bankers ran up a national bubble of debt, I agree with political scientist Mark Blyth. See his "Why Greece Isn't to Blame for the Crisis" (2015). See also Blyth's earlier *Austerity: The History of a Dangerous Idea* (2013).

here is the great retreat – while "undoing the demos," this new sort of "liberalism" is either unable or unwilling to believe "in the human capacity to craft and sustain a world that is humane, free, sustainable, and, above all, modestly under human control."[107]

[107] Brown, *Undoing the Demos*, pp. 220–222.

IO

What Is to be Done?

The human mind revolves around a story. Churches have litanies. Religions have a narrative ... It's the way we think. But we're selling [Democrats are selling] a set of issue positions. The same thing always comes back: People always like our [liberal] positions on the issues, and we always lose.

James Carville, in The New Republic (2004)

There is a liberal predicament of not telling, or not believing in, alpha stories. And it imposes during elections a disadvantage on the Democratic Party, which is, for the most part, liberal. And I am a liberal.

So, as Lenin asked, what's to be done? Actually, in a way, not much. This even though what we have learned so far positions us so that – as I will explain a little further on – we can at least appreciate what the difficulty is and act so as to confront it effectively. On that score, forewarned is forearmed.

Where Are We?

Here is how things stand. At the center of American politics, elections are contested by increasingly polarized candidates.[1] Technically speaking, rightists such as George W. Bush tell, or allude to, large and powerful

---

[1] A word about polarization. Many intellectuals and activists on the Right and the Left dwell, mentally, in entirely different worlds. For example, for incompatible interpretations of much that has happened in America during five centuries, see (on the Right) Larry Schweikart and Michael Allen, *A Patriot's History of the United States: From Columbus's Great Discovery to the War on Terror* (2007), and (on the Left) Howard Zinn, *A People's History of the United States: 1492 – Present* (2005). See especially Zinn's "Afterword," pp. 683–688, on how writing narrative history is inherently partisan.

alpha stories of hewing to tradition, to small government, and to capitalism. At the same time, leftists such as Barack Obama forego large-scale storytelling and promote instead philosophical pragmatism, which generates a series of possible solutions to a list of situations they regard as problematic.

It follows, in campaign face-offs, that liberals are handicapped because alpha stories sometimes provide a sense of ideological coherence that can sway a significant number of voters decisively.[2] After Michael Dukakis lost to Bush I in 1988, Democratic strategist Stanley Greenberg called on Democrats to "reorganize the disturbing 'facts' of American life into a coherent story about the nation's problems and its path of recovery."[3] After John Kerry lost to Bush II in 2004, Democratic strategist James Carville said much the same thing. Thus he captured the entire drama in the quotation which heads this chapter and which intimates that, even when Democrats promote attractive "issue positions," they lack a powerful story to tie those together.[4]

The Good News

The good news for liberals is that their strategists exaggerate the gravity of the storytelling handicap because, naturally, they want to win *all* elections. Meanwhile, campaign success seesaws back and forth between the two parties and their candidates; Republicans and Democrats alternate in the White House from time to time; and new majorities from one party occasionally replace old majorities of the other in either or both houses of Congress. And all of this unfolds somewhat evenly, because narratives are only one campaign resource among others. In fact, elections can be

[2] To assume the existence of a nexus between narratives and elections is to build on a large understanding that informs literature. Thus poet Arthur O'Shaughnessy's "Ode" (1874):

> We are the music-makers,
> And we are the dreamers of dreams ...
> With wonderful deathless ditties
> We build up the world's great cities.
> And out of a fabulous story,
> We fashion an empire's glory:
> One man with a dream, at pleasure,
> Shall go forth and conquer a crown;
> And three with a new song's measure
> Can trample an empire down.

[3] Stanley Greenberg, "Reconstructing a Democratic Vision," *The American Prospect* (Spring, 1990), pp. 82–89.

[4] Carville is quoted in Ryan Lizza, "Bad Message," *The New Republic* (November, 2004).

won by exploiting technical means, such as social media, for turning out friendly voters; they can be won by having charismatic candidates run against mere partisans; they can be won, at the congressional level, by adroit gerrymandering; they can be won when enough people tire of an unpopular war; and they can be won when a significant number of citizens start to feel – like when the financial system almost collapsed in late 2008 – that the time has come for a change.

Therefore the good news is really pretty good, although not exactly grounds for rejoicing, and it is that liberals are not going to lose election after election because they don't have a powerful narrative or several that reinforce one another. Leftists have much to offer policy-wise, and many voters lean in their direction. The moves, say, against privatizing Social Security and towards sanctioning gay marriages demonstrate that. In those circumstances, the game is not even close to being over.

On the other hand, the narrative gap exists; it isn't going away; it can deprive liberals of potential electoral strength; and it may occasionally cost them an election. In which case, why should people on the Left stand by passively, struggling like a horse hauling handicap weights in a race against another horse who carries none? Or, along with the strategists, why should liberals not strive for repeated rather than occasional wins? Paul Starr makes this point, implicitly, when he urges Democrats to ask how they might "achieve the organizational strength and intellectual coherence to create a *durable majority* [emphasis added] and lead the country in a progressive direction."[5]

To Close with a Tale

So the straightforward, common sense, practical question for people on the Left is this: what can be done about the storytelling gap in order to win *not all but more* elections than the Left does now? To the extent that stories are relevant to that end, what to do about the storytelling gap seems simple: close it. Therefore I should end this book by proposing at least a short version of a large story capable of resonating with liberal sentiments and inspiring the liberal camp.

I could say, just for instance – perhaps via anecdotes and homilies like in *The Reader's Digest*, via memorable characters like in *Huckleberry Finn*, and via heartwarming illustrations like those of Norman Rockwell – that a good society needs, now and into the future, considerable public

---

[5] Paul Starr, *Freedom's Power: The True Force of Liberalism* (2007), p. 220.

regulation of capitalism, ordinances for assuring a reasonable distribution of work and incomes, and respect for ecologically sound behavior as a cardinal social value. Moreover, all of this should be framed by passionate devotion to freedom, insistence on truly equal opportunities, love of country, and a willingness to share its burdens when necessary. If liberals would adopt such a story, the Right and the Left, each fortified by powerful narratives, could then (to mix metaphors slightly) ride out to campaign against each other on horses more equally matched than the ones they have been racing lately.

Puzzles and Problems

Well, yes. However, I won't tell a new story now – even the one just sketched – because doing so would not improve the situation. In truth, the liberal predicament is intractable. Accordingly, proposing a tale that would be available for liberals to regard as an alpha story for the Left will not move us closer to removing the handicap.

This is because the liberal predicament amounts to a "problem," where I am thinking of a "problem" not in the sense of liberals describing difficult circumstances but in the sense of "puzzles" and "problems" that I defined in Chapter 1. That is, when elements of a difficult situation can be adjusted so as to resolve the difficulty, such as when we assemble scattered pieces of a jigsaw puzzle, then the situation amounts to a "puzzle." But when the elements of a difficult situation cannot be adjusted so as to resolve the difficulty, such as when we cannot assemble pieces mingled accidentally from two different jigsaw puzzles, that situation amounts to a "problem." Problems in this sense don't have solutions for the moment, and perhaps never will.

Liberals Know They Need Stories
Several factors make liberalism's "predicament" into a "problem." The first is that liberals already know that their camp suffers electorally from not telling powerful stories. Therefore, thinkers like Paul Waldman in *Being Right is Not Enough: What Progressives Must Learn From Conservative Success* (2006),[6] and Geoffrey Nunberg in *Talking Right: How Conservatives Turned Liberalism Into a Tax-Raising, Latte-Drinking, Sushi-Eating, Volvo-Driving, New York Times-Reading, Body-Piercing, Hollywood-Living, Left-Wing Freak Show* (2007), and George

---

[6] Paul Waldman, *Being Right is Not Enough: What Progressives Must Learn from Conservative Success*, pp. 139–167.

Lakoff in *Whose Freedom?: The Battle Over America's Most Important Idea* (2007), and Drew Westen in *The Political Brain: The Role of Emotion in Deciding the Fate of the Nation* (2008), and Eric Alterman in *Kabuki Democracy: The System vs. Barrack Obama* (2011),[7] have noted and regretted the absence of liberal stories.

Furthermore, some of those writers and their colleagues – without my prodding – have already gone on to tell stories to fill in for those lacking, in the hope that their camp will adopt the new tales and proceed powerfully into the next election. To that end, large stories appear, for example, in Michael Lind's *The Next American Nation: The New Nationalism and the Fourth American Revolution* (1995); in Stanley Greenberg and Theda Skocpol's (eds.), *The New Majority: Toward a Popular Progressive Politics* (1997); in Joseph Stiglitz's *The Roaring Nineties: A New History of the World's Most Prosperous Decade* (2004); in Paul Waldman's *Being Right Is Not Enough* (2006); in Todd Gitlin's *The Bulldozer and the Big Tent: Blind Republicans, Lame Democrats, and The Revobery of American Ideals* (2007); in Thomas Friedman and Michael Mandelbaum's *That Used to be Us: How America Fell Behind in the World it Invented and How We Can Come Back* (2011); and in Charles Ferguson's *Predator Nation: Corporate Criminals, Political Corruption, and the Hijacking of America* (2012). Most recently, Eric Liu, in "What Every American Should Know," *The Atlantic* (2015), has even suggested that the best story for all Americans should be conveyed by a list – there is the list syndrome! – of 5,000 "names, phrases, dates, and concepts" which together constitute a "mirror for a new America" that will, in toto, instill in those familiar with it a liberal understanding of what makes America great.[8]

Ergo, liberals already know that storytelling is politically desirable. In which case they don't need me to remind them of that. And they have already proposed stories, some of them powerful, in order to catch up in

---

[7] Eric Alterman, *Kabuki Democracy: The System vs. Barack Obama*, pp. 151–158.

[8] In "What Every American Should Know," Liu recommends "a common culture" to America. But his view is avowedly partisan, because the culture he proposes is liberal (although he calls it "progressive"). He identifies approximately 5,000 items – from "Whiteness" to "The Federalist Papers" to "Organized labor" to "Reconstruction" to "Nativism" to "The Reagan Revolution" to "DARPA" to "The Almighty Dollar" and more, which together Liu describes as "the story of 'us'" – that he would teach in schools and elsewhere as the basis for such a culture. He argues that emphasizing multiculturalism would counter conservative notions of American history, which he regards as exaggerating the importance of Anglo-American traditions and praising too many dead white males.

this category with conservatives. In which case they don't need any story that I might suggest, because they already have candidates for the job.

The Audience Difficulty

But the "problem" is even more formidable than that, because it entails not just *proposing* but *accepting*. After all, some liberals have composed stories that they hope their compatriots will endorse and share. But their compatriots don't do that, or they don't do that strongly enough. Instead, as we have seen, liberal audiences do not much line up behind stories that are offered to them. Rather, when liberal authors suggest new tales – some based on philosophy and many spurred by outrage – none of those are widely endorsed. And none are repeated to the point where all Americans know where liberals stand.

The stories proposed by journalist Naomi Klein are a useful example of how liberals resist aggregation at the level of narratives. In *No Logo: Taking Aim at the Brand Bullies* (2000), Klein told a powerful story indicting callous and sometimes brutal corporations which practice globalization and exploit workers around the world. Then, in *The Shock Doctrine: The Rise of Disaster Capitalism* (2008), she condemned government-sponsored militarism and privatization as wasteful and morally unjust. And finally, in *This Changes Everything: Capitalism vs. The Climate* (2014), she insisted that climate warming is not about greenhouse gases but about capitalism, which is driven by its quest for private profits to generate those gases relentlessly and incessantly.[9]

In its own way, each of Klein's hard-hitting stories claims to describe urgent truths about the nature of modern life and might serve as an alpha story for liberals. Instead, such stories come and go. They may stir up short-term responses and partial repair of what Klein defines, in each book respectively, as huge dangers facing America or even the world today. But her stories have never gained the status of a tale capable of inspiring liberal passion and dedication over time – say, for an entire generation.

In short, there is an audience difficulty here. Liberals prefer not to adopt stories and act accordingly even when, spot on, someone spins for them a tale forcefully and eloquently. In this sense, to recall previous chapters,

[9] Naomi Klein, *This Changes Everything* (2014) could not discuss news reports from 2015, which described how Volkswagen, in 11,000,000 of its diesel vehicles, deliberately programmed pollution tracking devices to give the false impression that those vehicles pollute the world's air less than they do. See Karl Russell, Guilbert Gates, Josh Keller, and Derek Watkins, "How Volkswagen Is Grappling With Its Diesel Deception."

the political game of telling big stories is skewed against people who Max Weber defined as "modern." Weber claimed that those people are "disenchanted." As such, they are intellectually descended from Europeans who rejected the mythical, theological, transcendental, or metaphysical explanations that used to justify large institutions such as monarchy, the aristocracy, clerical orders, serfdom, the Crusades, cathedrals, public art, philosophy, and European education until, roughly speaking, "the Enlightenment." Later, as we saw, during the nineteenth and twentieth centuries Weber's modern people came to prefer scientific and pragmatic explanations for life's circumstances, this time not only rejecting most old stories but also not usually creating or adopting new ones.

On Projecting Stories

So liberals don't have large stories that unite their camp. And since people in that camp reject stories even when some are on offer, I won't propose a new story. However, I will also refrain from putting my oar in here because of a distinction that we should draw between *projecting* and *creating* great stories. A point of departure on this score is the fact, not always remarked, that conservatives do not *create* the alpha stories which they tell. Instead, they *inherit* those stories from the past, perhaps update and embellish them, and then *project* them into politics.

That is the significance of hallmark conservatives such as Edmund Burke and Barry Goldwater insisting that they have not discovered the truths they wish to promote. Thus Burke, in 1790, says:

We know that *we* have made no discoveries, and we think that no discoveries are to be made, in morality, nor many in the great principles of government, nor in the ideas of liberty, which were understood long before we were born.[10]

And thus Goldwater, in 1960, declares that "The laws of God, and of nature, have no dateline ... The challenge is not to find new or different truths, but to learn how to apply established truths to the problems of the contemporary world."[11]

This point is worth underscoring. Conservatives inherit stories and project them. In the process, they reject Judith Shklar's claim – with or without referring to her – that liberalism has, for several centuries, done exactly what it should do by continually and energetically opposing every sort of tyranny. Instead, they accuse liberals of failing to produce alpha

---

[10] Edmund Burke, *Reflections on the Revolution in France* (1790, 1955), p. 97.
[11] Barry Goldwater, *The Conscience of a Conservative* (1960), p. 5.

stories about life being linked to purpose, meaning, and virtue since the Enlightenment.

The argument here, as we saw in Chapter 6, starts by recalling that Western Europe was "Christian" before it became "enlightened." It follows, in right-wing opinion, that important Enlightenment ideas – such as the power of reason, the need for disenchantment, the separation of religion and state, and the cardinal importance of human dignity – arose out of Christian concepts and practices such as the papal Two Swords doctrine, which drew a line between spiritual and temporal authorities, and the Protestant critique of Catholic claims that priests possess a mystical power to mediate between God and their congregants.

From this point of view, Enlightenment *philosophes* such as Spinoza, Diderot, Voltaire, Rousseau, Hume, and Kant, who powerfully challenged Christian principles and practices, in doing so undermined a European sense of divine order and purpose that, over time, would have produced human progress without being goaded by radical ideas. Here was a crucial turning point in Western history, according to conservatives, because while Enlightenment thinkers chipped away at Christianity, they and their liberal descendants never managed to provide an acceptable replacement for Christianity's ethical narrative.

That is, according to conservatives, people on the Left never formulated a shared substitute for Christianity's alpha story of how God created the universe and human beings in it, and how in that universe, a loving relationship with God – as the Bible describes Him – is necessary to provide human beings with meaningful lives and firm morals.[12] Rightists buttress the charge by contending that, because the meaning of life is bound up with morals and values, and because such principles can come to us only from God, it is no wonder that liberals have failed and will probably continue to do so. Here is one reason why, as we noted several times, conservatives characteristically reject the concept of "humanism," whose faith in human "agency" assumes that people can act together effectively on their own without divine guidance.[13]

---

[12] Alasdair MacIntyre, *After Virtue: A Study in Moral Theory* (1984), 2nd edn, pp. 51–61.

[13] Conservatives criticize liberal intellectuals for not creating new alpha stories to explain the meaning of human life in general. What they speak less of is that market-driven societies, which are praised in the rightist alpha story, make it increasingly difficult for people to assess their own specific lives. On this score, see Richard Sennett, *The Corrosion of Character: The Personal Consequences of Work in the New Capitalism* (1998), pp. 15–31, which claims that many modern workers are frustrated by being unable to assign significance and value to their work. From literature, see also Tom Wolfe, *The Bonfire*

Creating Stories

In short, conservatives tell liberals that they must create new alpha stories. Modern society, they say, needs a sense of ultimate and inspiring purposes in life – especially when some people are so devoted to what they call reason and rationality that they lose a solid commitment to social order, consistency, and predictability. With this end in mind, conservatives feel uneasy about John Stuart Mill's liberal marketplace for ideas, wherein old-time verities are constantly – and, in conservative eyes, sometimes dangerously – challenged by new principles, inclinations, and lifestyles. Thus traditional virtues historian Gertrude Himmelfarb, in *On Looking Into the Abyss: Untimely Thoughts on Culture and Society* (1994),[14] and *New Criterion* editor Roger Kimball, in *Experiments Against Reality: The Fate of Culture in the Postmodern Age* (2002),[15] argue that Mill's enthusiasm for continual challenges to conventional beliefs and practices could undermine the reflexive and habitual sorts of behavior which Edmund Burke called "prejudices" and which may be necessary to maintain society.

Unintentionally, however, this demand points to a stubborn part of the liberal storytelling "problem" because behind the conservative call for liberals to *create* alpha stories there lies a question, seldom asked, about whether *anyone*, liberal or not, knows *how* to create a story for America so resonant that it will achieve alpha status for any large group of people. True, liberals have not created alpha stories. But if they have not, are they behaving irresponsibly or can it be that no one – including conservatives like Burke and Goldwater – knows how to create alpha stories?

To answer this question, we should consider alpha stories that we know of. If nothing else, the fact that they exist demonstrates that they can be created. But where did they come from, how did they arise, and what sets them off from lesser tales? What can we say, in fact, about the

---

of the Vanities (1988), pp. 236–241. Here, Sherman McCoy's seven-year-old daughter Campbell asks him to explain to her how he makes a living. He answers, struggling to use simple terms, that he *buys* and *sells* "bonds" for things like roads – which is not to say, exactly, that he *builds* roads. Each bond, says Sherman, is like "a slice of cake," so that when you "hand somebody a slice of the cake a tiny little bit comes off, like a little crumb, and you can keep that." Furthermore, "If you pass around enough slices of cake, then pretty soon you [Sherman] have enough crumbs to make a *gigantic* cake."

[14] Himmelfarb, "Liberty: One Very Simple Principle," in *On Looking into the Abyss*, pp. 74–106.

[15] Roger Kimball, "James Fitzjames Stephens v. John Stuart Mill," in Roger Kimball (ed.), *Experiments Against Reality: The Fate of Culture in the Postmodern Age* (2002), pp. 159–188.

origins and potency of two obvious conservative stories even though, as we have noticed, the story about permanent moral commandments sometimes contradicts the story about endless marketplace innovations?

Well, the first conservative alpha story is about God's love and justice and the traditions that point us towards behavior He approves. The basic outlines of this story took shape during several centuries. Many raconteurs such as St. Paul, the Four Evangelists, Constantine the Great, and St. Augustine contributed to it.[16] Later thinkers such as Thomas Aquinas, Martin Luther, and John Calvin enlarged and adjusted it. This story doesn't tell us much about how to create widely shared stories, though, because it is backed up by claims to divine revelation and therefore unlikely to be duplicated in our scientific day and age.

The second conservative story, about the virtues of a "free market" that supplies our needs and helps us to avoid government oppression, was born relatively recently and lacks transcendental origins. It therefore testifies to at least one successful and modern alpha gestation that might, in principle, be repeated. Furthermore, precisely because that modern story possesses such persuasive force – first as the division of labor, then as survival of the fittest, then as rugged individualism, then as free enterprise, then as neoliberalism, and now, backed by billionaire enthusiasts like Bill Gates, as so-called "philanthrocapitalism"[17] – we should ask how some thinkers managed, during the last several centuries, to create it.

We should ask. But so far, scholars who deal with stories – often perceptively and usefully – won't supply us with answers. This is because they write about *which* stories are present but not about *how* to compose others with similar impact. This is the situation in many academic fields

---

[16] James Carroll, in *Constantine's Sword: The Church and the Jews* (2002), shows how the Church established its doctrines gradually rather than in one flash of sudden understanding (that is, a sort of "founding moment.") Tom Holland's *In the Shadow of the Sword: The Birth of Islam and the Rise of the Global Arab Empire* (2012), shows how both Christianity and Islam took shape over several centuries, at least partly as instruments of imperial rule.

[17] Matthew Bishop and Michael Green, *Philanthrocapitalism: How the Rich Can Save the World* (2008). Intellectual historians may notice the similarity between today's charitable billionaires and Andrew Carnegie, who argued in "The Gospel of Wealth" (1889) that profiting endows the rich with wisdom as well as with money. For an analysis of how philanthrocapitalism may sometimes promote disastrous projects, see David Rieff, *The Reproach of Hunger: Food, Justice, and Money in the Twenty-First Century* (2015), pp. 210–229. On how philanthrocapitalism, in this case led by Mark Zuckerberg, isn't doing too well in the field of education either, especially in Newark's public schools, see Dale Russakoff, *The Prize: Who's in Charge of America's Schools?* (2015).

and works by typical practitioners. Their efforts, in good faith, show us that (so far, at least) alpha stories, such as the vision of a virtuous and efficient market, are quite mysterious products of human creativity.

Political Scientists

Thus, while focusing on dominant stories in public life, political scientist Rogers Smith, in *Stories of Peoplehood: The Politics and Morals of Political Membership* (2003), argues that only a combination of large and powerful tales can unite members of nations or peoples who want to live together in states that maintain security and foster prosperity. These tales he usefully distinguishes as "political" (dealing with defense, public order, civil rights, and so forth), "economic" (concerning production and distribution), and "ethically constitutive" (specifying traits that provide citizens with a sense of mutual identity and wellbeing).[18] However, Smith offers no instruction on how to create powerful stories when needed. Instead, he says that he doesn't know why some ethically constitutive stories are "compelling" and he concedes that we cannot know if those stories are "true" because they are not much "subject to tangible evidence."[19]

Frederick Mayer, in *Narrative Politics: Stories of Collective Action* (2014), is another political scientist who focuses on political stories. Using social choice theory, he explains that stories educate people about what is important to them and society. Stories thereby create common interests and encourage citizens to work together – not to "ride free" – to improve life in the community that they share with other citizens. Mayer observes, though, that we know little about how stories motivate behavior or engage some people's attention while other people remain indifferent. As we noted in Chapter 1, it is a fact that some stories are more powerful than others. For example, as Mayer says, Rachel Carson's story of dying robins "breathed life" into our understanding of "environmental degradation."[20] But no one, including Mayer, knows exactly how it did that.

---

[18] Rogers Smith, *Stories of Peoplehood: The Politics and Morals of Political Membership* (2003), pp. 19–71. Ethically constitutive stories (p. 98):

> present traits they emphasize as things having tremendous, often priceless ethical worth. To believe one's self to be a beloved child of God or a member of a superior race or the descendant of heroic ancestors or the bearer of a brilliant culture is to have a firm basis for a sense of meaning, place, purpose, and pride.

[19] *Ibid.*, pp. 98–100.
[20] Frederick Mayer, *Narrative Politics: Stories and Collective Action* (2014), p. 122.

Other Scholars

After political scientists come the rest. For example, in his "Politics as a Vocation" (1919), Max Weber discussed political "legitimacy" and declared that one of its sources is *the gift of grace* or charisma," where charisma is the special and authoritative – but inexplicable – ability of a leader to convince people to accept his or her "revelations" as true and pertinent to their lives.[21] Keeping this concept in mind one might argue that, somewhere and sometime in the future, a "charismatic" storyteller will fashion a new and liberal alpha story and manage to persuade other liberals to accept it as a roadmap to progress. If that will happen, the new story may become the grounds, in a democracy, for winning an election and animating a government. But in our quest to fathom the power of stories this concept does not help at all, because what it says – amplified by an elegant Greek term – is in plain English no more than that someone may eventually and unexpectedly appear with the requisite story. Furthermore, to posit the existence of "charisma" does not address the audience difficulty, because a "charismatic" leader like Adolf Hitler, promoting a sensational story, might succeed in Munich but not in Phoenix.

Also from sociology, in *Ideology and Utopia: An Introduction to the Sociology of Knowledge* (1936),[22] Karl Mannheim followed Karl Marx and noticed that some social entities (of class, religion, region, ethnicity, profession, and so on) develop "ideologies" (actually rationalizations) that justify their status, power, and privileges. We could apply Mannheim's insight to teachings of the Chamber of Commerce, the Business Roundtable, and many economists who, in America, do very well by endorsing capitalism and neoliberalism.[23] The difficulty here is that, although Mannheim and Marx both highlighted self-serving ideologies,

---

[21] Max Weber, *The Vocation Lectures* (2004), especially pp. 34–35.

[22] Karl Mannheim, *Ideology and Utopia: An Introduction to the Sociology of Knowledge* (1936, 1955), pp. 108–146.

[23] On doing well: Philip Mirowski [in *Never Let a Serious Crisis Go to Waste: How Neoliberalism Survived the Financial Meltdown* (2014), p. 299] used professors of English language and literature as a baseline and found that in 2009–2010 faculty mathematicians earned 7.2% more than them, psychology professors earned 8.9% more than them, and economists earned 41.2% more than them. One explanation for this disparity is that economists are providing a special service. Thus economist Robert Nelson, in *Economics as Religion: From Samuelson to Chicago and Beyond* (2001), p. xv, argues that economists serve capitalism less like scientists than like priests. That is, economists promote not *facts* but *desired behavior*. This centers (pp. 78–81) on promoting efficiency – as if pursuing efficiency, rather than other "values" less profitable to American capitalists, will generate human progress. See also Duncan Foley, *Adam's Fallacy: A Guide to Economic Theology* (2006).

which we might regard as alpha stories, neither explained how such stories come into being.

From psychology, Milgrim's *Obedience to Authority: An Experimental View* (1974), showed how, in a university laboratory, "teachers" were willing to administer painful and sometimes even fatal electrical shocks to "learners" in another room who delivered wrong answers concerning subjects about which they had been taught. That more than 60 percent of the "teachers" (ordinary people from New Haven) would deliberately injure "learners" (other ordinary people from New Haven) demonstrated obedience to the authority of the "experimenters" who supervised the proceedings. But that those "teachers" obeyed men in white coats (if that is what the supervisors wore) did not explain how authority – scientific, religious, parental, scholarly, political, or otherwise, and buttressed by stories – comes to be established.[24]

From philosophy, Michel Foucault claimed in 1977 that stories (or narratives, myths, or ideologies) reflect the state of power relationships in any given society and serve therein as "regimes of truth." As one configuration of power follows another over time, so do these regimes of truth, much like Thomas Kuhn's serial paradigms in science. Thus some great stories trump other stories and thereby allocate unequal amounts of status, income, and happiness among various groups in society.[25] Foucault helped us to recognize the special effect of powerful stories, but he spoke about where those stories are located and what they justify, rather than about how they are created.

Economist Deidre McClosky, in *The Rhetoric of Economics* (1985), observes that the marketplace story today – sometimes called neoclassical economics – rests not upon persuasive facts but upon powerful metaphors. Therefore, economists like Milton Friedman and Gary Becker – who may never visit factories or farms – teach us to think of production taking place in terms of, for example, "unseen hands," "markets," "models," "curves," "equilibrium," "elasticity," "liquidity preferences," "supply,"

---

[24] Milgrim's experimental results are congruent with a situation discussed by James Risen in *Pay Any Price: Greed, Power, and Endless War* (2014), "The War on Decency," pp. 163–201. In these pages, without referring to Milgrim, reporter Risen describes how Damien Corsetti – a PTSD-wracked veteran from the US Army's 519th Military Intelligence Battalion, who tortured prisoners at Bagram Prison in Afghanistan and Abu Ghraib in Iraq – obeyed orders in an interrogation program shaped by the presumably expert advice of psychologists paid as consultants by the CIA.

[25] Michel Foucault, "Truth and Power (1977)," in Michel Foucault (ed.), *Power/ Knowledge: Selected Interviews and Other Writings, 1972–1977* (1980), pp. 109–133.

and "demand."[26] How economists created and linked these persuasive metaphors, McClosky does not discuss.

Cognitive scientist Daniel Dennett, in *Breaking the Spell: Religion as a Natural Phenomenon* (2006), observes that the prevalence of religious beliefs and institutions in history suggests that religion in general may have evolutionary origins rather than transcendental justifications. Dennett extends this thought to note that every sort of religion is based on stories, that we all love stories, and that according to Elie Wiesel even God loves stories.[27] There are fascinating insights here. But Dennett does not ask why some people are indifferent to stories; he does not explore how the largest of stories arise; and he does not explain why some of them are more powerful than others.

Historian William McNeill stipulates that myths, which justify "coherent public action," are the basis for all human societies. He fears, however, that since the Enlightenment "myth-breaking" has exceeded "myth-making." In which case, after the era of FDR, Churchill, De Gaulle, Adenauer, Tito, and – less commendably – Stalin, the world needs new charismatic leaders who will combine elements of fact and fiction to hold nations together.[28] Until the requisite leaders arrive, argues McNeill, "historians, political scientists, and other academics" must fill in the gap, "proposing alternatives to accepted ideas."[29] In other words, academics have a special responsibility to create great new stories based on scholarly research, which so far has been a chief force for "myth-breaking." It is an inspiring assignment, but McNeill offers no hint about how his colleagues might construct such stories.

The Current Standoff

In sum, leading scholars may study great stories but never consider how to produce more of them. Well, we might say, they are focused on other issues. And they might have good reasons for addressing those issues. McNeil, however, without intending to, reminds us of our limitations in

---

[26] Only economists who spend little time in the real economy can declare, as Robert Lucas did five years before Wall Street began to collapse from brutal and deliberate misbehavior, that "macroeconomics ... has succeeded. Its central problem of depression prevention has been solved." See "Macroeconomic Priorities," his 2003 presidential address to the American Economic Association.

[27] Dennett, *Breaking the Spell*, pp. 252–253.

[28] William McNeill, "The Care and Repair of Public Myth," *Foreign Affairs* (Fall, 1982), pp. 5–6.

[29] *Ibid*, p. 6.

this realm when he argues that scholars should create stories to replace broken myths but doesn't tell us how to do that.[30] Therefore, once again, I will not try. In my terms, the liberal predicament is a "problem" and not a "puzzle." In which case, instead of trying to solve the problem, I believe that liberals should think practically about how best to live with it.

The Situation Now

To restate the matter: liberals are usually pragmatists who don't promote alpha stories in public life but recommend specific policy proposals instead. In Weberian terms they are, for the most part, modern people who place little faith in enchantment of any kind. Moreover, when some astute liberals occasionally suggest new and large stories around which their camp might unite in support of shared policy proposals, their target audience does not pay much attention and the new stories are not widely endorsed.

Standing opposite liberals are conservatives who, because they prefer tradition, do not think forward.[31] This means they do not create new alpha stories to take into account what has happened, and what goes on happening, to civilization since the Enlightenment.[32] Conservatives will continue to promote powerful stories they have inherited about virtuous traditions and effective markets. But these will not unite the nation because, in the name of science and pragmatism, many skeptics have already rejected the right-wing alpha stories that McNeil would regard as myths.

---

[30] Most scholars talk mainly to their colleagues rather than to the public. Therefore historian Jill Lepore (an exception to the rule), in *The Whites of Their Eyes: The Tea Party's Revolution and the Battle Over American History* (2010), pp. 68–69, observes that professional historians – unlike Columbia University's Richard Hofstadter, writing in the 1950s against what he called "the paranoid right" – make little effort nowadays to tell Americans an accurate story about the American Revolution that would demolish the partisan fable currently promoted by Tea Party enthusiasts.

[31] Thus William Buckley set the tone for post-World War II American conservatives when he proclaimed that *National Review* "stands athwart history, yelling Stop." See "Publisher's Statement," *National Review* (November 19, 1955), p. 5.

[32] About looking backwards, it is not surprising that, when times are terrible, some people will turn to old stories for insight and solace. See Herman Wouk, *The Language God Talks: On Science and Religion* (2011). Wouk, writing while deeply pious at age 94, shows how science, especially via its language of mathematics, empties the universe of "meaning." Then, pp. 169–180, he argues that meaning can be restored by the kind of story Wouk excerpts from his novel *War and Remembrance* (1978). That heart-rending tale centers on Arnold Jastrow, an imprisoned professor who delivers a sermon about the Book of Job while knowing that, on the next day, he will be taken from the Theresienstadt concentration camp in Czechoslovakia and transported to his death in Auschwitz.

This situation constitutes a strategic standoff. Each side is comfortable with its own practices, one hawking pragmatism and the other projecting stories.[33] Neither liberals nor conservatives, however, *do* new alpha stories if we mean by that *creating* stories. Furthermore, if we were to chart all of this, we would observe that when liberals try to create great new stories they fall short because no one knows how to do that, whereas if conservatives were to try to create great new stories they would probably fail for the same reason.

A final scholarly insight illuminates this point. While praising Jane Jacobs's *The Death and Life of Great American Cities* (1961), anthropologist James Scott remarks that no one knows how to plan and construct a great and successful city, even though we enjoy one when it arises over time from innumerable public and private actions, preferences, interactions, circumstances, and enterprises.[34] That is, we know such a city when we see it, and we appreciate its beauty and functionality. But we do not know how to create the same thing deliberately. It follows, although Scott does not say so, that even when we are capable of recognizing great political stories we may not know how to create them.

Consequences

In today's circumstances, the two sides are not likely to come together as Americans did eventually on Paine's disdain for monarchy in *Common Sense* and Lincoln's proclamation at Gettysburg that the Constitution and the Declaration of Independence are morally inseparable. Shared sentiments may support much social stability and many good works, therefore the nation might be better off for entertaining a wide-ranging consensus between liberals and conservatives about the nature of twenty-first-century life. But if, as conservatives claim, something extremely *useful* is missing here – a unifying story, rather than tumultuous pluralism, for the Age of Reason – it does not necessarily follow, even in anxious moments, that modern Americans will decide to believe in great conservative stories, which have been gravely challenged for

[33] In "Fact Finders: The Anti-Dogma Dogma," *The New Republic* (February 28, 2005), pp. 14–17, Jonathan Chait attributes this standoff to different epistemologies on the Left and Right, the former aiming at empirical pragmatism and the latter validated by ideological conclusions, which I have described as rooted in stories.

[34] James Scott, *Seeing Like a State: How Certain Schemes to Improve the Human Condition Have Failed* (1998), pp. 132–146.

two centuries, merely because those stories will, presumably, *work* for America.[35]

Instead, if offered something resembling Pascal's Wager,[36] then according to Weber modern men and women will want to know if the proposed story is *true*.[37] Moreover, if they will insist on asking, they are most likely to demand – unlike people of faith, who soldiered on after the Scopes Trial – an answer based on science rather than metaphysics or revelation.[38] In other words, in their post-Enlightenment world they will expect an adequate new alpha story to express a vision of sense and purpose flowing from what seem to be objective facts[39] rather than thought-experiment models and/or personal reflections about the incomparable

---

[35] This is the shortcoming of books like Alain de Botton, *Religion for Atheists: A Non-Believer's Guide to the Uses of Religion* (2013), which recommends retaining useful aspects of religious practice as if one can rescue the baby while throwing out the bathwater. Anthony Pagden, *The Enlightenment and Why It Still Matters*, (2013), pp. 406–408, is a more instructive guide when he observes that :

> By the mid-seventeenth century the entire structure on which all monotheistic beliefs rest, that the universe had been the creation of a divinity who continues to dictate every aspects of its being, had come to seem to many Europeans as threadbare as paganism had once seemed to Plato and Aristotle ... [Therefore] today most educated people, at least in the West, broadly accept the conclusion to which ... [the Enlightenment] led ... [which is that] it is possible to improve, through knowledge and science, the world in which we live ... [wherein] the laws by which humans order their lives ... [cannot] be anything other than human, intelligible, and changeable.

[36] The suspicion that no one can deliberately create alpha stories helps us to understand the anxiety that led to Pascal's Wager. In his *Pensees* (1660), Blaise Pascal argued that one should believe in God because, if He exists, atheists will spend their afterlives in Hell. In other words, if you don't have an alpha story, bet on one that promises an excellent payoff. Modern economists would say that, in his wager, Pascal made a rational decision to pursue "expected utility."

[37] The liberal insistence on truth is discussed by Sheldon Wolin, *Democracy, Inc.: Managed Democracy and the Specter of Inverted Totalitarianism* (2010), pp. 260–264, who argues that a democratic state democracy cannot make good decisions if public talk is riddled with even well-intentioned lies, and that citizens cannot think effectively if ideas are not shaped by intellectual integrity.

[38] This point is made in Greg Epstein, *Good Without God: What a Billion Nonreligious People Do Believe* (2009), pp. 9–12. See also Jerry Coyne, *Faith vs. Fact: Why Science and Religion Are Incompatible* (2015), p. 260:

> In the end, why isn't it better to find out how the world really works instead of making up stories about it, or accepting stories concocted centuries ago? And if we don't know the answers, why shouldn't we simply admit that we don't know, as scientists do regularly, and keep looking for answers using evidence and reason?

[39] The crucial importance of facts to modern, scientific thinking is discussed in David Wootton, *The Invention of Science: A New History of the Scientific Revolution* (2015), "Facts," pp. 251–309.

and the inscrutable.⁴⁰ Leaders on the Left will not fashion that story, and leaders on the Right will promote stories that skeptics have already rejected.⁴¹

This awkward state of affairs can be traced back at least to Charles Peirce and William James. Conservative blogger William Gairdner, in *The Great Divide: Why Liberals and Conservatives Will Never, Ever Agree* (2015), speaks for staunch rightists when he *argues* that leftists are too optimistic about human nature and therefore the two sides will never get together. But Dinesh D'Souza, who worked in the Reagan White House, inadvertently *demonstrates* why they won't join forces when he explains that – thank heavens – Ronald Reagan was not open-minded like liberals, who invite evidence that might change their minds. In fact, says D'Souza, Reagan was so firmly convinced of the validity of his principles that if his advisors told him that the facts were against him "Reagan's basic attitude was, 'Okay, get me new facts.' "⁴² There is the "tenacity" which Peirce and James, as philosophical pragmatists, long ago set aside in favor of the empiricism and science that liberals admire today.

Short-Term Stories

We come, then, with perhaps a sense of anticlimax for not finding a solution to the liberal predicament – that is, for not closing the storytelling gap – to some final observations. These are not complicated. And they are mainly about liberalism because that is where my sentiments lie. Moreover, I will emphasize what should be done on the Left because

---

⁴⁰ For such reflections, see David Hart, *The Experience of God: Being, Consciousness, Bliss* (2013), p. 234:

[God is] the logical order of all reality, the ground both of the subjective rationality of the mind and the objective reality of being, the transcendent and indwelling Reason of Wisdom by which mind and matter are both informed and in which both participate.

See also Brad Gregory, *The Unintended Reformation: How a Religious Revolution Secularized Society* (2012), pp. 30:

God is ... radically distinct from the universe as a whole, which he did not fashion by ordering anything already existent but rather created entirely ex nihilo. God's creative action proceeded neither by necessity nor by chance but from his deliberate love ... [therefore by love] God constantly sustains the world through his intimate, providential care ... Such a God is literally unimaginable and incomprehensible.

⁴¹ The situation is described in Thomas Frank, *Pity the Billionaire: The Hard-Times Swindle and the Unlikely Comeback of the Right* (2012), pp. 166–183, which claims that conservatives have a mistaken "story line" while liberals have none at all.

⁴² Dinesh D'Souza, *Letters to a Young Conservative* (2002), p. 69.

the Right already dominates public talk in the realm of narratives and doesn't need my help. Thus my observations suggest a practical strategy but do not attempt to predict whether or not liberals will adopt it. I can lead a horse to water, but I can't make that horse drink.

To begin with, as John Stuart Mill pointed out in *On Liberty*, every society needs people who are committed to social *order*. Think of the chaos in Syria. But every society also needs a party of *change*, which should promote new ideas and practices for the sake not of novelty but of improvement. Think of how America needed Rosa Parks and Martin Luther King, Jr. On this score, by constantly updating Paine's sense of outrage over oppressive arrangements that should be revised or abandoned, liberals can serve commendably as such a party in American life. To that end, when they become aware of the storytelling gap, Democrats should acknowledge that the gap cannot be overcome once and for all by adopting new alpha stories. They should, however, trust that it can be closed temporarily by telling campaign stories, designed minimalistically, to help propel liberal candidates into office.

Moving in this direction would require a strategy of telling one short-term story after another. This strategy would assume that composing and promoting powerful if temporary campaign messages, like Obama's message of hope and change in 2008, can momentarily unite enough voters to occasionally rout the party of order (conservative Republicans), which has difficulty breaking with the past. In this sense, marketing one-time stories, which may vary from election to election, can enable liberals to finesse the unbridgeable gap on perennial stories. It can permit pragmatists – who are inherent skeptics – to compete for the moment with idealists – who are long-term storytellers – at election time.

The relationship of these tales to alpha stories is crucial. As a matter of principle, a short-term story – say one that apocalyptically warns that if the President elected in 2016 is Republican, he or she will appoint right-wing zealots to the Supreme Court to join John Roberts, Samuel Alito, and Clarence Thomas – might achieve temporary credibility while never intended or understood by its creators to be true, like alpha stories, into a distant future or for all time.[43] Accordingly, liberals should concede that they can't fashion alpha stories of ultimate meaning. At the same time,

---

[43] Liberals seeking philosophical endorsement for short-term stories should consult Jean-Francois Lyotard, *The Post-Modern Condition: A Report on Knowledge* (1984), p. 60, where Lyotard says that "grand narratives" are no longer persuasive, therefore "the little narrative (*petit recit*) remains the quintessential form of imaginative invention."

they should make every effort to compose a different sort of story that will help them in the short run.

Of course, leftists should be realistic about trying to implement this strategy. Creating a campaign story for the coming election and getting Democratic candidates to rally around it are not easy matters. One reason for this is that American parties today are ill-equipped for such creativity. For example, in primary elections they have little control over what candidates will say, in which case fashioning a party-wide story in advance, which even the eventual nominee will support, is difficult if not impossible. This difficulty is expressed institutionally in that, roughly speaking, national nominating conventions used to discuss who the presidential nominee would be as a function of who might best promote a platform negotiated by powerful leaders at the convention. Yet for half a century now, both Republican and Democratic nominees are selected in primary elections before the convention, after which their supporting delegates write the platform however the candidate wants it. And when that happens, the platform is most likely to express a story highlighting the candidate rather than the party.[44]

Furthermore, although the Democratic Party is approximately a liberal party,[45] there are many kinds of liberals. Some are young, some are old; some are rich, some are poor; some are women, some are men; some are WASPs, some are African Americans; some are socialists, some are capitalists; some grow corn, some program computers; some mine coal, some ship books for Amazon. Therefore their personal interests often clash, and we cannot be sure that the disparate groups they form are capable of composing and then rallying to even short-term stories designed to serve some ends but not others.

Modern Messaging

Nevertheless, we should be optimistic. That is because, although they do not know how to create *alpha stories*, liberals have plenty of talent for fashioning *short-term stories*. They do this (as do conservatives) in many

---

[44] On the primacy of candidates over parties, see Martin Wattenberg, *The Rise of Candidate-Centered Politics: Presidential Elections of the 1980s* (1991). On the presidential nominee's very complex considerations concerning how to shape his or her campaign, see Samuel Popkin, *The Candidate: What It Takes to Win – and Hold – the White House* (2012).

[45] For recent statistics on who is more and less liberal in the Democratic Party, see http://www.gallup.com/poll/183686/democrats-shift-left.aspx.

realms of modern life, such as in Hollywood movies, public relations, press conferences, Broadway plays, advertisements, newspaper articles, and news broadcasts, and in the work of salesmen, speech writers, actors, lawyers, journalists, press secretaries, and agents with various clients. We may regard all these kinds of work (and all the works that they produce) as forms of modern messaging – which is actually advertising, broadly defined – on behalf of particular people, ideas, and products.

Such messaging is based on creative energies but also on a wealth of practical experience, which exploits a strategy that aims to tell stories to persuade people to buy or favor something or someone in the short run.[46] As such, there is no reason why, with an eye to this sort of messaging, Democratic campaign consultants, candidates, think-tankers, or activists cannot generate persuasive tales for every occasion. The main thing is to think not about eternity but about how liberals might effectively approach present circumstances at a particular moment, persuasively, confidently, and – crucially – together.

Some liberals might feel squeamish about doing this. They might feel that, in many cases, there is little to admire when advertisers and public relations people use potent messaging techniques to describe their clients' patriotism, their environmental sensitivity, their financial integrity, their altruism, their sincerity, and how to choose toothbrushes, beer, cars, soft drinks, aspirin, pizza, designer jeans, kitchen appliances, laundry soap, smartphones, running shoes, and so on. Let us leave such discouraging thoughts aside though, and consider, on behalf of worthy ends, several final observations.

To the extent that political stories can resemble advertisements – but in the best sense of that enterprise, with grace and wit – liberals should bear in mind that, in the commercial world, ads constitute a very powerful sort of storytelling in search of what "works" rather than what is "true." This does not mean that what works cannot embody elements of truth, which is what alpha stories claim to represent. What it does mean is that – when language is deliberately ratcheted up to be maximally persuasive, perhaps even accompanied by pictures and jingles – efficacy and veracity are not necessarily and fully linked. Here is a potential disjuncture that, in a way, lets liberals off the large-narrative hook by not obliging them to promote alpha stories which, as we saw, no one knows how to create anyway.

---

[46] Glenn Richardson's *Pulp Politics: How Political Advertising Tells the Stories of American Politics* (2008), 2nd edn., focuses mainly on short-term stories that are told in particular campaigns.

The implication here is clear. The immediate political story, modeled after advertisements – again, with grace and wit – will do just fine for leftists now, after which, when the next short-run circumstances appear, liberals will consider whether those are satisfactory or need repair. The goal is to compose, one election after another, attractive stories that are effective – rather than, in principle, a story that is true now and forever. And if that is the goal, then the techniques for achieving it are what refined and sophisticated messaging, at its best, can teach us.

This point is implicit in how Neil Postman described modern marketing via television in his classic *Amusing Ourselves to Death: Public Discourse in the Age of Show Business* (1985). "The truth or falsity of an advertiser's claim [story] is simply not an issue," he remarked:

A McDonald's commercial, for example is not a series of testable, logically ordered assertions. It is a drama – a mythology if you will – of handsome people selling, buying and eating hamburgers, and being driven to near ecstasy by their good fortune. No claims are made, except those the viewer projects onto or infers from the drama. One can like or dislike a television commercial, of course. But one cannot refute it.[47]

Postman had it exactly right. Liberalism needs drama. Thinkers on the Left, and the books they write, propose to us that modern society entails many sorts of oppressions, cruelties, and tyrannies – in Judith Shklar's terminology – some large and some small. Accordingly, in politics driven by philosophical pragmatism and its inherent humanism,[48] what electoral

---

[47] Neil Postman, *Amusing Ourselves to Death: Public Discourse in the Age of Show Business* (1985), p. 128.

[48] Again and again, liberals highlight difficulties in life and insist that citizens, sometimes via government, can come together to resolve those difficulties. For example, David Graeber, *Debt: The First 5,000 Years* (2012), p. 383:

To begin to free ourselves [from crushing individual and national debts encouraged and cultivated by modern banks and other financial actors], the first thing we need to do is to see ourselves again as historical actors, as people who can made a difference in the course of world events.

William Jennings Bryan made a similar argument in his "Cross of Gold" speech to the Democratic nominating convention in 1896. First, Bryan complained that bankers, and especially English bankers, had unfairly imposed in financial matters a gold standard on workers and farmers in America. Then he reminded the convention delegates that their freedom to act together was a precious right, which they must preserve and exercise. As he said (and here was his humanism):

This nation is able to legislate for its own people on every question, without waiting for the aid or consent of any other nation [England] on earth ... It [whether or not to replace the gold standard with free coinage of silver] is the issue of 1776 over again. Our ancestors ... had the courage to declare their political independence of every other nation; shall we, their descendants ... declare that we are less independent than our forefathers?

competition calls for is that subjugations, inequalities, exaggerations, exploitations, dominations, and servitudes will be condemned dramatically. To that end, liberals need to exploit the fact that advertising and public relations techniques are neutral with regard to content. Because that is so, Democrats should use those techniques in the short run, boldly and shrewdly, to promote liberal insights very strongly.

So here is a final observation, which complements what some liberal writers say should be done to improve their camp's electoral chances. Political alpha stories – which Republicans dispense consciously or unconsciously, explicitly or implicitly – help to make right-wing candidates attractive, especially to people who feel that those stories, with timeless appeal, can bring order and purpose to American lives and communities. Because conservatives are ahead on this score, liberals should create small tales aimed at immediate projects, define them as urgent, share them with compatriots, and clothe them for dissemination with especially powerful rhetoric. Such is the road to best competing electorally for so long as liberals lack alpha stories and, realistically speaking, will continue to do so.

Postscript
(June 8, 2016)

By winning several primary elections on June 7, 2016, Hillary Clinton assured herself a majority of pledged delegates to the Democratic nominating convention scheduled to convene in Philadelphia in July. Perhaps most importantly, on June 7 she defeated Bernie Sanders in the California Democratic primary. Yet the approximately 56–44% margin of her victory there showed that many rank-and-file members of her party were still cool to her candidacy. Therefore pundits were intensely curious about what impact these June events might have first on Clinton's nomination campaign and later on the national election in November.

I decided, though, that a more general issue should be addressed here, because *Politics Without Stories* presented a thesis about political narratives rather than speculation about who might win any particular election. Consequently, readers who followed news reports about caucuses and primary elections in the first half of 2016, after most of this book was written and sent to press, may wonder how what happened in the liberal camp – between Clinton and Sanders competing for delegates on their way to the Democratic nominating convention – did or did not fit into what I have described as the liberal predicament. It is too early for me to draw firm conclusions about that, but here are some plausible lines of analysis.

The Candidates

Hillary Clinton projected no narrative about America's current situation. She did not tell a tale about where the country was, how it got there, and how, if necessary, life in America could be improved. Instead, to use James

Kloppenberg's term, she was "philosophically pragmatic," promoting many policy proposals touching upon foreign affairs, minority rights in America, feminism, poverty, pre-school education, environmental difficulties, the banking system, immigration reform, political fundraising, and more. She therefore resembled Democrats like Rahm Emmanuel, Charles Schumer, and Barak Obama, who I cited as examples of liberals who promote lists of governmental projects.[1]

Against the story that Sanders told – we will come to that in a moment – Clinton spoke to Democrats about how she was a realist, about how well informed she was on political issues, about how being knowledgeable helped her to understand what government can and cannot do, about how she could translate what she knew about public affairs into effective public policies, and about how, if elected, she would do in Washington what she promised to do there during the primaries. As evidence of her being qualified for the office of President, she frequently cited her experiences as a United States Senator and then Secretary of State. On these grounds, she seemed to many Democratic leaders and journalists worthy of being her party's nominee.

Bernie Sanders

In contrast to Clinton, Sanders was a storyteller. In effect, he revived the New Deal story which used to serve many Democrats. His updated version of it, framed by references to Franklin Roosevelt's achievements and his antipathy to wealthy foes, appeared in stump speeches by Sanders, and in major addresses like that delivered at Georgetown University in November of 2015.[2] It also appeared in his book *The Speech* (2011),[3] which was based on his 2010 filibuster before the Senate against a budget bill and which, approved by Barack Obama, extended tax cuts initiated by George W. Bush for rich Americans.

In a few words, Bernie Sanders offered to voters a powerful story of financial corruption ruining America for at least a generation. It was not an alpha story, and I will explain that point more fully in a moment. But it touched – among other things – upon wealth flowing mainly to rich Americans while millions of ordinary citizens lost jobs, homes, and

---

[1] Political scientists Jacob Hacker and Paul Pierson describe Clinton as a pragmatist in "Clinton's Bold Vision, Hidden in Plain Sight?" *New York Times* (March 17, 2016).

[2] See Sanders, "My Vision for Democratic Socialism in America."

[3] Bernie Sanders, *The Speech: A Historic Filibuster on Corporate Greed and the Decline of Our Middle Class* (2011).

businesses; upon the Supreme Court permitting huge private political expenditures via the Court's decision in *Citizens United vs. Federal Election Commission* (2010); upon the fact that bankers and brokers who were implicated in financial swindles leading up to the Crash of 2008 were not, for the most part, fined or imprisoned; and upon the impropriety of politicians – serving or retired – receiving large speaking fees or campaign contributions from institutions like Cisco, General Electric, the Pharmaceutical Care Management Association, Deutsche Bank, and Goldman Sachs, whose officers hope that politicians will enact laws favoring their institutions.

Alongside his story, Sanders little emphasized the classic conundrums of foreign affairs: matters of diplomacy and war. This was probably because he assumed that the chief threat to America's wellbeing was the undue influence of plutocrats and started at home. Therefore, the events taking place outside the country that Sanders did speak of – apart from the war in Iraq (which he voted against in 2003) – were mostly linked to globalization, free trade agreements, outsourcing, deindustrialization and the like. These, he explained, are all driven, or supported, by Americans who would rather profit from such industrial and commercial arrangements than work politically to assure the survival and wellbeing of ordinary people struggling with economic hardship in towns and cities across the land.

The Basic Difference

The basic difference between Clinton and Sanders showed up as early as February 5, 2016, in the New Hampshire debate between them. When both candidates were asked by the debate's moderator what they would first do after hypothetically entering the White House, Sanders said he would push immediately for campaign finance reform, because unlimited political contributions perpetuate the economic injustices that he described and condemned in his campaign speeches. Not surprisingly, Clinton answered by running through a list of projects, many commendable, from among those that she promoted, again and again in her rallies.[4] The inference was clear: Sanders was a storyteller, while Clinton was a serial pragmatist. Or, in Isaiah Berlin's terms, Clinton was a fox with many aims, and Sanders was a hedgehog focused mainly on one goal.

---

[4] See www.nytimes.com/2016/02/05/us/politics/transcript-of-the-democratic-presidential-debate.html?_r=0.

Speaking of Realism

When Clinton and her surrogates portrayed Sanders as "unrealistic," they were extending a point of some historical importance. When a Democratic candidate for President says that she will do what is feasible in Washington, she is, in effect, participating in the great liberal retreat (see Chapter 9) away from the vibrant, across-the-board optimism that even in hard times inspired many of FDR's Democrats – as in his 1933 Inaugural Address declaration that "We have nothing to fear but fear itself."

In this sense, Hillary Clinton was fearful. She probably believed what Al From, Bill Clinton, Al Gore, Sam Nunn, Charles Robb, Will Marshall, Tom Daschle, Joe Lieberman, and other members of the Democratic Leadership Council (1985–2011) believed a generation ago. Such men were convinced that after Ronald Reagan twice captured the White House, Democratic candidates in order to win elections and "get things done" in Washington should act less like FDR and more like Republicans. Thus they should enact the North American Free Trade Agreement (NAFTA), dismantle national welfare programs, multiply prisons and expand incarceration, repeal the Glass-Steagall Banking Act and, in general, disdain economic populism.

Labels here are not important, so we can regard this sort of *détente* with such Republican ideas as either the DLC world view or neoliberalism. Whichever, it assumed that Bernie Sanders' story – which called for large-scale changes, not all of them precisely defined, in the way in which Government and Democrats went about their business of who gets what, when, and how – was unrealistic and dangerous. But to make this charge was to refrain from campaigning about what *should* be done by the national government and to settle instead for advocating intricate micro-steps concerning what – before an election that might shake up the gridlock plaguing Washington – *might* be done.[5]

To demonstrate this point with a thought experiment, we can ask why the Clinton campers who accused Sanders of being unrealistic did not draw up a list of Franklin Roosevelt's programs and agencies – such as Social Security, the Wagner Labor Relations Act, the Tennessee Valley Authority, the Securities and Exchange Commission, the Civilian Conservation Corps, federal deposit insurance, the Fair Labor Standards Act, the Public Works Administration, the Glass-Steagall Banking Act, and agricultural subsidies – and then consider whether, if FDR had

---

[5] On how *little* might be done, see the political science articles collected in James Thurber and Antoine Yoshinaka (eds.), *American Gridlock: The Sources, Character, and Impact of Political Polarization* (2015).

suggested them during his campaign in 1932, "realistic" observers would have foreseen their enactment in the following years. For Clinton's most visible supporters, such an exercise was outside the box. It was as if they no longer really admired the New Deal and the optimism that accompanied it, even while – from time to time, and for the sake of appearances – they praised various New Deal projects, such as Social Security, for being signature accomplishments of twentieth-century Democrats and liberals.

The Democratic Party

By late May of 2016, on behalf of "realism" and "experience" 171 Democratic congressmen had endorsed Clinton while Sanders was endorsed by only 9. Furthermore, Clinton was supported by 40 Democratic senators while Sanders was supported by 2, including himself; Clinton was backed by 17 Governors while no Governor backed Sanders; and Clinton was recommended by 279 members of the Democratic National Committee while only 31 recommended Sanders. With the solidarity of such jobholders at stake, it was to be expected that, among superdelegates to the Democratic nominating convention, Clinton led in endorsements by 520 to 43.[6]

In scholarly literature, an insight into how such lopsided scores arise can start from understanding – along with political scientist V. O. Key – that political parties consist of three components: the party in its elected officials, in its formal organization, and in the electorate.[7] Roughly speaking this means that, in 2016, two sectors of the Democratic Party were composed of people who actively participated in the political game that was being played. They occupied positions of more or less power, income, and status, ranging from Precinct Captain to County Chairperson, from State Legislator to National Committeewoman, from Member of Congress to, perhaps, President of the United States. To retain those positions, such people tended to ally themselves to others who played the game successfully, and the leader among Democrats in that respect was Hillary Clinton. Elsewhere, however, the same party in the electorate consisted of voters who were associated, if at all, mainly with various civil society groups – of retirees, workers, minorities, teachers, co-religionists,

---

[6] See https://en.wikipedia.org/wiki/List_of_Democratic_Party_superdelegates,_2016 (accessed on May 30, 2016.) Not every source offered exactly the same numbers. Thus www.bloomberg.com/politics/graphics/2016-delegate-tracker/ (accessed on May 30, 2016) claimed that Clinton led Sanders in superdelegates by 541 to 43.

[7] The three-sector model of American political parties appeared originally in V. O. Key, *Politics, Parties, and Pressure Groups* (1942).

feminists, bowlers, surfers, stamp collectors, and so on. Some of these were interested in public policy and others were not. Of course, most voters on the Left felt that they were liberal Democrats or leaning in that direction. But they did not usually have a personal stake in the outcome of any particular election. Accordingly, they did not live in a world of profitable political alliances, permanent or shifting, but they responded mainly to what they heard candidates say, or what they heard about those candidates from acquaintances, news reports, and social media.

In these circumstances, when crowds of left-leaning voters attended Sanders rallies and applauded his attack on the 1 percent, what he said was a direct threat to the Democratic Party organization and its elected officials. After all, by encouraging ordinary citizens to vote and make a "revolution," Sanders was calling for a new political game, perhaps with new rules and new players. And that was something which two energetic and articulate sectors of the Democratic Party, each with income and status to lose, feared day and night. The Republican Party establishment confronted a similar challenge in the charismatic but erratic figure of Donald Trump and was similarly anxious. But tensions in that party are not my subject, so I will not explore them here.

Stories

Within the framework of what I explained in earlier chapters about the liberal predicament as a long-range electoral disadvantage, two final observations about Democratic storytelling are warranted. On the one hand, Secretary Clinton said essentially what John Dewey said in the 1930s and 1940s, which was that her sort of pragmatism (wary empiricism) was safer than storytelling (exciting ideology). If that were true, the story that Sanders proclaimed was – in Clinton's view – dangerous for being unrealistic, and it was unrealistic for being likely to hamper efforts by Clinton and her allies, if elected, to achieve in Washington what she described in her campaign as feasible goals. Many liberal pundits, led by Paul Krugman, were sympathetic to Clinton's argument along these lines.[8]

---

[8] On Krugman against Sanders, see Krugman, "How Change Happens," *New York Times* (January 22, 2016), and Krugman, "Learning from Obama," *New York Times* (April 1, 2016). Thomas Frank, *Listen, Liberal: Or, What Ever Happened to the Party of the People?* (2016), promotes the opposite point of view, which is that Secretary Clinton and her colleagues don't care much about ordinary Americans and have abandoned the party's former commitment to economic justice.

On the other hand, Senator Sanders was essentially doing – albeit without the benefit of my advice – what I suggested in Chapter 10 that liberals should do to win not every election but more of them than otherwise. He was not promoting an alpha story that projected permanent truths. He was, instead, framing short-term events. To that end, his story was tailored to recent and present circumstances. It reflected hard times for some and prosperity for others, and it flowed from what I described in Chapter 7 as "liberal outrage."

On this score, figuratively at least, Sanders took pages from, say, Naomi Klein, Marc Mauer, Alan Wolfe, Rachel Carson, Hedrick Smith, Barbara Ehrenreich, William Greider, Elizabeth Warren, Garrett Hardin, Andrew Bacevich, Wendy Brown, and Joseph Stiglitz. Then, having found his voice, Sanders clothed his story in graceful and passionate prose. And finally, he promoted it energetically, powerfully, and repeatedly. In short, Sanders fashioned a tale for 2016 and stayed firmly on message, proclaiming that story repeatedly so that voters would know where, in his opinion, the country stood and how he proposed, *a la* Judith Shklar, to combat what he described as large inequities and subjugations in America today.

I recommended that kind of storytelling to liberals in Chapter 10. I made no claim, however, that any particular story would work for Democrats this year. Politics is too complicated for that. Therefore I was not surprised that Sanders convinced only part of the liberal camp to adopt his story. Perhaps he should have started campaigning earlier in order to promote that story more extensively. Perhaps some Democrats, and especially office holders, regarded his story as too radical for them to embrace. Perhaps in the telling, Sanders did not evoke sentiments of group identity – like Clinton did – among, for example, women and African-Americans. And perhaps some Clinton supporters saw the seventy-four-year-old Sanders as frail and judged him – the "democratic socialist" – to be slightly wacky.

The Bottom Line

In the 2016 contest between the Secretary and the Senator, Hillary Clinton was on Barack Obama's side of the storytelling gap. Following his example, she offered to Democrats what many of them regarded as comfortable and familiar intimations of pragmatism. She was mostly hawking half-loaves, to the point where her pragmatism was more incremental than transformational. Nevertheless, by early June – after primaries and caucuses in all fifty states - it seemed quite certain that in July, at her party's national convention, she would receive its nomination to run for President.

Consequently, and taking into account the main contentions I advanced in *Politics Without Stories*, two questions arose. On the one hand, would offering pragmatism to America suffice after July to carry the Secretary to victory in November? In a year marked by considerable anti-establishment sentiment, to commend her own Washington skills might not excite many voters. However, Clinton would certainly attack Donald Trump personally and repeatedly in the hope of arousing widespread disdain for him. So maybe playing up her competence while questioning his would provide sufficient electoral traction for her. On the other hand, would the Secretary, at the Democratic convention or afterwards, decide to inject into her campaign dramatic elements of the story that Sanders promoted? After all, here was a tale that had thrilled many Democrats in the Spring and could galvanize them in the Fall. To cultivate the enthusiasm of such people, who earlier in the year had shown little interest in Clinton's list of pragmatic proposals, might put her over the top.

Because of their relevance to my thesis about storytelling, and because I was worried about who might win the election, these questions intrigued me. But I decided, in this year of strange events and unusual candidates, not to address them here. As wise men from Niels Bohr to Yogi Berra have observed, it is hard to predict accurately, and it is especially hard to predict the future accurately.

References

Ackerman, Bruce, *The Decline and Fall of the American Republic* (Cambridge, MA: Harvard University Press, 2010).

Adler, Les, and Thomas Paterson, "Red Fascism: The Merger of Nazi Germany and Soviet Russia in the American Image of Totalitarianism, 1930s–1950s," *American Historical Review* (April, 1970), pp. 1046–1064.

Akerlof, George, and Robert Shiller, *Phishing for Phools: The Economics of Manipulation and Deception* (Princeton: Princeton University Press, 2015).

Allison, John, *The Financial Crisis and the Free Market Cure: Why Pure Capitalism is the World Economy's Only Hope* (New York: McGraw-Hill, 2013).

Alter, Jonathan, *The Center Holds* (New York: Simon and Schuster, 2013).

Alterman, Eric, *Kabuki Democracy: The System Vs. Barack Obama* (New York: Nation Books, 2011).

Alterman, Eric, *Why We're Liberals: A Handbook for Restoring America's Most Important Ideals* (New York: Penguin, 2009).

Ambrose, Stephen, *Citizen Soldiers: The US Army from the Normandy Beaches to the Surrender of Germany* (New York: Simon and Schuster, 1998).

American Civil Liberties Union, "Close Guantanamo" (2016), at www.aclu.org/close-guantanamo.

Armey, Richard, and Matt Kibbe, *Give Us Liberty: A Tea Party Manifesto* (New York: HarperCollins, 2010).

Arrow, Kenneth, *Social Choice and Individual Values*, 2nd edn. (New Haven: Yale University Press, 1963).

Aschoff, Nicole, *The New Prophets of Capital* (New York: Verso, 2015).

Associated Press, "House Unable to Override Veto of Obamacare Repeal" (February 2, 2016), at www.cbsnews.com/news/house-unable-to-override-veto-of-obamacare-repeal/.

Bacevich, Andrew, *Breach of Trust: How Americans Failed Their Soldiers and Their Country* (New York: Picador, 2013).

Washington Rules: America's Path to Permanent War (New York: Metropolitan Books, 2011).

Bakan, Joel, *The Corporation: The Pathological Pursuit of Profit and Power* (New York: Free Press, 2005).

Baltz, Dan, *Collision 2012: Obama Vs. Romney and the Future of Elections in America* (New York: Viking, 2013).

Barber, Benjamin, *Consumed: How Markets Corrupt Children, Infantilize Adults, and Swallow Citizens Whole* (New York: Norton, 2008).

   The Conquest of Politics: Liberal Philosophy in Democratic Times (Princeton: Princeton University Press, 1988).

Barlett, Donald, and James Steele, *The Betrayal of the American Dream* (New York: Public Affairs, 2012).

Barofsky, Neil, *Bailout: How Washington Abandoned Main Street While Rescuing Wall Street* (New York: Free Press, 2013).

Barry, Brian, *The Liberal Theory of Justice: A Critical Examination of the Doctrines in "A Theory of Justice" by John Rawls* (New York: Oxford University Press, 1973).

Bartels, Larry, "The Irrational Electorate," *The Wilson Quarterly* (Autumn, 2008), pp. 44–50.

   Unequal Democracy: The Political Economy of the New Gilded Age (Princeton: Princeton University Press, 2008).

Barzun, Jacque, "Culture High and Dry," in Jacque Barzun (ed.), *The Culture We Deserve* (Middletown, CT: Wesleyan University Press, 1989), pp. 3–22.

Becker, Carl, *The Declaration of Independence: A Study in the History of Ideas* (New York: Harcourt, Brace, 1922).

   The Heavenly City of the 18th Century Philosophers (New Haven: Yale University Press, 1932).

Beckworth, Francis, and Michael Bauman (eds.), *Are You Politically Correct? Debating America's Cultural Standards* (Buffalo, NY: Prometheus, 1993).

Beeman, Richard, *Plain, Honest Men: The Making of the American Constitution* (New York: Random House, 2010).

Bell, Daniel, *The Cultural Contradictions of Capitalism* (New York: Basic Books, 1976).

   The End of Ideology: On The Exhaustion of Political Ideas in the Fifties (Glencoe, IL: Free Press, 1960).

Bell, Daniel (ed.), *The Radical Right* (Garden City, NY: Doubleday, 1963).

Bellah, Robert, Richard Madsen, William Sullivan, Ann Swidler, and Steven Tipton, *Habits of the Heart: Individualism and Commitment in American Life* (New York: Perennial, 1986).

Bennett, William, *Why We Fight: Moral Clarity and the War on Terrorism* (New York: Doubleday, 2002).

Bentham, Jeremy, *A Fragment on Government* (orig. 1776; London: Oxford University Press, 1951).

   The Principles of Morals and Legislation (orig. 1789; New York: Harper, 1948).

Berlinski, David, *The Devil's Delusion: Atheism and its Scientific Pretensions* (New York: Basic Books, 2009).

Berman, Marshall, *The Reenchantment of the World* (Ithaca: Cornell University Press, 1981).

Bernays, Edward, *Propaganda* (New York: H. Liveright, 1928).

Bernstein, Richard, *The Pragmatic Turn* (Cambridge, MA: Polity, 2010).

Bilmes, Linda, and Joseph Stiglitz, *The Three Trillion Dollar War: The True Cost of the Iraq War* (New York: Norton, 2008).

Bishop, Bill, *The Big Sort: Why the Clustering of Like-Minded America is Tearing Us Apart* (Boston: Mariner, 2009).

Bishop, Matthew, and Michael Green, *Philanthrocapitalism: How the Rich Can Save the World* (New York: Bloomsbury, 2008).

Blom, Philipp, *A Wicked Company: The Forgotten Radicalism of the European Enlightenment* (New York: Basic Books, 2010).

Bloom, Allen, *The Closing of the American Mind: How Higher Education Has Failed Democracy and Impoverished the Souls of Today's Students* (New York: Simon and Schuster, 1987).

Bluestone, Barry, and Bennett Harrison, *The Deindustrialization of America: Plant Closings, Community Abandonment, and the Dismantling of Basic Industry* (New York: Basic Books, 1982).

Blumberg, Paul, *The Predatory Society: Deception in the American Marketplace* (New York: Oxford University Press, 1989).

Blythe, Mark, *Austerity: The History of a Dangerous Idea* (New York: Oxford University Press, 2013).

"Why Greece Isn't to Blame for the Crisis," *Foreign Affairs* (July 7, 2015), at www.foreignaffairs.com/ articles/greece/2015-07-07/pain-athens.

Boerma, Linda, "Obama Reflects on His Biggest Mistake as President," *CBS News* (July 12, 2012), at www.cbsnews.com/news/obama-reflects-on-his-biggest-mistake-as-president/.

Boxer, Barbara, *Strangers in the Senate: Politics and the New Revolution of Women and America* (Washington, DC: National Press Books, 1994).

Boyer, William, *Myth America: Democracy vs. Capitalism* (New York: Roman and Littlefield, 2003).

Brinkley, Alan, "Liberalism and Belief," in Neil Jumonville and Kevin Mattson (eds.), *Liberalism for a New Century* (Berkeley: University of California Press, 2007), pp. 75–89.

Liberalism and Its Discontents (Cambridge, MA: Harvard University Press, 1998).

The End of Reform: New Deal Liberalism in Recession and War (New York: Vintage, 1996).

Brody, David, *The Teavangelicals: The Inside Story of How the Evangelicals and the Tea Party are Taking Back America* (Grand Rapids, MI: Zondervan, 2012).

Brokaw, Tom, *The Greatest Generation* (New York: Random House, 1998).

Brookhiser, Richard, *The Way of the WASP: How It Made America, and How It Can Save It, So to Speak* (New York: Free Press, 1991).

Brown, Wendy, *Undoing the Demos: Neoliberalism's Stealth Revolution* (New York: Zone Books, 2015).

Bruce, Tammy, *The Death of Right and Wrong: Exposing the Left's Assault On Our Culture and Values* (New York: Three Rivers Press, 2003).

Bryan, William Jennings, "Cross of Gold Speech," *American History From Revolution to Reconstruction and Beyond* (1896), at www.let.rug.nl/usa/documents/1876-1900/william-jennings-bryan-cross-of-gold-speech-july-8-1896.php.

Buckley, William, "Publisher's Statement" and "Credenda," *National Review* (November 19, 1955), pp. 5–6.

Burbick, Joan, *Gun Show Nation: Gun Culture and American Democracy* (New York: New Press, 2006).

Burgin, Angus, *Great Persuasion: Reinventing Free Markets Since the Depression* (Cambridge, MA: Harvard University Press, 2012).

Burke, Edmund, *Reflections on the Revolution in France* (orig. 1790; New York: Liberal Arts Press, 1955).

Burnham, James, *Suicide of the West: The Meaning and Destiny of Liberalism* (Chicago: Regnery, 1985).

Bush, George, "Address Accepting the Presidential Nomination at the Republican National Convention in New Orleans" (August 18, 1988), at www.presidency .ucsb.edu/ws/?pid=25955.

Bush, George W., "Address to the Nation on the Terrorist Attacks" (September 20, 2001), at http://georgewbush-whitehouse.archives.gov/news/releases/2001/09/ 20010920-8.html.

Bush, George W., "Inaugural Address" (January 20, 2001), at www.presidency. ucsb.edu/ws/?pid=25853.

Bush, Jeb, and Clint Bolick, *Immigration Wars: Forging an American Solution* (New York: Threshold Editions, 2014).

Callahan, David, *The Moral Center: How We Can Reclaim Our Country from Die-Hard Extremists, Rogue Corporations, Hollywood Hacks, and Pretend Patriots* (New York: Harcourt, 2006).

Cannon, Lou, *President Reagan: The Role of a Lifetime* (New York: Public Affairs, 2000).

Carnegie, Andrew, "The Gospel of Wealth," in Edward Kirkland (ed.), *The Gospel of Wealth and Other Timely Essays* (Cambridge: Harvard University Press, 1962), pp. 14–29.

Carr, Nicholas, *The Shallows: What the Internet is Doing to Our Brains* (New York: Norton, 2011).

Carroll, James, *Constantine's Sword: The Church and the Jews* (Boston: Houghton Mifflin, 2002).

Carson, Rachel, *Silent Spring* (Boston: Houghton Mifflin, 1962).

Carter, Jimmy, *Living Faith* (New York: Times Books, 1998).

Carter, Stephen, "Evolutionism, Creationism, and Treating Religion as a Hobby," *Duke Law Journal* (December, 1987), pp. 977–996.

The Culture of Disbelief: How American Law and Politics Trivialize Religious Devotion (New York: Anchor, 1994).

Cassirer, Ernest, *The Philosophy of the Enlightenment* (orig. 1932; Boston: Beacon, 1955).

Cato Institute, "The Milton Friedman Prize for Advancing Liberty" (2016), at www.cato.org/friedman-prize.

Chait, Jonathan, "Fact Finders: The Anti-Dogma Dogma," *The New Republic* (February 28, 2005), pp. 14–17.

The Big Con: The True Story of How Washington Got Hoodwinked and Hijacked by Crackpot Economics (Boston: Houghton Mifflin, 2007).

Chamberlain, Paul, *Can We Be Good Without God? A Conversation About Truth, Morality, Culture, & a Few Other Things That Matter* (Downers Grove, IL: InterVarsity Press, 1996).

Ciepley, David, *Liberalism in the Shadow of Totalitarianism* (Cambridge, MA: Harvard University Press, 2007).

Citizens United vs. Federal Election Commission, 558 US 310 (January 21, 2010).

Club of Rome, *The Limits to Growth: A Report of the Club of Rome's Project on the Predicament of Mankind* (New York: Universe Books, 1972).

Coates, Wilson, and Hayden White, *The Emergence of Liberal Humanism: An Intellectual History of Western Europe* (New York: McGraw-Hill, 1966).

  The Ordeal of Liberal Humanism: An Intellectual History of Western Europe (New York: McGraw-Hill, 1970).

Cohen, Lizabeth, *A Consumers' Republic: The Politics of Mass Consumption in Postwar America* (New York: Vintage, 2003).

Cohen, Richard, "The Enigmatic War," *Washington Post* (June 23, 2014), www.washingtonpost.com/opinions/richard-cohen-a-hundred-years-later-world-war-i-remains-enigmatic/2014/06/23/ae1cf484-fb0d-11e3-8176-f2c941cf35f1_story.html.

Colson, Charles, *A Dance With Deception: Revealing the Truth Behind the Headlines* (Dallas: Word, 1993).

Commager, Henry, *Jefferson, Nationalism, and the Enlightenment* (New York: George Braziller, 1975).

  The Empire of Reason: How Europe Imagined and America Realized the Enlightenment (New York: Doubleday, 1977).

Common Cause, "Money In Politics" (2016), at www.commoncause.org/issues/money-in-politics/.

Connelly, James, *The Modern Liberal Jungle: A Guide for Americans* (Lexington, KY: CreateSpace Independent Publishing Platform, 2012).

Coontz, Stephanie, *The Way We Never Were: American Families and the Nostalgia Trap* (New York: Basic Books, 1992).

Coulter, Ann, *Treason: Liberal Treachery From the Cold War to the War on Terrorism* (New York: Crown Forum, 2003).

Coyne, Jerry, *Faith vs. Fact: Why Science and Religion Are Incompatible* (New York: Viking, 2015).

Craig, William Lane, *Reasonable Faith: Christian Truth and Apologetics* (Wheaton, IL: Crossway, 2008).

Crick, Bernard, *In Defense of Politics* (orig. 1962; Chicago: University of Chicago Press, 1993).

Croly, Herbert, *The Promise of American Life* (New York: Macmillan, 1909).

Crotty, William (ed.), *Winning the Presidency, 2012* (Boulder: Paradigm, 2013).

Crouch, Colin, *The Strange Non-Death of Neoliberalism* (Cambridge, MA: Polity, 2011).

Cuomo, Mario, "Religious Belief and Public Morality: A Catholic Governor's Perspective" (1984), reprinted in Mario Cuomo, *More Than Words: The Speeches of Mario Cuomo* (New York: St. Martin's, 1993), pp. 32–51.

Dahl, Robert, *How Democratic is the American Constitution?* (New Haven: Yale University Press, 2001).

Dallek, Robert, *Nixon and Kissinger: Partners in Power* (New York: HarperCollins, 2007).

Dean, Jodi, *Democracy and Other Neoliberal Fantasies: Communicative Capitalism and Left Politics* (Durham: Duke University Press, 2009).

Deaver, Michael (ed.), *Why I Am a Reagan Conservative* (New York: Harper, 2005).

De Botton, Alain, *Religion for Atheists: A Non-Believer's Guide to the Uses of Religion* (New York: Pantheon, 2013).

De Crevecoeur, J. Hector St. John, *Letters from an American Farmer* (orig. 1782; New York: Dutton, 1957).

Delay, Tom, *No Retreat, No Surrender: One American's Fight* (New York: Sentinel, 2007).

De Maistre, Joseph, *On God and Society* (Chicago: Henry Regnery, 1959).

Demint, Jim, *The Great American Awakening: Two Years that Changed America, Washington, and Me* (Nashville, TN: B&H Publishing Group, 2011).

Dennett, Daniel, *Breaking the Spell: Religion as a Natural Phenomenon* (New York: Penguin, 2006).

Dershowitz, Alan, *Rights From Wrongs: The Origins of Human Rights in the Experience of Injustice* (New York: Basic Books, 2005).

De Tocqueville, Alexis, *Democracy in America*, Vol. 2 (orig. 1840; New York: Vintage, 1945).

Dewey, John, *Freedom and Culture* (New York: Putnam's Sons, 1939).

Dewey, John, *Individualism Old and New* (New York: Prometheus, 1999).
    Liberalism and Social Action (orig. 1935; New York: Capricorn, 1963).
    The Public and Its Problems: An Essay in Political Inquiry (New York: Henry Holt, 1927).
    The Quest for Certainty: A Study of the Relation of Knowledge and Action (New York: Minton, Balch, 1929).

Dickens, Charles, *A Tale of Two Cities* (orig. 1859; New York: Dover, 1998).

Dionne, E. J., "Foreword," in Neil Jumonville and Kevin Mattson (eds.), *Liberalism for a New Century* (Berkeley: University of California Press, 2007), pp. vii–xvii.
    Our Divided Political Heart: The Battle for the American Idea in an Age of Discontent (New York: Bloomsbury, 2012).

Disraeli, Benjamin, *Coningsby, or the New Generation* (orig. 1844; New York: Signet, 1962).

Donohue, *The New Freedom: Individualism and Collectivism in the Social Lives of Americans* (New Brunswick, NJ: Transaction Books, 1990).

D'Souza, Dinesh, *Letters to a Young Conservative* (New York: Basic Books, 2002).
    The End of Racism: Principles for a Multi-Racial Society (New York: Free Press, 1995).
    The Enemy at Home: The Cultural Left and Its Responsibility for 9/11 (New York: Doubleday, 2007).
    What's So Great About Christianity (Carol Stream, IL: Tyndale House Publishers, 2007).

Dukakis, Michael S., "'A New Era of Greatness for America': Address Accepting the Presidential Nomination at the Democrative National Convention in Atlanta" (July 21, 1988), at www.presidency.ucsb.edu/ws/?pid=25961.

Durrenmatt, Friedrich, *The Physicists* (orig. 1962; New York: Grove Press, 2010).

Dworkin, Ronald, *Justice for Hedgehogs* (Cambridge, MA: Harvard University Press, 2011).

Edmunds, David, *Would You Kill the Fat Man? The Trolley Problem and What Your Answer Tells Us About Right and Wrong* (Princeton: Princeton University Press, 2014).

Edsall, Thomas, and Mary Edsall, *Chain Reaction: The Impact of Race, Rights, and Taxes on American Politics* (New York: Norton, 1992).

Ehrenreich, Barbara, *Nickel and Dimed: On (Not) Getting By In America* (New York: Metropolitan Books, 2001).

Eisenach, Eldon, *Sacred Discourse and American Nationality* (New York: Rowman and Littlefield, 2012).

　The Lost Promise of Progressivism (Laurence, KS: University Press of Kansas, 1994).

Eisenhower, Dwight, "First Inaugural Address" (January 20, 1953), at http://avalon.law.yale.edu/20th_century/eisen1.asp.

Ellis, Joseph, *Founding Brothers: The Revolutionary Generation* (New York: Vintage, 2001).

Emanuel, Rahm, and Bruce Reed, *The Plan: Big Ideas For America* (New York: Public Affairs, 2006).

Epstein, Edward, *News From Nowhere: Television and the News* (New York: Vintage, 1974).

Epstein, Greg, *Good Without God: What a Billion Nonreligious People Do Believe* (New York: Harper, 2009).

Evans, Christopher, *Liberalism Without Illusions: Renewing an American Christian Tradition* (Waco, TX: Baylor University Press, 2010).

Fallows, James, "The Passionless Presidency: The Trouble with Jimmy Carter's Administration," *The Atlantic Monthly* (May, 1979), at www.theatlantic.com/ past/unbound/flashbks/pres/fallpass.htm.

Falwell, Jerry, *Listen America!* (Garden City, NY: Doubleday,1980).

　The New American Family: The Rebirth of the American Dream (Dallas: Word, 1992).

Fandos, Nicholas, "US Foreign Arms Deals Increased Nearly $10 Billion in 2014," *New York Times* (25 December, 2015), at www.nytimes.com/2015/12/26/world/middleeast/us-foreign-arms-deals-increased-nearly-10-billion-in-2014.html?_r=0.

Fast, Howard, (ed.), *The Selected Work of Tom Paine and Citizen Tom Paine* (New York: Modern Library, 1945).

Faux, Jeff, *The Servant Economy: Where America's Elite is Sending the Middle Class* (New York: Wiley, 2012).

Federal News Service, "Transcript of the Second Debate Between President Obama and Republican Nominee Mitt Romney" (October 16, 2012), at www.npr.org/2012/10/16/163050988/transcript-obama-romney-2nd-presidential-debate.

"Transcript of the Democratic Presidential Debate," *New York Times* (February 5, 2016), at www.nytimes.com/2016/02/05/us/politics/transcript-of-the-democratic-presidential-debate.html?_r=0.

Ferguson, Charles, *Predator Nation: Corporate Criminals, Political Corruption, and the Hijacking of America* (New York: Crown, 2012).

Feulner, Edwin, *Getting America Right: The True Conservative Values Our Nation Needs Today* (New York: Three Rivers, 2007).

Fioramonti, Lorenzo, *Gross Domestic Problem: The Politics Behind the World's Most Powerful Number* (New York: Zed Books, 2013).

Fiorina, Morris, *Retrospective Voting in American National Elections* (New Haven: Yale University Press, 1981).

Fish, Stanley, *Is There a Text in This Class? The Authority of Interpretive Communities* (Cambridge, MA: Harvard University Press, 1980).

    There's No Such Thing as Free Speech, and It's a Good Thing, Too (New York: Oxford University Press, 1994).

Flynn, Daniel, *Why the Left Hates America: Exposing the Lies That Have Obscured Our Nation's Greatness* (New York: Crown, 2004).

Foley, Duncan, *Adam's Fallacy: A Guide to Economic Theology* (Cambridge, MA: Harvard University Press, 2006).

Foner, Eric, *The Story of American Freedom* (New York: Norton, 1998).

Foucault, Michel, "Truth and Power (1977)," in Michel Foucault (ed.), *Power/Knowledge: Selected Interviews and Other Writings, 1972–1977* (New York: Vintage, 1980), pp. 109–133.

Fox, Justin, *The Myth of the Rational Market: A History of Risk, Reward, and Delusion on Wall Street* (New York: Harper, 2009).

Frank, Thomas, *Listen, Liberal: Or, What Ever Happened to the Party of the People?* (New York: Metropolitan Books, 2016).

    Pity the Billionaire: The Hard-Times Swindle and the Unlikely Comeback of the Right (New York: Metropolitan Books, 2012).

    The Winner-Take-All Society: Why the Few at the Top Get So Much More Than the Rest of Us (New York: Penguin, 1996).

    What's The Matter with Kansas? How Conservatives Won the Heart of America (New York: Metropolitan Books, 2004).

Frankel, Charles, *The Case for Modern Man* (New York: Harper and Brothers, 1956).

Freeman, Charles, *The Closing of the Western Mind: The Rise of Faith and the Fall of Reason* (New York: Vintage, 2005).

Freud, Sigmund, *Group Psychology and the Analysis of the Ego* (London: The International Psychoanalytical Press, 1922).

    The Ego and the Id (London: Hogarth, 1927).

Friedan, Betty, *The Feminine Mystique* (New York: Dell, 1963).

Friedman, Milton, *Capitalism and Freedom* (Chicago: University of Chicago Press,1962).

    "The Social Responsibility of Business is to Increase its Profits," *New York Times* (September 13, 1970), at www.colorado.edu/student groups /libertarians /issues/friedman-soc-resp-business.html.

Friedman, Milton, and Rose Friedman, *Free To Choose: A Personal Statement* (New York: Harcourt, Brace, 1979, 1990).

Friedman, Thomas, "More Poetry Please," *New York Times* (November 1, 2009), at www.nytimes. com/2009/11/01/opinion/01friedman.html.

Friedman, Thomas, and Michael Mandelbaum, *That Used To Be Us: How American Fell Behind the World We Invented – and How We Can Come Back* (New York: Farr, Straus, and Giroux, 2011).

Fromm, Eric, *The Sane Society* (New York: Rinehart, 1955).

Gabler, Mel, and Norma Gabler, *What Are They Teaching Our Children?* (Wheaton, IL: Victor Books, 1985).

Gairdner, William, *The Great Divide: Why Liberals and Conservatives Will Never, Ever Agree* (New York: Encounter Books, 2015).

Galbraith, John Kenneth, *The Affluent Society* (New York: Mentor, 1958).

Galilei, Galileo, *Dialogue Concerning the Two Chief World Systems, Ptolemaic & Copernican*, 2nd edn. (orig. 1632; Berkeley: University of California Press, 1967).

Galston, William, *Liberal Purposes* (New York: Cambridge University Press, 1991).

Gardner, Howard, *Frames of Mind: The Theory of Multiple Intelligences* (New York: Basic Books, 1983).

Gay, Peter, *The Enlightenment: An Interpretation, Vol. II: The Science of Freedom* (New York: Knopf, 1969).

Gelbspan, Ross, *Boiling Point: How Politicians, Big Oil and Coal, Journalists, and Activists Have Fueled a Climate Crisis – and What We Can Do to Avert Disaster* (New York: Basic Books, 2005).

  The Heat is On: The Climate Crisis, The Cover Up, The Prescription (Cambridge, MA: Perseus, 1998).

Gibson, John, *The War on Christmas: How the Liberal Plot to Ban the Sacred Christian Holiday Is Worse Than You Thought* (New York: Sentinel, 2005).

Gibson, Rosemary, and Janardan Singh, *The Battle Over Health Care: What Obama's Reform Means for America's Future* (New York: Rowman and Littlefield, 2012).

Gilder, George, *Wealth and Poverty* (New York: Basic Books, 1981).

Gilens, Martin, *Affluence and Influence: Economic Inequality and Political Power in America* (Princeton: Princeton University Press, 2012).

Gillespie, Michael, *The Theological Origins of Modernity* (Chicago: University of Chicago Press, 2008).

Gingrich, Newt, *To Save America: Stopping Obama's Secular–Socialist Machine* (Washington, DC: Regnery, 2011).

  Window of Opportunity: A Blueprint for the Future (New York: Tom Dougherty, 1984).

Gingrich, Newt, and Richard Armey, *Contract with America: The Bold Plan by Rep. Newt Gingrich, Rep. Dick Armey, and the House Republicans to Change the Nation* (New York: Times Books, 1994).

Ginsberg, Benjamin, *The American Lie: Government by the People and Other Political Fables* (Boulder: Paradigm, 2007).

Gitlin, Todd, *The Bulldozer and the Big Tent: Blind Republicans, Lame Democrats, and the Recovery of American Ideals* (Hoboken, NJ: John Wiley, 2007).

  The Sixties: Years of Hope, Days of Rage (New York: Bantam, 1993).

GlobalFirePower.com, "Defense Budget By Country" (2016), at www.globalfirepower.com/defense-spending-budget.asp.

Goldberg, Jonah, *Liberal Fascism: The Secret History of the American Left, From Mussolini to the Politics of Change* (New York: Crown Forum, 2009).

Goldwater, Barry, *The Conscience of a Conservative* (Shepherdsville, KY: Victor, 1960).

Goldwin, Robert (ed.), *Left, Right, and Center: Essays on Liberalism and Conservatism in the United States* (Chicago: Rand McNally, 1966).

Goodman, Paul, *Growing Up Absurd* (New York: Vintage, 1960).

Goodwin, Neva, Frank Ackerman, and David Kiron (eds.), *The Consumer Society* (Washington, DC: Island Press, 1997).

Gore, Al, *The Assault on Reason* (New York: Penguin, 2007).

Graeber, David, *Debt: The First 5,000 Years* (New York: Melville House, 2012).

Gray, John, *Enlightenment's Wake: Politics and Culture at the Close of the Modern Age* (New York: Routledge, 1995).

Gregory, Brad, *The Unintended Reformation: How a Religious Revolution Secularized Society* (Cambridge, MA: Harvard University Press, 2012).

Green, Philip, *Deadly Logic: The Theory of Nuclear Deterrence* (New York: Schocken, 1968).

Greenberg, Stanley, "Reconstructing a Democratic Vision," *The American Prospect* (Spring, 1990), pp. 82–89, at http://prospect.org/article/reconstructing-democratic-vision.

Greenberg, Stanley, and Theda Skocpol (eds.), *The New Majority: Toward a Popular Progressive Politics* (New Haven: Yale University Press, 1997).

Greenblatt, Stephen, *The Swerve: How the World Became Modern* (New York: Norton, 2011).

Greenfeld, Kent, *The Myth of Choice: Personal Responsibility in a World of Limits* (New Haven: Yale University Press, 2011).

Greenhouse, Steven, *The Big Squeeze: Tough Times for the American Worker* (New York: Anchor, 2008).

Gregory, *The Unintended Reformation* (Cambridge, MA: Harvard University Press, 2012).

Greider, William, *One World, Ready or Not: The Manic Logic of Global Capitalism* (New York: Touchstone, 1997).

Gross, Neil, *Why Are Professors Liberal and Why Do Conservatives Care?* (Cambridge, MA: Harvard University Press, 2013).

Ground Zero, *Nuclear War: What's In It for You?* (New York: Pocket Books, 1982).

Grunwald, Michael, *The New New Deal: The Hidden Story of Change in the Obama Era* (New York: Simon and Schuster, 2012).

Gutting, Gary, "Can Wanting to Believe Make Us Believers?" New York Times (October 7, 2014), at http://opinionator.blogs. nytimes.com/2014/10/05/can-wanting-to-believe-make-us-believers/?_php=true &_type=blogs &_r=0].

Hacker, Jacob, and Paul Pierson, "Clinton's Bold Vision, Hidden in Plain Sight?" *New York Times* (March 17, 2016) at www.nytimes.com/2016/03/17/opinion/campaign-stops/clintons-bold-vision-hidden-in-plain-sight.html?_r=0.

"No Cost for Extremism: Why the GOP Hasn't (Yet) Paid for Its March to the Right," *The American Prospect* (Spring, 2015) at http://prospect.org/article/no-cost-extremism.

Off Center: The Republican Revolution and the Erosion of American Democracy (New Haven: Yale University Press, 2005).

Winner-Take-All Politics: How Washington Made the Rich Richer – and Turned Its Back on the Middle Class (New York: Simon and Schuster, 2011).

Haidt, Jonathan, *The Righteous Mind: Why Good People Are Divided by Politics and Religion* (New York: Pantheon, 2012).

Hamilton, Alexander, John Jay, and James Madison, *The Federalist* (New York: Modern Library, 1937).

Hamilton, Clive, *Requiem for a Species: Why We Resist the Truth About Climate Change* (New York: Routledge, 2010).

Hammer, Stefanie, "The Role of Narrative in Political Campaigning: An Analysis of Speeches by Barack Obama," *National Identities*, 12:3 (September, 2010), pp. 269–290.

Hannity, Sean, *Deliver Us From Evil: Defeating Terrorism, Despotism, and Liberalism* (New York: Regan Books, 2004).

Hardin, Garrett, "The Tragedy of the Commons," *Science* (December 13, 1968), pp. 1243–1248.

Harris, Sam, *The End of Faith: Religion, Terror, and the Future of Reason* (New York: Norton, 2005).

Hart, David, *The Experience of God: Being, Consciousness, Bliss* (New Haven: Yale University Press, 2013).

Hart, Gary, *A New Democracy: A Democratic Vision for the 1980s and Beyond* (New York: William Morrow, 1982).

Hartmann, Thom, *Screwed: The Undeclared War Against the Middle Class* (San Francisco: Berrett-Koehler, 2007).

Hartz, Louis, "Goals for Political Science: A Discussion," *American Political Science Review* (December, 1951), pp. 1001–1005.

Hartz, Louis, *The Liberal Tradition in America* (New York: Harvest, 1955).

Harvey, David, *A Brief History of Neoliberalism* (New York: Oxford University Press, 2005).

Hayek, Friedrich (ed.), *Collectivist Economic Planning: Critical Studies on the Possibilities of Socialism* (London: George Rutledge, 1935).

The Road to Serfdom (Chicago: University of Chicago Press, 1944).

HealthReformVotes.org, "How Members of Congress Voted on Health Reform: Roll Call Votes on Significant Health Reform Legislation" (2016), at www.healthreformvotes.org.

Hecht, Jennifer, *Doubt: A History* (New York: HarperOne, 2004).

Heclo, Hugh, "Issue Networks and the Executive Establishment," in Anthony King (ed.), *The New American Political System* (Washington, DC: The American Enterprise Institute, 1978), pp. 87–124.

Henry, Jules, *Culture Against Man* (New York: Vintage, 1965).

Hetherington, Marc, and Jonathan Weiler, *Authoritarianism and Polarization in American Politics* (New Haven: Yale University Press, 2009).

Hibbing, John, Kevin Smith, and John Alford, *Predisposed: Liberals, Conservatives, and the Biology of Political Differences* (New York: Routledge, 2014).

Himmelfarb, Gertrude, *One Nation, Two Cultures* (New York: Knopf, 1999).

Hirsch, Fred, *Social Limits to Growth* (Cambridge, MA: Harvard University Press, 1976).

Hirschman, Albert, *The Rhetoric of Reaction: Perversity, Futility, Jeopardy* (Cambridge, MA: Harvard University Press, 1991).

Hitchens, Christopher, *God is Not Great: How Religion Poisons Everything* (New York: Twelve, 2009).

Hobsbawm, E. J., *Nations and Nationalism Since 1780* (New York: Harvest, 1990).

Hofstadter, Richard, *The Paranoid Style in American Politics and Other Essays* (New York: Vintage, 1964).

Hoggan, James, and Richard Littlemore, *Climate Cover-Up: The Crusade to Deny Global Warming* (Vancouver: Greystone Books, 2009).

Holland, Tom, *In the Shadow of the Sword: The Birth of Islam and the Rise of the Global Arab Empire* (New York: Anchor, 2012).

Hoover, Herbert, *American Individualism* (New York: Doubleday, Page, and Company, 1922).

Hoover, Herbert, "Principles and Ideals of the United States Government" (October 22, 1928), at http://millercenter.org/president/speeches/speech-6000.

Huckabee, Mike, *Do The Right Thing: Inside the Movement That's Bringing Common Sense Back to America* (New York: Penguin, 2008).

Huntington, Samuel, *American Politics: The Promise of Disharmony* (Cambridge, MA: Harvard University Press, 1981).

The Clash of Civilizations and the Remaking of World Order (New York: Simon and Schuster, 1996).

Hyde, Henry, "The Importance of Transcendent Moral Values," in Michael Deaver (ed.), *Why I Am a Reagan Conservative* (New York: Harper, 2005).

Ingersoll, Robert, *What's God Got To Do With It?: Robert Ingersoll On Free Thought, Honest Talk, and the Separation of Church & State* (Hanover, NH: Steerforth Press, 2005).

Isaac, Jeffrey, *The Poverty of Progressivism: The Future of American Democracy in a Time of Liberal Decline* (New York: Roman and Littlefield, 2003).

Israel, Jonathan, *A Revolution of the Mind: Radical Enlightenment and the Intellectual Origins of Modern Democracy* (Princeton: Princeton University Press, 2010).

Isserman, Maurice, and Michael Kazin, *America Divided: The Civil War of the 1960s* (New York: Oxford University Press, 1999).

Jacobs, Jane, *The Death and Life of Great American Cities* (New York: Vintage, 1961).

Jacobs, Lawrence, and Theda Skocpol, *Health Care Reform and American Politics* (New York: Oxford University Press, 2012).

Jacoby, Russell, *The End of Utopia: Politics and Culture in an Age of Apathy* (New York: Basic Books, 1999).

Jacoby, Susan, *The Age of American Unreason* (New York: Vintage, 2009).

James, William, "What Pragmatism Means," in William James (ed.), *Pragmatism: A New Name for Some Old Ways of Thinking* (New York: Longmans, Green, 1907).

Jefferson, Thomas, "Jefferson's Wall of Separation Letter" (January 1, 1802), at www.constitution.org/tj/sep_church_state.htm.

Jefferson, Thomas, *Notes on the State of Virginia* (orig. 1785; New York: Harper Torchbooks, 1964).

Johnson, Lyndon B., "Remarks at the University of Michigan" (May 22, 1964), at www.lbjlib.utexas.edu/johnson/archives.hom/speeches.hom/640522. asp.

Johnson, Simon, and James Kwak, *13 Bankers: The Wall Street Takeover and the Next Financial Meltdown* (New York: Vintage, 2011).

Jones, Daniel, *Masters of the Universe: Hayek, Friedman, and the Birth of Neoliberal Politics* (Princeton: Princeton University Press, 2012).

Judt, Tony, *Thinking the Twentieth Century* (London: Vintage, 2013).

Jumonville, Neil and Kevin Mattson (eds.), *Liberalism for a New Century* (Berkeley: University of California Press, 2007).

Kabaservice, Geoffrey, *Rule and Ruin: The Downfall of Moderation and the Destruction of the Republican Party, From Eisenhower to the Tea Party* (New York: Oxford University Press, 2012).

Kagan, Robert, and William Kristol (eds.), *Present Dangers: Crisis and Opportunity in American Foreign and Defense Policy* (San Francisco: Encounter, 2000).

Kahn, Paul, *Putting Liberalism in its Place* (Princeton: Princeton University Press, 2005).

Kahneman, Daniel, *Thinking, Fast and Slow* (New York: Penguin, 2012).

Kassner, Tim, *The High Price of Materialism* (Cambridge, MA: MIT Press, 2002).

Katznelson, Ira, *Fear Itself: The New Deal and the Origins of Our Time* (New York: Liveright, 2013).

Kaye, Harvey, *The Fight for The Four Freedoms: What Made FDR and the Greatest Generation Truly Great* (New York: Simon and Schuster, 2014).

Kazin, Michael, *American Dreamers: How the Left Changed a Nation* (New York: Knopf, 2011).

Kennan, George, "The Sources of Soviet Conduct," *Foreign Affairs* (July, 1947), pp. 53–63.

Kennedy, D. James, "Reclaiming America for Christ," in D. James Kennedy, Gary Bauer, John Ashcroft, *et al.* (eds.), *Reclaiming America for Christ* (Fort Lauderdale, FL: Coral Ridge Ministries, 1996), pp. 1–9.

Kennedy, D. James, *What If America Were a Christian Nation Again?* (Nashville, TN: Thomas Nelson, 2003).

Kennedy, John, "Acceptance of Party Nomination at Commodore Hotel, New York" (September 14, 1960), at www.presidency.ucsb.edu/ws/?pid=74012.

"Address to the Greater Houston Ministerial Association" (September 12, 1960), at www.jfklibrary.org/Asset-Viewer/ALL6YEBJMEKYGMCntnSCvg.aspx.

"Commencement Address at Yale University" (1962), at www.presidency. ucsb.edu/ws/?pid=29661.

Kennedy, Robert, "Remarks at the University of Kansas" (March 18, 1968), at www.jfklibrary.org/Research/Research-Aids/Ready-Reference/RFK-Speeches/Remarks-of-Robert-F-Kennedy-at-the-University-of-Kansas-March-18-1968.aspx.

Kernell, Samuel, *Going Public: New Strategies of Presidential Leadership*, 4th edn. (Washington, DC: Congressional Quarterly Press, 2006).

Kerry, John, *A Call to Service: My Vision For a Better America* (New York: Penguin, 2003).

Kertzer, David, *The Pope Against the Jews: The Vatican's Role in the Rise of Modern Anti-Semitism* (2001).

Kesler, Charles, *I Am the Change: Barack Obama and the Crisis of Liberalism* (New York: Broadside Books, 2012).

Key, V. O., *Politics, Parties, and Pressure Groups* (New York: Thomas Crowell, 1942).

Kimball, Roger (ed.), *Experiments Against Reality: The Fate of Culture in the Postmodern Age* (New York: Ivan Dee, 2002).

Kimball, Roger, "James Fitzjames Stephens v. John Stuart Mill," in Roger Kimball (ed.), *Experiments Against Reality: The Fate of Culture in the Postmodern Age* (New York: Ivan Dee, 2002), pp. 159–188.

Kimball, Roger, *Tenured Radicals: How Politics Has Corrupted Our Higher Education* (New York: HarperPerennial, 1990).

Kimball, Roger, *The Long March: How the Cultural Revolution of the 1960s Changed America* (New York: Encounter Books, 2000).

King, Anthony (ed.), *The New American Political System* (Washington, DC: The American Enterprise Institute, 1978).

King, Martin Luther, Jr., *Why We Can't Wait* (New York: Signet, 1964).

Kingdon, John, *Agendas, Alternatives, and Public Policies* (Boston: Little, Brown, 1984).

Klein, Naomi, *No Logo: Taking Aim At the Brand Bullies*, rev. edn. (New York: Picador, 2002).
    The Shock Doctrine: The Rise of Disaster Capitalism (New York: Picador, 2008).
    This Changes Everything (New York: Simon and Schuster, 2014).

Kloppenberg, James, "In Retrospect: Louis Hartz's The Liberal Tradition in America," *Reviews in American History* (September, 2001), pp. 460–476.
    Reading Obama: Dreams, Hope, and the American Political Tradition (Princeton: Princeton University Press, 2011).

Kornhauser, William, *The Politics of Mass Society* (Glencoe, IL: Free Press, 1959).

Kotz, Nick, *Wild Blue Yonder: Money, Politics, and the B-1 Bomber* (New York: Pantheon, 1988).

Kristol, Irving, "Business and the New Class (1975)," in Irving Kristol (ed.), *Neoconservatism: The Autobiography of an Idea* (New York: Ivan Dee, 1999), pp. 205–210.

Kristol, William, "The 1993 Kristol Memo on Defeating Health Care Reform," *Talking Points Memo* (September 24, 2013), at http://talkingpointsmemo.com/edblog/the-1993-kristol-memo-on-defeating-health-care-reform.

Kronman, Anthony, *Education's End: Why Our Colleges and Universities Have Given Up on the Meaning of Life* (New Haven: Yale University Press, 2007).

Krugman, Paul, "Hating Good Government," *New York Times* (January 19, 2015), at www.nytimes.com/2015/01/19/opinion/paul-krugman-hating-good-government.html?_r=0.

"How Change Happens," *New York Times* (January 22, 2016), at www.nytimes.com/2016/01/22/opinion/how-change-happens.html?_r=0.

"Imaginary Health Care Horrors," *New York Times* (March 30, 2015), at www.nytimes.com/2015/03/30/opinion/paul-krugman-imaginary-health-care-horrors.html?_r=0.

"Learning From Obama," *New York Times* (April 1, 2016), at www.nytimes.com/2016/04/01/opinion/ learning-from-obama.html?_r=0.

"The President Is Missing," *New York Times* (April 20, 2011), at www.nytimes.com/2011/04/11/opinion/11krugman.html.

"Zombies of 2016," *New York Times* (April 24, 2015), at www.nytimes. com/2015/04/24/opinion/paul-krugman-zombies-of-2016.html?_r=0.

Krutch, Joseph Wood, *The Modern Temper: A Study and a Confession* (orig. 1929; New York: Harvest, 1957).

Kuhn, Thomas, *The Structure of Scientific Revolutions* (Chicago: University of Chicago, 1962).

Kuttner, Robert, *Everything For Sale: The Virtues and Limits of Markets* (New York: Knopf, 1998).

LaHaye, Tim, *Faith of Our Founding Fathers: A Comprehensive Study of America's Christian Foundations* (1990).

Lakoff, George, *Whose Freedom?* (New York: Picador, 2007).

Lasch, Christopher, *Haven in a Heartless World: The Family Besieged* (New York: Basic Books, 1977).

Laswell, Harold, *Psychopathology and Politics* (Chicago: University of Chicago, 1930).

Leach, William, *Land of Desire: Merchants, Power, and the Rise of a New American Culture* (New York: Vintage, 1993).

Lekachman, Robert, *The Age of Keynes* (New York: Vintage, 1968).

Lepore, Jill, *The Whites of Their Eyes: The Tea Party's Revolution and the Battle Over American History* (Princeton: Princeton University Press, 2010).

Leuchtenburg, William, *Franklin Roosevelt and the New Deal: 1932–1940* (New York: Harper and Row, 1962).

Levendusky, Matthew, *The Partisan Sort: How Liberals Became Democrats and Conservatives Became Republicans* (Chicago: University of Chicago, 2009).

Levine, Lawrence, *The Opening of the American Mind: Canons, Culture, and History* (Boston: Beacon, 1996).

Levine, Peter, *The New Progressive Era: Toward a Fair and Deliberative Democracy* (New York: Rowman and Littlefield, 2000).

Levinson, Sanford, *An Argument Open To All: Reading "The Federalist" in the Twenty-First Century* (New Haven: Yale University Press, 2015).

Framed: America's 51 Constitutions and The Crisis of Governance (New York: Oxford University Press, 2012).

(ed.), *Torture: A Collection* (New York: Oxford University Press, 2004).

Lilla, Mark, "The Great Disconnect," *New York Times* (September 30, 2012), at www.nytimes.com/2012/09/30/books/review/the-great-disconnect.html?_r=0.

The Stillborn God: Religion, Politics, and the Modern West (New York: Vintage, 2008).

Limbaugh, Rush, *The Way Things Ought to Be* (New York: Pocket Books, 1994).

Lind, Michael, *The Land of Promise: An Economic History of the United States* (New York: Harper, 2012).

Lippmann, Walter, *Public Opinion* (orig. 1922; New York: Free Press, 1965).

Lipset, Seymour Martin, *Political Man: The Social Bases of Politics* (Garden City, NY: Doubleday, 1960).

Liu, Eric, "What Every American Should Know," *The Atlantic* (July 3, 2015), at www.theatlantic.com/ politics/archive /2015/07/what-every-american-should-know/397334/.

Lizza, Ryan, "Bad Message," *The New Republic* (November, 2004), at www.newrepublic.com/article/bad-message.

Lowi, Theodore, *The End of Liberalism: Ideology, Policy, and the Crisis of Public Authority* (New York: Norton, 1969).

Lucas, Robert, "Macroeconomic Priorities," *American Economic Review*, (2003) 93(1), pp. 1–14, at http://pages.stern.nyu.edu/~dbackus/Taxes/Lucas%20priorities%20AER%2003.pdf.

Lukes, Steven, *Liberals and Cannibals: The Implications of Diversity* (New York: Verso, 2003).

Lutz, William, *Double-Speak* (New York: Harper and Row, 1989).

Lynn, Barry, *Cornered: The New Monopoly Capitalism and the Economics of Destruction* (New York: Wiley, 2010).

Lyotard, Jean-Francois, *The Post-Modern Condition: A Report on Knowledge* (Minneapolis: University of Minnesota, 1984).

MacArthur, John, *The Selling of "Free Trade": NAFTA, Washington, and The Subversion of American Democracy* (New York: Hill and Wang, 2000).

Macedo, Stephen, *Liberal Virtues: Citizenship, Virtue, and Community in Liberal Constitutionalism* (New York: Oxford University Press, 1990).

MacIntyre, Alasdair, *After Virtue*, 2nd edn. (Notre Dame: Notre Dame University, 1984).

Magnet, Myron, *The Dream and the Nightmare: The Sixties' Legacy to the Underclass* (New York: William Morrow, 1993).

The Founders at Home: Building America, 1735–1817 (New York: Norton, 2013).

Mann, James, *The Obamians: The Struggle Inside the White House to Redefine American Power* (New York: Penguin, 2012).

Mann, Thomas, and Norman Ornstein, *It's Even Worse Than It Looks: How the American Constitutional System Collided With the New Politics of Extremism* (New York: Basic Books, 2012).

Mannheim, Karl, *Ideology and Utopia: An Introduction to the Sociology of Knowledge* (orig. 1936; New York: Harcourt, Brace, 1955).

Maraniss, David, "First Lady Launches Counterattack," *Washington Post* (January 28, 1998), at www.washingtonpost.com/wp-srv/politics/special/clinton/stories/hillary 012898.htm.

Marcell, David, *Progress and Pragmatism: James, Dewey, Beard, and the American Idea of Progress* (Westport, CN: Greenwood, 1974).

Marcuse, Herbert, *One Dimensional Man: Studies in the Ideology of Advanced Industrial Society* (Boston: Beacon, 1964).

Marsden, George, *The Twilight of the American Enlightenment* (New York: Basic Books, 2014).

Marshall, George, *Don't Even Think About It: Why Our Brains Are Wired to Ignore Climate Change* (New York: Bloomsbury, 2014).

Mauer, Marc, *Race to Incarcerate* (New York: Free Press, 1999).

May, Henry, *The Enlightenment in America* (New York: Oxford University Press, 1976).

Mayer, Frederick, *Narrative Politics: Stories and Collective Action* (New York: Oxford University Press, 2014).

Mayer, Jane, *Dark Money: The Hidden History of the Billionaires Behind the Rise of the Radical Right* (New York: Doubleday, 2016).

McCarty, Nolan, Keith Poole, and Howard Rosenthal, *Polarized America: The Dance of Ideology and Unequal Riches* (Cambridge, MA: MIT Press, 2008).

McClosky, Deidre, *The Rhetoric of Economics* (Madison: University of Wisconsin, 1985).

McConnell, Mitch, "Top GOP Priority: Make Obama a One-Term President," *National Journal* (September 23, 2010), at www.nationaljournal.com/member/ magazine/top-gop-priority-make-obama-a-one-term-president-20101023.

McNeill, William, "The Care and Repair of Public Myth," *Foreign Affairs* (Fall, 1982), pp. 1–13.

Menand, Louis (ed.), *Pragmatism: A Reader* (New York: Random House, 1997).

Menand, Louis, *The Metaphysical Club: A Story of Ideas in America* (New York: Farrar, Straus, Giroux, 2002).

Meyer, Frank, "Conservatism," in Robert Goldwin (ed.), *Left, Right, and Center: Essays on Liberalism and Conservatism in the United States* (Chicago: Rand McNally, 1966).

Milgrim, Stanley, *Obedience to Authority: An Experimental View* (New York: Harper and Row, 1974).

Mill, James, *An Essay on Government* (orig. 1820; New York: Liberal Arts Press, 1955).

Mill, John Stuart, *On Liberty* (orig. 1859; New York: Liberal Arts Press, 1956).

Miller, David, *On Nationality* (New York: Oxford University Press, 1995).

Miller, James, *Democracy is In the Street: From Port Huron to the Siege of Chicago* (New York: Simon and Schuster, 1988).

Miller, Mark Crispin, *The Bush Dyslexicon: Observations on a National Disorder* (New York: Norton, 2002).

Miller, Stephen, *Conversation: A History of a Declining Art* (New Haven: Yale University Press, 2007).

Miroff, Bruce, *Pragmatic Illusions: The Presidential Politics of John F. Kennedy* (New York: Longman, 1979).

Mirowski, Philip, *Never Let a Serious Crisis Go to Waste: How Neoliberalism Survived the Financial Meltdown* (New York: Verso, 2014).

Morgan, Edmund, *American Slavery, American Freedom* (New York: Norton, 1975).

Mondak, Jeffery, *Personality and the Foundations of Political Behavior* (New York: Cambridge, 2010).

Mooney, Chris, *The Republican Brain: The Science of Why They Deny Science – and Reality* (New York: Wiley, 2012).

Moreton, Bethany, *To Serve God and Wal-Mart: The Making of Christian Free Enterprise* (Cambridge, MA: Harvard, 2009).

Murray, Charles, *Losing Ground: American Social Policy, 1950–1980* (New York: Basic Books, 1984).

Myers, David, *The American Paradox: Spiritual Hunger in an Age of Plenty* (New Haven: Yale, University Press, 2000).

Nagel, Thomas, "A Philosopher Defends Religion," *New York Review of Books* (September 27, 2012), at www.nybooks.com/articles/archives/2012/sep/27/philosopher-defends-religion/?pagination=false.

Nelson, Robert, *Economics as Religion: From Samuelson to Chicago and Beyond* (University Park, PA: Pennsylvania State University, 2001).

New York Times, "Welfare Queen' Becomes Issue in Reagan Campaign," *New York Times* (February 15, 1976), p. 51.

Newman, Katherine, *Falling From Grace: The Experience of Downward Mobility in the American Middle Class* (New York: Vintage, 1988).

Newport, Frank, "Democrats in the US Shift to the Left," *Gallup* (June 18, 2015), at www.gallup.com/poll/183686/democrats-shift-left.aspx.

Niebuhr, H. Richard, *The Kingdom of God in America* (New York: Harper and Row, 1937).

Nixon, Richard, and Nikita Khrushchev, "The Kitchen Debate" (1949), at http://teachingamericanhistory.org/library/document/the-kitchen-debate/.

Noah, Timothy, *The Great Divergence: America's Growing Inequality Crisis and What We Can Do About It* (New York: Bloomsbury, 2013).

Noble, David, *Debating the End of History: The Marketplace, Utopia, and the Fragmentation of Intellectual Life* (Minneapolis: University of Minnesota, 2012).

Noel, Hans, *Political Ideologies and Political Parties in America* (New York: Cambridge, 2013).

Novak, Michael, *The Spirit of Democratic Capitalism* (New York: Simon and Schuster, 1982).

Nunberg, Geoffrey, *Talking Right: How Conservatives Turned Liberalism into a Tax-Raising, Latte-Drinking, Sushi-Eating, Volvo-Driving, New York Times-Reading, Body-Piercing, Hollywood-Loving, Left-Wing Freak Show* (New York: Public Affairs, 2006).

Obama, Barack, *Change We Can Believe In: Barack Obama's Plan to Renew America's Promise* (New York: Three Rivers Press, 2008).

Dreams From My Father (New York: Crown, 2004).

"First Inaugural Address" (January 20, 2009), at www.presidency.ucsb.edu/ws/?pid=102827.

"Remarks by the President at a Campaign Event in Roanoke, Virginia" (July 13, 2012), at www.whitehouse.gov/the-press-office/2012/07/13/remarks-president-campaign-event-roanoke-virginia.

"Remarks of President Barack Obama – State of the Union Address As Delivered" (January 13, 2016), at www.whitehouse.gov/the-press-office/2016/01/12/remarks-president-barack-obama-%E2%80%93-prepared-delivery-state-union-address.

"Second Inaugural Address" (January 21, 2013), at www.whitehouse.gov/the-press-office/2013/01/21/inaugural-address-president-barack-obama.

"State of the Union Address" (January 12, 2016), at www.whitehouse.gov/sotu.

The Audacity of Hope: Thoughts on Reclaiming the American Dream (New York: Canongate, 2006).

Obenshain, Kate, *Divider-in-Chief: The Fraud of Hope and Change* (Washington, DC: Regnery, 2012).

Olson, Mancur, *The Rise and Decline of Nations: Economic Growth, Stagflation, and Social Rigidities* (New Haven: Yale University Press, 1982).

O'Keefe, Ed, "What Jeb Bush Meant When He Said the US Should Not Have a Multicultural Society," *Washington Post* (September 23, 2015), at www.washingtonpost.com/news/post-politics/wp/2015/09/23/what-jeb-bush-meant-when-he-said-the-u-s-should-not-have-a-multicultural-society/.

O'Neill, William, *Coming Apart: An Informal History of America in the 1960s* (New York: Quadrangle, 1971).

OpenSecrets.org, "Ranked Sectors" (2016), at www.opensecrets.org/lobby/top.php?showYear%20=2009&indexType=c.

O'Reilly, William, *No Spin Zone: Confrontations with the Powerful and Famous in America* (New York: William Morrow, 2001).

Oreskes, Naomi, *Merchants of Doubt: How a Handful of Scientists Obscured the Truth on Issues from Tobacco Smoke to Global Warming* (New York: Bloomsbury, 2011).

O'Shaughnessy, Arthur, "Ode," *Poetry Foundation* (1874), at www.poetryfoundation.org/poem/242554.

Pagden, Anthony, *The Enlightenment and Why It Still Matters* (New York: Random House, 2013).

Page, Benjamin, and Robert Shapiro, *The Rational Public: Fifty Years of Trends in Americans' Policy Preferences* (Chicago: University of Chicago, 1992).

Paget, Karen, "Citizen Organizing: Many Movements, No Majority," *The American Prospect* (Summer, 1990), pp. 115–128, see http://prospect.org/article/citizen-organizing-many-movements-no-majority.

Paine, Thomas, "Common Sense (1776)," in Howard Fast (ed.), *The Selected Work of Tom Paine and Citizen Tom Paine* (New York: Modern Library, 1945), pp. 3–54.

Paine, Thomas, "The Age of Reason (1793)," in Howard Fast (ed.), *The Selected Work of Tom Paine and Citizen Tom Paine* (New York: Modern Library, 1945), pp. 285–330.

Palley, Thomas, *Plenty of Nothing: The Downsizing of the American Dream and the Case for Structural Keynesianism* (Princeton, NJ: Princeton University Press, 1998).

Papal Encyclicals Online, "Syllabus Condemning the Errors of the Modernists" (1907), at www.papalencyclicals.net/Pius09/p9syll.htm.

Parker, Robert, *Flesh Peddlers and Warm Bodies: The Temporary Help Industry and its Workers* (New Brunswick, NJ: Rutgers University Press, 1994).

Patel, Raj, *The Value of Nothing: Why Everything Costs So Much More Than We Think* (New York: Harper Perennial, 2009).

Paterson, Thomas, *Informing the News: The Need for Knowledge-Based Journalism* (New York: Vintage, 2013).

Paul, Rand, *The Tea Party Goes to Washington* (New York: Center Street, 2011).

Perkins, Frances, *The Roosevelt I Knew* (New York: Harper and Row, 1964).

Pew Research Centre, "Most Say Government Policies Since Recession Have Done Little to Help Middle Class, Poor" (March 4, 2016), at www.people-press.org/2015/03/04/most-say-government-policies-since-recession-have-done-little-to-help-middle-class-poor/.

Philander, S. George, *Is the Temperature Rising? The Uncertain Science of Global Warming* (Princeton: Princeton University Press, 1998).

Phillips-Fein, Kim, *Invisible Hands: The Businessmen's Crusade Against the New Deal* (New York: Norton, 2009).

Pinker, Steven, "College Makeover," *Slate* (November 16, 2005).

Pirsig, Robert, *Zen and the Art of Motorcycle Maintenance: An Inquiry into Values* (New York: Bantam, 1975).

Popielarz, Pamela, and Zachery Neal, "The Niche as a Theoretical Tool," *Annual Review of Sociology* (August, 2007), pp. 65–84.

Popkin, Samuel, *The Candidate: What It Takes to Win – and Hold – the White House* (New York: Oxford University Press, 2012).

    The Reasoning Voter: Communication and Persuasion in Presidential Campaigns (Chicago: University of Chicago, 1994).

Postman, Neil, *Amusing Ourselves to Death: Public Discourse in the Age of Show Business* (New York: Penguin, 1985).

    The End of Education: Redefining the Value of School (New York: Knopf, 1996).

Potter, Wendell and Nick Penniman, *Nation on the Take: How Money Corrupts Our Politics and What We Can Do about It* (New York: Bloomsbury, 2016).

Prinz, Jese, *Beyond Human Nature: How Culture and Experience Shape Our Lives* (New York: Penguin, 2012).

Purcell, Edward, *The Crisis of Democratic Theory: Scientific Naturalism and the Problem of Value* (Lexington, KY: University Press of Kentucky, 1973).

Purdum, Todd, *An Idea Whose Time Has Come: Two Presidents, Two Parties, and the Battle for the Civil Rights Act of 1964* (New York: Henry Holt, 2014).

Rae, Douglas, "Maximum Justice and an Alternative Principle of General Advantage," *American Political Science Review* (June, 1975).

Rakove, Jack (ed.), *The Unfinished Election of 2000: Leading Scholars Examine America's Strangest Election* (New York: Basic Books, 2001).

Rapoport, Anatol, *Strategy and Conscience* (Harper and Row, 1964).

Rauschenbusch, Walter, *A Theology for the Social Gospel* (orig. 1917; Louisville, KY: Westminster John Knox Press, 1997).

Rawls, John, *A Theory of Justice* (Cambridge, MA: Harvard University Press, 1971).

    Political Liberalism: Expanded Edition (New York: Columbia University Press, 2005).

Reagan, Ronald, "A Time for Choosing" (1964), at www.reagan.utexas.edu/archives/reference/timechoosing.html.

"Farewell Address to the Nation" (1989), at www.reagan.utexas.edu/archives/speeches/1989/011189i.htm.

"First Inaugural Address" (1981), at www.presidency.ucsb.edu/ws/?pid=43130.

"News Conference" (August 12, 1989), at www.reaganfoundation.org/reagan-quotes-detail.aspx?tx=2079.

"Second Inaugural Address" (1985), at http://avalon.law.yale.edu/20th_century/reagan2.asp.

Reich, Charles, *The Greening of America* (New York: Random House, 1970).

Reich, Robert, *Beyond Outrage: What Has Gone Wrong With Our Economy and Our Democracy, and How to Fix It* (New York: Vintage, 2012).

Reason: Why Liberals Will Win the Battle for America (New York: Vintage, 2005).

Supercapitalism: The Battle for Democracy in an Age of Big Business (2007).

Ricci, David, *Good Citizenship in America* (New York: Cambridge University Press, 2004).

The Tragedy of Political Science: Politics, Scholarship, and Democracy (New Haven: Yale University Press, 1983).

The Transformation of American Politics: The New Washington and the Rise of Think Tanks (New Haven: Yale University Press, 1993).

Why Conservatives Tell Stories and Liberals Don't: Rhetoric, Faith, and Vision on the American Right (Boulder: Paradigm, 2011).

Richards, Jay, *Money, Greed, and God: Why Capitalism is the Solution and Not the Problem* (New York: HarperOne, 2009).

Richardson, Glenn, Jr., *Pulp Politics: How Political Advertising Tells the Stories of American Politics*, 2nd edn. (New York: Roman and Littlefield, 2008).

Rieff, David, *The Reproach of Hunger: Food, Justice, and Money in the Twenty-First Century* (New York: Simon and Schuster, 2015).

Risen, James, *Pay Any Price: Greed, Power, and Endless War* (New York: Houghton Mifflin Harcourt, 2014).

Ritzer, George, *The McDonaldization of Society: An Investigation into the Changing Character of Contemporary Social Life* (Thousand Oaks, CA: Pine Forge Press, 2000).

Robertson, Pat, *America's Dates with Destiny* (Nashville, TN: Thomas Nelson, 1986).

Robin, Corey, *The Reactionary Mind: Conservatism From Edmund Burke to Sarah Palin* (New York: Oxford University Press, 2011).

Rodgers, Daniel, *Age of Fracture* (Cambridge, MA: Harvard University Press, 2011).

Romney, Mitt, "Full Transcript of the Mitt Romney Video," *Mother Jones* (September 19, 2012), at www.motherjones.com/politics/2012/09/full-transcript-mitt-romney-secret-video.

Romney, Mitt, "Romney's Speech in Pennsylvania Today" (September 19, 2012), at http://race42016.com/2012/07/17/romneys-speech-in-pennsylvania-today/.

Roosevelt, Franklin D., "Acceptance Speech for the Renomination for the Presidency" (July 27, 1936), at www.presidency.ucsb.edu/ws/?pid=15314.

Roosevelt, Franklin D., "Address at Oglethorpe University in Atlanta Georgia" (May 22, 1932), at www.presidency.ucsb.edu/ws/?pid=88410.

"First Inaugural Address" (March 4, 1933), at www.bartleby.com/124/pres49.html.

"Four Freedom's Speech" (January 6, 1941), at http://docs.fdrlibrary.marist.edu/od4frees.html.

"Speech at Madison Square Garden" (October 31, 1936), at http://millercenter.org/president/speeches/speech-3307.

"State of the Union Message" (January 11, 1944), at www.presidency.ucsb.edu/ws/?pid=16518.

"The Commonwealth Club Address" (September 23, 1932), at www.presidency.ucsb.edu/ws/?pid=88391.

"The Forgotten Man" (April 7, 1932), at http://newdeal.feri.org/speeches/1932c.htm.

Rorty, Richard, *Achieving our Country* (Cambridge, MA: Harvard University Press, 1998).

Contingency, Irony, and Solidarity (New York: Cambridge University Press, 1989).

Philosophy and the Mirror of Nature (Princeton: Princeton University Press, 1979).

Rosenblum, Nancy (ed.), *Liberalism and the Moral Life* (Cambridge, MA: Harvard University, 1989).

Ross, E. A., *Sin and Society: An Analysis of Latter-Day Iniquity* (orig. 1907; Charleston, SC: BiblioLife, 2010).

Rostow, Walt, *The Stages of Economic Growth: A Non-Communist Manifesto* (New York: Cambridge University Press, 1960).

Roszak, Theodore, *The Making of a Counter Culture: Reflections on the Technocratic Society and the Youthful Opposition* (Garden City, NY: Anchor, 1969).

Rowe, Edward, *Save America!* (Old Tappen, NJ: Fleming H. Revell Co., 1976).

Russakoff, Dale, *The Prize: Who's in Charge of America's Schools?* (New York: Houghton Mifflin Harcourt, 2015).

Russell, Karl, Guilbert Gates, Josh Keller, and Derek Watkins, "How Volkswagen Is Grappling With Its Diesel Deception," *New York Times* (March 24, 2016), at www.nytimes.com/interactive/2015/business/international/vw-diesel-emissions-scandal-explained.html?_r=0.

Ryan, Alan, *The Making of Modern Liberalism* (Princeton: Princeton University Press, 2012).

Sabato, Larry (ed.), *Barack Obama and the New America: The 2012 Election and the Changing Face of Politics* (New York: Rowman and Littlefield, 2013).

Sandel, Michael, *Democracy's Discontent: America in Search of a Public Philosophy* (Cambridge, MA: Harvard University Press, 1996).

Justice: What's The Right Thing to Do? (New York: Farrar, Straus, and Giroux, 2009).

Liberalism and the Limits of Justice: A Critical Examination of the Principle Doctrines in "A Theory of Justice" by John Rawls (New York: Cambridge University Press, 1982).

"The Procedural Republic and The Unencumbered Self," *Political Theory* (February, 1984), pp. 81–96.

What Money Can't Buy: The Moral Limits of Markets (New York: Farrar, Straus, and Giroux, 2012).

Sanders, Bernie, "My Vision For Democratic Socialism in America," *In These Times* (November 19, 2015), at www.inthesetimes.com/article/18623/bernie_ sanders_democratic_socialism_georgetown_speech.

The Speech: A Historic Filibuster on Corporate Greed and the Decline of Our Middle Class (New York: Nation Books, 2012).

Santorum, Rick, *It Takes a Family: Conservatism and the Common Good* (Wilmington, DE: Intercollegiate Studies Institute, 2005).

Savage, Michael, *Liberalism is a Mental Disorder* (Nashville, TN: Thomas Nelson, 2005).

Schell, Jonathan, *The Fate of the Earth* (New York: Avon, 1982).

Schlesinger, Arthur, Jr., "The Liberal Opportunity," *The American Prospect* (March, 1990), pp. 10–18.

The Vital Center: Our Purposes and Perils on the Tightrope of American Liberalism (Boston: Houghton Mifflin, 1949).

Schmidt, Alvin, *The Menace of Multiculturalism: Trojan Horse in America* (Westport, CN: Praeger, 1997).

Schneider, Stephen, and Tim Flannery, *Science as a Contact Sport: Inside the Battle to Save the Earth's Climate* (Washington, DC: National Geographic, 2009).

Schor, Juliet, *Born to Buy: The Commercialized Child and the New Consumer Culture* (New York: Scribner, 2004).

Schumer, Chuck (Charles), *Positively American: How Democrats Can Win in 2008* (New York: Rodale, 2007).

Schumpeter, Joseph, *Capitalism, Socialism, and Democracy*, 3rd edn. (New York: Harper, 1950).

Schwartz, Barry, *The Costs of Living: How Market Freedom Erodes the Best Things in Life* (New York: Norton, 1994).

The Paradox of Choice: Why More is Less (New York: Harper Perennial, 2004).

Schweikart, Larry, and Michael Allen, *A Patriot's History of the United States: From Columbus's Great Discovery to the War on Terror* (New York: Sentinel, 2007).

Scitovsky, Tibor, *The Joyless Economy: An Inquiry Into Human Satisfaction and Consumer Dissatisfaction* (New York: Oxford University Press, 1976).

Scott, James, *Seeing Like a State: How Certain Schemes to Improve the Human Condition Have Failed* (New York: Routledge, 1998).

Seabury, Samuel, *A View of the Controversy Between Great Britain and Her Colonies* (London: Richardson and Urquhart, 1775), at http://anglicanhistory.org/usa/seabury/farmer/03.html.

Self, Robert, *All in the Family: The Realignment of American Democracy Since the 1960s* (New York: Hill and Wang, 2012).

Sen, Amartya, *The Idea of Justice* (Cambridge, MA: Harvard University Press, 2011).

Sennett, Richard, *The Corrosion of Character: The Personal Consequences of Work in the New Capitalism* (New York: Norton, 1998).

Shafer, Byron, *Nationalism: Myth and Reality* (New York: Harvest, 1955).

Shklar, Judith, "The Liberalism of Fear," in Nancy Rosenblum (ed.), *Liberalism and the Moral Life* (Cambridge, MA: Harvard University, 1989), pp. 21–38.

Shlaes, Amity, *The Forgotten Man: A New History of the Great Depression* (New York: Harper, 2007).

Shor, Boris, "Polarization in American State Legislatures," in James Thurber and Antoine Yoshinaka (eds.), *American Gridlock: The Sources, Character, and Impact of of Political Polarization* (New York: Cambridge University Press, 2015), pp. 203–221.

Siedentop, Larry, *Inventing the Individual: The Origins of Western Liberalism* (Cambridge, MA: Harvard University Press, 2014).

Simon, Herbert, *Administrative Behavior*, 4th edn. (New York: Free Press, 1997).

Singer, Peter, *The President of Good and Evil: Taking George W. Bush Seriously* (New York: Dutton, 2004).

Skidelsky, Robert, and Edward Skidelsky, *How Much is Enough? Money and the Good Life* (New York: Other Press, 2012).

Skowronek, Stephen, *Presidential Leadership in Political Time*, 2nd edn. (Lawrence, KS: University Press of Kansas, 2011).

Smelser, Neil and Jeffrey Alexander (eds.), *Diversity and Its Discontents: Cultural Conflict and Common Ground in Contemporary Society* (Princeton: Princeton University, 1999).

Smith, Adam, *The Wealth of Nations* (orig. 1776; New York: Modern Library, 1994).

Smith, Hedrick, *Who Stole the American Dream?* (New York: Random House, 2012).

Smith, Jason Scott, *Building New Deal Liberalism: The Political Economy of Public Works, 1933–1956* (New York: Cambridge University Press, 2009).

Smith, Rogers, "Beyond Tocqueville, Myrdal, and Hartz: The Multiple Traditions in America," *American Political Science Review* (September, 1993), pp. 549–566.

  Stories of Peoplehood: The Politics and Morals of Political Membership (New York: Cambridge University Press, 2003).

Smith, Steven, *The Disenchantment of Secular Discourse*, (Cambridge, MA: Harvard University Press, 2010).

Sowell, Thomas, *Basic Economics: A Common Sense Guide to the Economy*, 4th edn. (New York: Basic Books, 2010).

  "Trickle Down" Theory and "Tax Cuts for the Rich" (Stanford, CA: Hoover Institution Press, 2012).

SpeechNow.Org v. Federal Election Commission, United States Court of Appeals for the District of Columbia Circuit, No. 08-5223 (March 26, 2010).

Starkman, Dean, *The Watchdog That Didn't Bark: The Financial Crisis and the Disappearance of Investigative Reporting* (New York: Columbia University Press, 2014).

Starr, Paul, *Freedom's Power: The True Force of Liberalism* (New York: Basic Books, 2007).

    Remedy and Reaction: The Peculiar American Struggle Over Health Care Reform (New Haven: Yale University Press, 2011).

Steger, Manfred, and Ravi Roy, *Neoliberalism: A Very Short Introduction* (New York: Oxford University Press, 2010).

Stein, Judith, *Pivotal Decade: How the United States Traded Factories for Finance in the Seventies* (New Haven: Yale University Press, 2010).

Stewart, Matthew, *Nature's God: The Heretical Origins of the American Republic* (New York: Norton, 2014).

Stiglitz, Joseph, *The Price of Inequality: How Today's Divided Society Endangers Our Future* (New York: Norton, 2012).

    The Roaring Nineties (New York: Penguin, 2004).

Strasser, Susan, *Satisfaction Guaranteed: The Making of the American Mass Market* (Washington, DC: Smithsonian Institution Press, 1989).

Sumner, William Graham, *What Social Classes Owe to Each Other* (orig. 1883; Caldwell, Idaho: Caxton Printers, 1961).

Sunstein, Cass, *The Second Bill of Rights: FDR's Unfinished Revolution and Why We Need it More Than Ever* (New York: Basic Books, 2004).

Suskind, Ron, *Confidence Men: Wall Street, Washington, and the Education of a President* (New York: Harper, 2011).

    "Faith, Certainty and the Presidency of George W. Bush," *New York Times* (October 17, 2004), at www.nytimes.com/2004/10/17/magazine/faith-certainty-and-the-pre sidency-of-george-w-bush.html.

Taylor, Charles, *A Secular Age* (Cambridge, MA: Harvard University Press, 2007).

Thaler, Richard, and Cass Sunstein, *Nudge: Improving Decisions About Health, Wealth, and Happiness* (New Haven: Yale University Press, 2008).

Thurber, James, and Antoine Yoshinaka (eds.), *American Gridlock: The Sources, Character, and Impact of Political Polarization* (New York: Cambridge University Press, 2015).

Trilling, Lionel, *The Liberal Imagination: Essays on Literature and Society* (Garden City, NY: Doubleday Anchor, 1953).

Truman, Harry, "The Truman Doctrine" (March 12, 1947), at http://avalon.law. yale.edu/20th_century/trudoc.asp.

Tsongas, Paul, *The Road From Here: Liberalism and Realities in the 1980s* (New York: Knopf, 1981).

Tuschman, Avi, *Our Political Nature: The Evolutionary Origins of What Divides Us* (Amherst, NY: Prometheus, 2013).

Twain, Mark, *A Connecticut Yankee in King Arthur's Court* (orig. 1889; New York: Oxford University Press, 1997).

Viguerie, Richard, *The New Right: We're Ready to Lead* (Falls Church, VA: Viguerie Company, 1980).

Viorst, Milton, *Fire in the Streets: America in the 1960s* (New York: Simon and Schuster, 1979).

Von Mises, Ludwig, "Economic Calculation in the Socialist Commonwealth (1920)," in Friedrich Hayek (ed.), *Collectivist Economic Planning: Critical Studies on the Possibilities of Socialism* (London: George Rutledge, 1935), pp. 87–130.

Wachtel, Paul, *The Poverty of Affluence: A Psychological Portrait of the American Way of Life* (Philadelphia: New Society Publishers, 1989).

Waldman, Paul, *Being Right is Not Enough: What Progressives Must Learn From Conservative Success* (New York: Wiley, 2006).

Wallison, Peter, *Hidden in Plain Sight: What Really Caused the World's Worst Financial Crisis and Why It Could Happen Again* (San Francisco: Encounter Books, 2015).

Walton, *One Nation Under God* (Washington, DC: Third Century Publishers, 1975).

Walzer, Michael, *Spheres of Justice* (New York: Basic Books, 1983).

Wanniski, Jude, *The Way the World Works* (New York: Touchstone, 1978).

Warren, Elizabeth, "Elizabeth Warren Speech Text," *Huffington Post* (September 5, 2012), at www.huffingtonpost.com/2012/09/05/elizabeth-warren-speech-text_n_1850597.html?view=print&comm_ref=false.

Wattenberg, Martin, *The Rise of Candidate-Centered Politics: Presidential Elections of the 1980s* (Cambridge, MA: Harvard University Press, 1991).

Waxman, Chaim (ed.), *The End of Ideology Debate* (New York: Touchstone, 1969).

Weber, Max, "Science as a Vocation" (1917), in Max Weber (ed.), *The Vocation Lectures* (Indianapolis, IN: Hackett, 2004), pp. 1–31.

The Vocation Lectures (Indianapolis, IN: Hackett, 2004).

Weldon, T. D., *The Vocabulary of Politics* (Baltimore: Penguin Books, 1953).

West, Cornel, *The American Evasion of Philosophy: A Geneology of Pragmatism* (Madison: University of Wisconsin Press, 1989).

Westen, Drew, *The Political Brain: The Role of Emotion in Deciding the Fate of the Nation* (New York: Public Affairs, 2008).

Whitehead, John, *The Stealing of America* (Westchester, IL: Crossway Books, 1983).

Wieseltier, Leon, "Crimes Against Humanities," *The New Republic* (September 3, 2013) at www.newrepublic.com/article/114548/leon-wieseltier-responds-steven-pinkers-scientism.

Wikipedia, "List of Democratic Party Superdelegates, 2016" *Wikipedia* (April 6, 2016), at https://en.wikipedia.org/wiki/List_of_Democratic_Party_superdelegates,_2016.

Will, George, "Rewriting History on the Filibuster," *Washington Post* (December 22, 2012).

Williams, Bernard, *Truth and Truthfulness* (Princeton: Princeton University Press, 2002).

Wills, Garry, *Lincoln at Gettysburg: The Words That Remade America* (New York: Simon and Schuster, 1992).

Wilson, James Q., *The Moral Sense* (New York: Free Press, 1993).

Wolf, Naomi, *Give Me Liberty: A Handbook for American Revolutionaries* (New York: Simon and Schuster, 2008).

The Beauty Myth: How Images of Women Are Used Against Women (New York: William Morrow, 1991).

Wolfe, Alan, *The Future of Liberalism* (New York: Vintage, 2010).

Wolfe, Tom, *The Bonfire of the Vanities* (New York: Bantam, 1988).

Wolffe, Richard, *The Message: The Reselling of President Obama* (New York: Twelve, 2013).

Wolin, Sheldon, *Democracy Inc.: Managed Democracy and the Specter of Inverted Totalitarianism* (Princeton: Princeton University Press, 2010).

Wootton, David, *The Invention of Science: A New History of the Scientific Revolution* (New York: HarperCollins, 2015).

Wouk, Herman, *The Language God Talks: On Science and Religion* (Boston: Little, Brown, 2011).

Wuthnow, Robert, "The Culture of Discontent," in Neil Smelser and Jeffrey Alexander (eds.), *Diversity and Its Discontents: Cultural Conflict and Common Ground in Contemporary Society* (Princeton: Princeton University, 1999).

"The Moral Minority," *The American Prospect* (December 19, 2001), at https://prospect.org/article/moral-minority.

Young, James, *Reconsidering American Liberalism: The Troubled Odyssey of the Liberal Idea* (Boulder, CL: Westview, 1996).

Zinn, Howard, *A People's History of the United States: 1492 – Present* (New York: HarperPerennial, 2005).

Index